Psychodynamic Psychotherapy in SOUTH AFRICA

Psychodynamic Psychotherapy
in SOUTH AFRICA

contexts, theories and applications

EDITED BY Cora Smith, Glenys Lobban and Michael O'Loughlin

WITS UNIVERSITY PRESS

Published in South Africa by:

Wits University Press
I Jan Smuts Avenue
Johannesburg

www. witspress.co.za

Published edition© Wits University Press 2013
Compilation© Edition editors 2013
Chapters© Individual contributors 2013

First published 2013

ISBN 978-1-86814-603-1 (print)
ISBN 978-1-86814-604-8 (digital)

Edited by Lee Smith
Cover design and layout by Hothouse South Africa
Printed and bound by Interpak Books

Contents

Editors

CORA SMITH PhD is an Adjunct Professor in the Division of Psychiatry, Department of Neurosciences, School of Clinical Medicine and Faculty of Health Sciences, University of the Witwatersrand, Johannesburg. She is also the Chief Clinical Psychologist of the Child, Adolescent and Family Unit at the Charlotte Maxeke Johannesburg Academic Hospital. She has extensive clinical experience in state hospitals and community clinics. She is responsible for the psychological training of Masters Clinical Psychology Interns, Psychiatry Registrars and Child Psychiatry Fellows. She has published a number of articles in journals and chapter collections and has presented many papers in South Africa and at international conferences.

GLENYS LOBBAN PhD is in full-time private practice in New York City. She is a graduate of the New York University Postdoctoral Program in Psychoanalysis and Psychotherapy and an Adjunct Clinical Supervisor, Clinical Psychology Doctoral Program, City University of New York. She was born in South Africa and also holds a Master's degree in Psychology from the University of the Witwatersrand, Johannesburg. She has published a number of articles in psychoanalytic journals and collections in the United States and has presented many papers in the United States and internationally. She wrote three chapters for *With Culture in Mind: Psychoanalytic Stories,* edited by Muriel Dimen and published by Routledge in 2011.

MICHAEL O'LOUGHLIN PhD, Professor at Adelphi University, New York, is on the faculty of Derner Institute of Advanced Psychological Studies and in the School of Education. He is a clinical and research supervisor in the PhD programme in Clinical Psychology and on the faculty of the Postgraduate Programs in Psychoanalysis and Psychotherapy at Adelphi. He published *The Subject of Childhood* in 2009 and edited *Imagining Children Otherwise: Theoretical and Critical Perspectives on Childhood Subjectivity* with Richard Johnson in 2010. He is editor of two volumes, *Psychodynamic Perspectives on Working with Children, Families and Schools* and *The Uses of Psychoanalysis in Working with Children's Emotional Lives,* both of which will be published in 2013 by Jason Aronson. His interests include the working through of intergenerational and collective trauma, the social origins of psychosis and schizophrenia, and the emotional lives of children. He is currently Co-Chair of the Association for the Psychoanalysis of Culture and Society and Treasurer of the Joint Psychoanalytic Conference. He is a research affiliate at Austen Riggs Center, where he conducts research on psychosis in collaboration with Marilyn Charles.

Contributors

GIADA DEL FABBRO PhD is the Senior Clinical Psychologist at the Child, Adolescent and Family Unit, Department of Neurosciences, University of the Witwatersrand, Johannesburg. She also holds an MSc in Forensic Psychology from the University of Kent at Canterbury, United Kingdom. She has several publications in the field of forensic psychology as well as in the area of clinical psychology.

GILL EAGLE PhD is a Full Professor at the University of the Witwatersrand, Johannesburg, and previous Head of the Department of Psychology. She sits on several university committees. She has focused her academic and research work in the two fields of trauma studies and masculinity studies and has published numerous journal articles and book chapters in these areas. She co-edited *Psychopathology and Social Prejudice* (2002) and co-authored *Traumatic Stress in South Africa* (2010). She is particularly interested in the application of psychoanalytic ideas to socio-political issues in South Africa.

YVETTE ESPREY is a Clinical Psychologist in private practice in Johannesburg, South Africa. She holds Master's degrees in Industrial and Clinical Psychology from the University of the Witwatersrand, Johannesburg. She previously held the position of Head Psychologist at Tara H Moross Psychiatric Hospital, and has worked as a lecturer at the Universities of Cape Town and the Witwatersrand. She has specific interests in psychoanalytic theory, borderline personality disorders, trauma, and the intersection of race and psychotherapy. She teaches both locally and overseas, and has presented numerous papers at local and international conferences.

VANESSA HEMP MA is currently in private practice in Johannesburg, South Africa. Prior to this, as the Senior Clinical Psychologist at Tara H Moross Psychiatric Hospital she was responsible for training Clinical Psychology Interns. She initiated and coordinated the HIV/AIDS orphans group psychotherapy outreach programme at Tara-Alex Eastbrook Clinic.

GAVIN IVEY PhD is an Associate Professor and the coordinator of the PhD Programme at the University of the Witwatersrand, Johannesburg. He is the current editor of the journal *Psychoanalytic Psychotherapy in South Africa*. He is a member of the Institute for Psychodynamic Child Psychotherapy, where he runs seminars on WR Bion's contribution to psychoanalysis. He has published papers on psychoanalytic theory and therapy in *The International Journal of Psychoanalysis*, *British Journal of Psychotherapy*, *British Journal of Medical Psychology*, *American Journal of Psychotherapy* and *Psychotherapy: Theory/Research/Practice/ Training*.

TINA SIDERIS PhD is a Clinical Psychologist in private practice in Johannesburg, South Africa. She has combined theoretical work, field research, clinical practice and activism in work on gender-related violence in South Africa. She was a founding member in 1994 of Masisukumeni Women's Crisis Centre in Mpumalanga province of South Africa, which provides counselling and legal services to women and children who have survived rape and domestic violence. She has consulted to organisations in South Africa, Mozambique and Denmark on issues related to violence, trauma, inter-organisational collaboration and organisational development. She has presented papers at local and international conferences and published articles in edited collections and in peer reviewed journals, including *AGENDA*, *African Studies*, *Psychoanalytic Psychotherapy in South Africa* and *Psychoanalysis, Culture and Society*.

SALLY SWARTZ PhD is an Associate Professor in the Psychology Department of the University of Cape Town. She also practises psychotherapy. She is currently the Deputy Dean of the Faculty of Humanities at the University of Cape Town. She was formerly the Head of the Department of Psychology at the University of Cape Town. She has published widely in the areas of psychotherapy and the history of psychiatry in South Africa. She has a particular interest in the challenges of working as a psychoanalytic psychotherapist in South Africa, and her work explores the effects of race, class and gender divides on experiences of trauma and healing.

Acknowledgements

The editors would like to thank all the contributors to this book who have shared their work and insights so generously.

We would also like to acknowledge our appreciation to Professor Ahmed Wadee for his unfailing support and generous financial assistance towards the publication of this book from the Wadee Trust. In addition we are grateful for the financial support from the Faculty of Health Sciences at the University of the Witwatersrand, Johannesburg.

Thanks are also due to the staff of Wits University Press for their guidance and assistance.

We are also indebted to Lisa Aarons Platt for her assistance with the graphic design of the cover.

Finally we would like to thank our clients and patients for sharing their life stories, trusting us with their vulnerabilities and teaching us so much.

Editors: Cora Smith
       Glenys Lobban
       Michael O'Loughlin

ACRONYMS AND ABBREVIATIONS

CBT	cognitive behavioural therapy
CCW	community care worker
EMDR	Eye Movement Desensitisation and Reprocessing
NHI	National Health Insurance
OASSSA	Organisation for Appropriate Social Services in South Africa
PTSD	Post-traumatic Stress Disorder
SAPS	South African Police Service
SASH	South African Stress and Health study
TFCBT	trauma-focused CBT
TRC	Truth and Reconciliation Commission

Introduction

With this book we hope to broaden knowledge about how psychodynamic psychotherapy, as well as psychoanalytic concepts and theories are practised and applied in the context of contemporary South Africa. The chapters include a wide range of psychodynamic work undertaken by clinical psychologists working in university settings, state hospitals, community projects, private practice and research. The aim is to provide the reader with an experience of the current debates, clinical issues, therapeutic practice and nature of research that is representative of the work being done in South Africa.

There are a handful of qualified psychoanalysts practising in South Africa at present. Although the South African Psychoanalytic Association was accredited as an official International Psychoanalytical Association study group in 2009, with the ultimate aim of training psychoanalysts in accordance with international standards, only a very few privileged South Africans will be able to pursue such training or afford to undergo the experience of psychoanalysis. The vast majority of South Africans will only have access to briefer forms of psychotherapy, some of which is psychodynamically informed. Most of the psychoanalytically oriented psychotherapy conducted in South Africa is done by clinical psychologists who have been trained at a university offering a psychodynamically oriented Master's degree in Clinical Psychology.[1]

It is within this context of psychodynamic applications that the contributors to this book have written about their work and experience. The approaches described draw on several theoretical models, reflecting the pluralism in the field today. The book is a collective effort by experienced therapists, clinicians, trainers, teachers, clinical supervisors, consultants and researchers working in the field of diversity as it applies to the South African context.

The work described in this volume is situated within the context of post-apartheid South Africa, with all the complexities, hopes, dreams and even disillusionments that have emerged in our fledgling and fragile democracy. With this socio-political history in mind, it is important for clinicians to understand that issues of race, disparity, inequality, complicity, reparation, reconciliation, cultural diversity, difference and trauma permeate our practice of psychodynamic interventions. These issues require personal reflection, academic debate, theoretical interrogation and sensitive adaptation in clinical practice. It is also hoped that the book will provide an opportunity for engagement with these pertinent issues for all therapists who practise in diverse political, racial, religious and multicultural settings.

The book is structured into three main sections but each chapter stands as an autonomous and independent piece of work. The first section introduces contemporary issues about race, identity, disavowal and otherness viewed within an intersubjective theoretical frame. Chapter 1 explores the implications of working within a relational psychoanalytic frame in a post-colonial setting in which difference, being other and othering, is inevitably a constitutive part of trauma.

The chapter acknowledges the question of the usefulness of psychoanalytic theory in a post-colonial setting and the often noted shame and envy of local practitioners who lack pure psychoanalytic training and practise 'pale' reflections of the real thing. The chapter challenges South African psychoanalytic practice both in terms of its professional identity and its experience of having fundamental value in the country's desperate need to address pervasive trauma and violence. The need to go beyond naming difference in identity, not as a final recognition but as a process toward a shared humanity, is discussed with a focus on the politics of naming. Finally, the chapter argues for a celebration of a deeply African hybridisation of psychoanalytic practice in our pursuit of raced, gendered transformative spaces, which requires an understanding of otherness and a will to reach across the divide.

Chapter 2 deals with race and the role it plays in the South African post-apartheid psychotherapy room. The chapter interrogates the challenges that arise in the silences and disavowals that take place in the therapeutic relationship in a country that holds a position in history which defined its interactions according to racially defined legislation. Arguing that it is not whether race and racism enter the psychotherapeutic dyad, but rather when and how we notice it, the chapter examines race as an active third in the intersubjective therapeutic encounter. Chapter 3 describes a compelling personal journey of discovering a mixed-race ancestry in post-apartheid South Africa and how race and culture shape subjectivity and identity. The chapter brings into focus the personal experiences of racialised subjectivity and how these are often inflected through a lens which privileges whiteness. The chapter offers insightful reflections for the practice of psychotherapy and interesting theoretical contributions toward the formation of identity and subjectivity.

The second section of the book deals broadly with psychodynamic perspectives in trauma; the impact of violence on attachment, family function and individual survival; and the psychotherapeutic dilemmas these conditions raise for psychodynamically oriented therapists. Chapter 4 offers an experience-near encounter of clinical cases that are representative of the difficulties faced in psychodynamic psychotherapy in the mental health services of the public sector in post-apartheid South Africa. The chapter describes the stark realities of everyday life for most South Africans, where apartheid still casts a long shadow over citizens who continue to struggle with disrupted family constellations, violence and trauma, competing cultural practices and diverse epistemologies of meaning. The use of psychoanalytically informed psychotherapy in assisting patients and therapists to deal with their painful legacies is richly described in four psychotherapy encounters. These cases not only challenge notions of idealised psychoanalytic practice in the South African context, but also bring into focus contemporary global debates around theoretical purism and plurality as well as the general financial pressure to produce shorter-term interventions.

Chapter 5 notes that because the levels of exposure to a wide range of trauma in South Africa are so high, the country unfortunately represents a natural laboratory in which to observe the impact of trauma. The chapter is based on a wealth of clinical and theoretical experience and cogently argues that psychodynamic theory is helpful in formulating trauma impact, in informing interventions and in working with multicultural belief systems. While offering a comprehensive understanding of historical, collective and pervasive traumatisation in the South African context, the chapter offers reflections on the facility of psychodynamically informed trauma work to engage with prejudice in trauma survivors, and to assist therapists in dealing with their own experiences of such work.

The third section of this book deals with a range of highly relevant social issues currently the focus of psychodynamic psychotherapy and application in the South

African context. These include the complex relationship between psychoanalysis and traditional healing, the politics and psychodynamics of gendered violence, the challenge of running psychodynamic group therapy community projects with South African AIDS orphans, the intergenerational and psychodynamic processes in the proliferation of serial murder in post-apartheid South Africa and the psychodynamic potential for reparative therapy in contemporary South Africa.

Chapter 6 deals with the complex relationship between classical psychoanalytic theory and practice and traditional healing in the South African context. Focusing on the integrationist trend in contemporary psychoanalytic theory and technique, this chapter invites an investigation of the essential commonalities and differences between indigenous African healing and psychoanalytic treatment. The recognition of common factors at play between the two modalities is debated in juxtaposition with the divergent philosophical frameworks underpinning both views. The chapter offers insightful debate and grapples with incompatibilities transcending popular politically correct arguments.

Chapter 7 is based on doctoral research with African men in rural South Africa, using intersubjective and object relations theory to explore the impact of changes in gender relations in post-apartheid South Africa. The chapter focuses on violence perpetrated by men against women with whom they are intimately involved and questions the continuity of violence in the context of social and political transformation in the advent of South Africa's new democracy. While the new constitutional order endorses gender equality, neither the structural foundations of inequality nor the ideology which makes access to power an ideal has been dismantled, rendering many men with potential feelings of loss and envy when gender rights are evoked. The perplexing question of why intimate violence might intensify under these conditions is broached and the dilemmas of applying psychodynamic understandings to practice in the context of poor and marginalised groups of people are examined.

Chapter 8 describes both forensic work and doctoral research with serial killers in post-apartheid South Africa, with its unique social, cultural and political heritage. The curious phenomenon of serial murder emerging with significance only in post-apartheid democratic South Africa is discussed in the context of the political landscape of the country and the obvious differences in infrastructure within a developing country. The chapter includes interviews with two serial killers, illustrating the important role played by contextual and cultural elements in the way serial murder manifests with regard to victim selection and modus operandi.

Chapter 9 reflects on the difficult challenges encountered in running psychotherapy groups with AIDS-orphaned children and their caregivers in community settings during a political period of AIDS denialism in South Africa's health service delivery. The chapter describes the complexities and difficulties in managing the psychodynamic processes that unfold and the need to contain adult–child interactions which often avoid overwhelming affect as a way of coping and produce potentially destructive enactments. The unspoken issues of race and racism in dealing with group dynamics with children who struggle with their conceptualisations of white persons, white privilege and assumed white lack of empathy are discussed. The chapter engages the anti-group phenomena and the negative impact these dynamics have on the group processes that unfold. Finally, the difficulties in maintaining the psychotherapeutic frame to facilitate the therapy without alienating the clinic staff and the population in the community setting are elucidated.

Chapter 10 provides a rich encounter in understanding and working psychodynamically with social history by engaging the notion of reclaiming genealogy, memory and history and the opportunities for reparative psychotherapy these offer. By permitting a push to forget the past and look to the future, South Africans may run the risk of creating a privileged version of history that leaves stories untold, trauma unprocessed and skeletons lurking in the nation's closet. The chapter offers an insight into how psychoanalytic thinking might contribute to the reformation of South Africa as a nation through the dissemination of psychoanalytic ideas in mental health, community care structures and school settings. By including examples from other parts of the world, the reader is offered a more global perspective of the subtle and sometimes hidden consequences of history. The chapter concludes with the notions of evocative pedagogy and regenerative curricula as ways of providing psychodynamic applications to children and youth on pathways to healing.

FUTURE CONSIDERATIONS FOR PSYCHODYNAMIC PRACTICE

The way forward for psychoanalytic practice in the South African context will be determined by three crucial factors. First, the changes in the structure of healthcare service and delivery that are imminent in the proposed National Health Insurance (NHI) will directly influence the shape and nature of psychoanalytically oriented practice that can be offered. Second, the role of training institutions with regard to the training and teaching of psychoanalytic theory, research and clinical applications will be vital in providing psychoanalytic models that are relevant. Third, the willingness of local clinical colleagues to embrace robust contemporary models of psychoanalytic psychotherapy that are relevant to the South African context is essential if we are to develop a positive psychological identity as psychodynamic practitioners.

In the interests of distributive justice and the right of access to healthcare, South Africa is in the process of introducing an NHI system – to be phased in over the next several years – which aims to ensure that everyone has access to appropriate, efficient and quality healthcare services (NHI, 2011). The thrust of the NHI is to provide improved access to health services and in particular mental healthcare services, for all South Africans. The restructuring of mental healthcare services and how they are distributed, structured and formulated will have a profound impact on how psychodynamic psychotherapy will be practised in the future.

South Africa is classified as a middle-income country with a high disease burden, dual disease pattern, and large discrepancies between socio-economic groups. There are currently 5 651 registered applied psychologists and 126 community service psychologists in South Africa (HPCSA, 2011) for an estimated population of 50.5 million people. At present only 529 psychologists (10%) work in the public health sector (DoH, 2011). Overall, we are very under-resourced with regard to registered psychologists and human resource capacity to provide crucially needed psychological services (Burns, 2011).

For a comprehensive and effective psychological service to become available to all South Africans within the NHI, the current number of psychologists working with the public sector will need to be increased. In order to provide mental healthcare for all South Africans it is clear that the NHI and its proposed partnerships with the private sector will favour short-term psychotherapy models that are evidence based and sensitive to diverse cultural practices, racial and ethnic identifications, religious affiliations, gender issues and sexual orientations, in accordance with the South African Constitution. This implies that the majority of psychodynamic psychotherapy practice which currently takes place in the private sector will need to find a home in the public sector under the NHI. If we as agents of psychodynamic thinking and practice wish for our profession to survive this structural shift, we will need to adapt to shorter-term models of psychoanalytically oriented psychotherapy practice and theoretical models that reflect the rich and diverse context in which we live. It is more likely that as South Africans we will need to develop an approach to teaching, training and practising psychodynamic psychotherapy that is unique to our multicultural and resource-constricted homes, and not pursue approximations and imitations of idealised psychoanalytic practice more suited to developed countries with first-world resources and economies.

Training institutions in clinical psychology such as universities and internship centres are for the most part cognisant of the need for appropriate contextual models but many retain a nostalgic wish for idealised psychoanalytic practice that is inappropriate to our local context, leaving their students feeling unnecessarily inadequate and insufficient in their skills and abilities. Universities are uniquely placed to promote and support the very necessary research required to provide evidence-based legitimacy for psychoanalytically oriented practice as well as to provide affirmation for positive role models of local psychodynamic practice that are not relegated to second-class status in comparison to their first-world cousins. While some training institutions embrace the quest for supporting and promoting transformation candidates so that previously disadvantaged students are represented in clinical courses, there remain some institutions that lack commitment to this ideal. Without robust representation of racial, cultural, gender and religious diversity reflective of the country's demography in our clinical programmes, psychoanalytic thinking, conceptualisation and application will remain inaccessible to the majority of people.

Finally, our colleagues that practise long-term psychoanalytically oriented psychotherapy in the private sector have much to offer in their reading groups, private practices and clinical supervision, but only in so far as they are able to adapt these skills to our changing context and embrace contemporary psychoanalytic theoretical models that privilege context, as the needs of our country demand.

It is only through our collective efforts in adapting psychodynamic ideas, concepts and principles to our country's contemporary political landscape with a sensitivity to cultural difference and the effects of economic and political hardship that we as psychodynamic practitioners can be effective and relevant in our therapeutic endeavours and interventions. South Africans need to complete the healing process started by the Truth and Reconciliation Commission by focusing on the psychosocial wounds of our nation inflicted by a legacy of racism, sexism and engineered inequality. I believe that psychoanalytic ideas can facilitate an honest and open dialogue that addresses unspoken issues and feelings – both within and between racial groupings in South Africa – that have emerged as part of our racialised history and, more recently, in our disappointment at the failure to transform and deliver on the promise of our rainbow democracy.

Although this book has a strong focus on South African issues, it is not parochial in its offerings. Many of the issues raised have international relevance in the crisis facing psychoanalysis in a world plagued by the tyranny of managed healthcare and the demand for instant results. The need for shorter-term therapy models and evidence-based interventions is as acute in global practice as it is locally. Equally, the theoretical debates regarding context, intersubjectivity, the analytic third, racism, prejudice, multicultural sensitivity, cultural relativism, trauma and the ethical dilemmas that these issues raise, are pertinent to all therapists who practise within a psychoanalytic frame. It is hoped that this book will contribute to the contemporary theoretical debates in the international community of psychoanalytic practice.

A NOTE ON CONFIDENTIALITY

It is crucial that the privacy of all clients and patients discussed in this book is protected. In each case the identifying details have been altered or disguised to protect the confidentiality of the individuals involved. Those patients or cases drawn from academic teaching hospitals were requested to permit their material to be used for teaching or publication in accordance with the Code of Ethics of the profession and the regulations of the academic hospitals. Clients or patients from private practices were individually approached for consent and those cases from research projects were processed through the Ethics Research Committees of their respective universities. The contributors to this book are indebted to their patients and clients for permitting their experiences to be shared in the spirit of advancing knowledge. The contributors acknowledge the privilege of learning from their patients and clients and the valuable lessons they have been taught by them.

Cora Smith

NOTE

1   There are some counselling and educational psychologists, psychiatrists and social workers who practise psychodynamic psychotherapy in the country.

REFERENCES

Burns, JK (2011) The mental health gap in South Africa: Human rights issue. *The Equal Rights Review*, 6: 99–113.

DoH (Department of Health) (2011) *HRH Strategy for the Health Sector: 2012/13 – 2016/17.* Accessed from http://www.info.gov.za/view/DownloadFileAction?id=152486 on 27 October 2012.

HPCSA (Health Professional Counsel of South Africa) (2011) *HPCSA: iRegister.* Accessed from www.hpcsa.co.za/statististics.php on 12 October 2011.

NHI (National Health Insurance) (2011) *National Health Insurance: Healthcare for all South Africans.* Accessed from http://www.doh.gov.za on 9 November 2012.

SECTION

I

SUBJECTIVITY AND IDENTITY

NAMING AND OTHERNESS: South African intersubjective psychoanalytic psychotherapy and the negotiation of racialised histories[1]

Sally Swartz

Why are encounters across difference often so complicated and prone to misunderstanding and painful experience of shame and exclusion? And why, worldwide, is there such violent acting out around difference – persecution of Jews, Christian crusades against Islam, genocide of one tribe by another in Rwanda? Being other, democrat or dictator, Muslim or Christian, poor or rich, black or white, living in the northern or southern hemisphere, gay or straight, married or single, man, woman or child, HIV+ or dying of starvation or healthy, the differences between us proliferate and continue to be marked in public discourse, named, every second, on all public media, and also privately, in our hearts and bones. In the decade since 9/11, notions of justice, national safety and retribution constantly rehearse an us–them divide. Genocides and the use of rape of women and children as a weapon of war erode daily our capacity to believe in a shared humanity, an underlying sameness between us all.

Given this extraordinary world context, it is not remarkable that there has been increasing concern about the ways in which psychoanalytic theory and practice might have been blind to, or perpetuated, prejudice in different ways. Theorising gender and sexuality, race and class, cultural difference and religious or spiritual values in the psychoanalytic space is no longer seen as an 'extra' set of variables to be taken into account, but as fundamental to the dialogue with the unconscious. The intersubjective and relational turn in psychoanalysis, embedded as it is in postmodern concepts of fluid and shifting identities, underwritten by powerful social systems, has been helpful in sharpening the focus on identity and difference and their effects on relational transformation. Within the psycho-analytic community broadly, there is a deepening movement towards political engagement (Benjamin, 2009). This involves a number of possible activities, ranging from *pro bono* consultation in public clinics, support for frontline activists working with disadvantaged and vulnerable groups, and engagement with psychoanalytic theory to ensure that it opens doors and embraces complexity, to taking a public stand against discrimination and the silencing of the disenfranchised, wherever it happens.

In South Africa, experiences of deeply entrenched and racialised divisions between communities past and present continue to shape the negotiation of power in therapeutic spaces, and affect participants' capacity to engage freely with the exploration of unconscious communication. This chapter will begin to unpack some of the implications of working in relational ways in a post-colonial setting in which difference, being other and othering, is always a constitutive part of trauma. It will begin with a discussion of subjectivity and the politics of naming and being named, of doing and repeating dark things with words. It will sketch aspects of the unnameable and its contagious unconscious life. It will end with some comments on orthodoxy, hybridity and carnival and the creation of raced, gendered transformative spaces.

THIRDNESS IN THE THIRD WORLD

The argument begins with a broad constituting context for working with otherness in post-colonial settings. The first issue concerns the meaning for South African clinicians of being 'post'-colonial. South Africa, politically, is no longer a colony, but as in all previously colonised states, structures arising from the colonial condition live on. The one pertinent to this chapter concerns the meaning of diaspora for psychoanalytic practitioners. South Africa does not have well-established psychoanalytic training, and very few fully qualified psychoanalysts practise here. Despite this, psychoanalysis as a theory remains an idealised model of mind and practice. In relation to psychoanalysts in the northern hemisphere, those working with psychoanalytic theory in clinical practice in South Africa are in a subordinate position, because we are unanalysed and therefore lack the experience that would confer on us the possibility of speech. We work daily with a body of theory with no rights of negotiation about its fundamental assumptions. The shame of the unanalysed state, the lack of 'pure' training, filters into our study groups and professional societies as an affective marker of our inequality, and this in turn colours our attempts to describe our work (Swartz, 2007a). Just as the colonised subject mimics the master, taking on his culture and language, so too do psychoanalytic psychotherapists assume the psychoanalytic mask, gesture, posture and vocabulary, but at some level the knowledge of aping, as opposed to being, continues to haunt our self-representation (Fanon, 1967).

The shame that affects post-colonial clinicians about their etiolated access to 'pure' knowledge, training and experience, and their brave attempts to cobble together a pale reflection of it (always in the hope of some day being able to go to London or Chicago or New York to do the 'real' thing), have had powerful consequences. Writing from South Africa has found a confident voice in relation to our particular struggles – working with black clients, trauma, torture and violence, for example (see Eagle, 2005; Lazarus & Kruger, 2004). There is also a body of literature accumulating around an examination of whiteness, white guilt, and the perversities of practice that were created by the apartheid state (for example, see Straker, 2004). While benefits have accrued as a result of this soul-searching, there have also been costs, mainly in the ways in which 'whiteness' studies essentialise difference. However, there is a relative silence about the foundations of psychoanalytic theory and its usefulness in post-colonial settings. We bow to the authority as we receive it, instead of celebrating its inevitable, deeply African, hybridisation. Hybrid theory, like miscegenation, is coloured in the South African context with phobic anxiety about contamination and impurity (Swartz & Ismail, 2001).

Secondly, being 'post'-colonial has left clinicians in a divided society, with a legacy of class, race and gender inequality, a history of violation and trauma that complicates both speaking and hearing (Kottler, 1996). Many qualified clinicians in South Africa are unable to have a mother tongue conversation with the majority of people in the country, have little idea of what it might be like to live without proper housing, electricity and running water, and without easy access to ordinary medical care. There is now evidence that South Africans living in very poor communities will seek psychotherapy if it is available at an affordable fee (Waumsley & Swartz, 2011). Despite this new development, relatively long-term therapies remain a middle-class, often white, luxury commodity.

There are therefore challenges for South African psychoanalytic practitioners both in terms of its disciplinary identity and its fundamental value in the country's ongoing desperate need to address widespread trauma and violence. Both challenges involve an understanding of otherness and a will to reach across the divides it creates. Failure to rise to these challenges will maintain a rigidity in capacity for reflective functioning, and a potential collapse into splitting, idealisation and projection, the primitive defences that protect 'us' from 'them'. In short, what threatens our work is the collapse of the analytic third, the space in which reverie replaces enactment (Ogden, 1994).

'IRREDUCIBLE SUBJECTIVITY'

The debates about the inevitable presence of analysts' subjectivity in the analytic process have been well rehearsed in the past decade, and accompany a fundamental acceptance not only that scientific neutrality and objectivity are impossible, but also that this state of affairs is not necessarily problematic. However we choose to inhabit our moment-by-moment being, we have no choice but to participate in it. Bakhtin calls this having 'no alibi' and, as Holquist suggests, this 'means I have a stake in everything that comes my way' (1990: 153). Bakhtin (1993) is pointing to the situated and participatory nature of being as the centrepiece for understanding lifeworlds. The debate has moved without much ado into new theories – those of mutual influence, intersubjectivity, the tension between empathy and the recognition of difference, and the expanding definition of projective identification to describe co-created conscious and unconscious states, to name a few of the developments enriching current psychoanalytic thinking.

However, an understanding of the operation of otherness in the therapeutic dyad and its challenges to the analytic third (which is essentially an intersubjective phenomenon) must first tackle the notion of subjectivity itself, and its relationship to language and, in particular, to naming. The Oxford English Dictionary defines 'subjectivity' as 'consciousness of one's perceived states'; 'a conscious being'. The sense it entails then is not only of an inner life, but awareness of it, a capacity to reflect on it. A second meaning given is 'the quality or condition of viewing things exclusively through the medium of one's own mind or individuality; the condition of being dominated by or absorbed in one's personal feelings, thoughts, concerns, etc.; hence, individuality, personality'. The connotations of the latter are clearly negatively coloured in some respects, carrying the sense of narcissistic preoccupation or influence that objectivists would once have wished be put aside in order that a clear vision be achieved.

These definitions point to two issues relevant to this discussion. One is the existence of subjectivity as a function of awareness (as opposed, for example, to a state of being, a feeling state). This allows the possibility that subjectivity is brought into existence by scrutiny – in fact, by being subject to awareness. The second is the tension between subjective awareness and the capacity to imagine the world through the eyes of another. Kohut (1971) argues that access to subjectivity exists only through introspection, and is always hidden to whoever is outside one's own skin. Empathy is an act of imagination and a means of collecting data – a 'resonance of alikeness' (Schwaber, 1990: 229) – an oscillation between subjectivities (Teicholz, 1999).

However, as soon as mental life reaches representation, in either spoken or written language, it becomes an *object* for scrutiny. In addition to this, as one interior life encounters others, through conversation and colliding bodies, an intact experience of one's own subjectivity remains so for as long as it does not disturb expectation. While there is indeed a 'resonance of alikeness', a seamless connection and kinship, subjectivity is shared. It becomes an *object* at the same moment that it becomes *other*.

This is precisely the point at which theorising subjectivity must take account of power, which I believe always entails an insertion of difference, of otherness, into communication. The marking of difference in conversation entails power in a wide variety of ways – through disagreement, assertion of authority over another, through discursive claims to knowledge, and gate-keeping of access to different experience. My concern in this chapter is to look at the therapeutic implications of working in contexts in which otherness is the inevitable point of departure, where this saturates early contact, and yet where a 'resonance of alikeness' is an important prerequisite for fundamental transformation. The argument asks the question: is empathy (in a Kohutian sense) – the oscillation between two subjectivities – possible when difference confers a fluid, shifting but ever-present otherness on every encounter?

REPRESENTING SUBJECTIVITY AND THE POWER OF NAMING

What happens when one subjectivity encounters another, so that there is a moment-by-moment experience of communication? It is impossible for two bodies to share a space and not communicate, even if no words are spoken. Our age, race, gender, culture and some things about our characteristic ways of being communicate before we open our mouths. We resonate with perceived affective states in those near us. Complex systems of representation, only subliminally available to conscious thought, organise this experience. This layer of communicative capacity is deeply integrated into psychoanalytic theory, and the technical term 'projective identification' partly defines the area. Ogden suggests that it is a process in which 'feeling states corresponding to the unconscious fantasies of one person (the projector) are engendered in and processed by another person (the recipient)' (1982: 1). The process of being made to experience another's world in a visceral way has been broadly recognised as an important analytic tool, but one that often defies description (Bion, 1963; Bollas, 1987). The unworded interplay of bodily communication is a significant component in 'moments of meeting', central to the mutative effects of the analytic encounter (Stern et al., 1998: 906).

Then there is language. In relation to subjectivity, language is a double-edged sword: it is the 'cool web' that 'winds us in' (Graves, 2000: 283), organising experience into tolerable pockets, giving a syntax, linking object and action; it represents experience in ways that offer access to meaning; it does nothing less than reformulate experience in order to make living possible. It makes objects of subjects, it separates us from 'blooming buzzing confusion' (James, 1981: 462). On the other hand, language does allow experience to be relived and communicated. For example, trauma seeps into and colours language, transmitting itself from one body to another. Recent research suggests that trauma debriefing (retelling the traumatic event in detail) may actively damage clients by flooding their already hyper-alert and overactive bodies with intolerable affect (Van der Kalk, 1996). In the wake of the London bombing in 2005, counsellors were advised not to do trauma debriefing, as this has potentially harmful effects precisely because of its capacity to re-evoke experience. 'Secondary trauma' describes effects on the listener of saturation in narratives of violence. This may result from an inward awakening of previous trauma in the listener, with the narrative simply a precipitant; but the effects are nonetheless of trauma shared between two bodies as a result of a conversation. We know therefore that communication between subjectivities is not only possible, but profoundly part of being human. Its effects are not always benign.

So far this argument has described the transmission of often powerful affective states between subjectivities. Putting the shared experience into words in ways that feel apt then might be said to constitute a sense of 'understanding' that is transformational. All of this belongs in the realm of sameness, of the 'resonance of alikeness' to which Schwaber refers.

Many acts of communication, however, whatever their intention, have the effect of marking difference, of othering. As Judith Butler argues, 'to be named by another is traumatic: it is an act that precedes my will' (1997: 38). The naming of one person by another – as black or white, Jew or Muslim, lesbian, or disabled, for example – is a 'founding subordination', an act of power with potentially damaging effects. It is an act of interpellation that converts an individual into merely a representative of a group (Guralnik & Simeon, 2010).

In South Africa, the work of the Truth and Reconciliation Commission (TRC) was premised on the belief that to name victims and perpetrators, and to hear the narratives of both, would bring about the possibility of healing. Often the idea of forgiveness was woven into the tapestry (Gobodo-Madikizela, 2003). In many ways, the TRC was a therapeutic encounter on a massive scale, designed specifically to allow subaltern voices of the *apartheid* past to speak. It was an extraordinary moment, acknowledged worldwide, but not unfettered by pre-designed roles (perpetrator, victim, political affiliation). The intersubjective complications of forgiveness implicate privilege. The act of forgiving in a conversation between perpetrator and victim issues from a position of power, however momentarily it is held. This unsettles the free flow of dialogue, invokes uncomfortable notions of who, after all, is 'innocent', and never allows the sentence 'I forgive you for being my victim', thereby creating a layer of otherness in 'the forgiven', ironically shackled in the very moment of release.

However, Butler also argues that naming creates 'the scene of agency' (1997: 38). She goes on:

> The terms by which we are hailed are rarely the ones we choose (and even when we try to impose protocols on how we are to be named, they usually fail); but these terms we never really choose are the occasion for something we might still call agency, the repetition of an originary subordination for another purpose, one whose future is partially open. (1997: 38)

Agency, for Butler, constitutes itself therefore around definition of difference, which fits well with Jessica Benjamin's (1990) argument that the encounter with otherness and the survival of these differentiating moments is not only inevitable, but also essential to true mutuality or 'recognition'. As Benjamin (1990: 84) notes, 'our deepest desires for freedom and communion become implicated in control and submission' as long as there is no recognition of the other. Recognition of difference creates the possibility of two separate subjectivities, and builds the structure through which a 'resonance of alikeness' might eventually be built.

Butler argues that 'there is no purifying language of its traumatic residue' but also 'no way to work through trauma except through the arduous effort it takes to direct the course of its repetition. It may be that trauma constitutes a strange kind of resource, and repetition, its vexed but promising instrument' (1997: 38). Some words will still, in spite of ourselves, 'stubbornly resist' submitting to appropriation for the purpose of the speaker, carrying always an intention from another context, 'as if they put themselves in quotation marks against the will of the speaker' (Butler, 1997: 77). Language carries history; its associative matrix constantly binds us to narratives of erasure or violence, in the same moment as it veils us from them. Words like 'Holocaust', 'genocide', 'rape' and 'apartheid' name events that repeat and will never be undone.

Engaging intersubjectively with the fullness of history and difference, with the aim of creating the possibility of transformation, might therefore entail breaking though language as 'a cool web' in which lines of domination and subordination precede us in words, sentences and their associations. This suggests ways of talking that subvert and disrupt the 'hearable' mainstream (Bernard-Donals, 1998). The challenge is to make a co-constructed intersubjective space, an analytic space in which naming is an occasion for curiosity, and where difference in identity is used not as a final recognition, but as a signal to go beyond – towards a shared humanity. Naming will be a shared, not a unilateral, activity and the sting of history, of deep antagonisms and violent division will be challenged by a playful suspension of the weight of the past in the analytic third. Space must be made for our own unconscious anxieties – unique to every individual – to be brought to awareness, beyond prescribed discursive positions dictated by gender, race, class.

Recognition of subjectivity is carried in language through agency, the 'I' or 'you' in a sentence, coupling around verbs and adverbs of comparison in ways that allow both the 'I' and the 'you' to survive intact. The cool web of domination deeply entwined in language itself must be negotiated if mutual recognition is to take place. Such a negotiation is made possible through play. We need to create an analytic space in which our patients 'try on', 'dress up in', our interpretations. Bollas argues that 'our errors of association, corrected by the analysand – or "destroyed" through use of them – assist in the ordinary essential deconstruction of analytical certainty' (1992: 132). He advocates 'the reliable deconstruction' of analytic authority, such that we become 'democratic representatives in the assembly of consciousness rather than monarchs of an imposed truth' (1992: 133). Winnicott suggests that:

> psychotherapy takes place in the overlap of two areas of playing, that of the patient and that of the therapist. If the therapist cannot play, then he [sic] is not suitable for the work. If the patient cannot play, then something needs to be done to make the patient become able to play, after which psychotherapy may begin. (1971: 63)

There is a powerful convergence between the rich, subversive and playful energy of unconscious communication and Bakhtin's notion of carnival. For Bakhtin, carnivals throw together 'the profane and the sacred, the lower and the higher, the spiritual and the material' (1984: 285–286). They incorporate political, religious and social commentary, colourfully enacting the grotesque and the taboo, the revered and the feared in an embodied, often parodic display that escapes the repressive effects of dominant discourse. Carnivals are quintessentially celebrations of otherness, and this is why they may provide a paradigm within which to explore the possibility of giving voice to otherness in the analytic space. Drawing on Bakhtin's notion of carnival, it can be argued that, paradoxically, in foregrounding otherness and celebrating alterity, dominant hegemonic discourses are temporarily opened to the new and strange – the mad, the culturally exotic, the sexually experimental, the regressed. Hwa Yol Jung describes the carnivalesque as 'the most radical aspect of the dialogics of difference because it serves as a *non-violent technique of social transformation* by maximal display of the body' (his emphasis, 1998: 104).

Carnivals involve crowds and clowns; multiple messages and many voices. Kristeva talks about the need to 'disturb the syntactic chain', to attack the 'unity of the speaking subject' (1985: 215). The purpose of this is to break open the foreclosed subject, to let in what is 'heterogeneous in sense' (1985: 217). Syntax itself creates coherence and the purpose of disrupting it is to 'make language stammer' (Deleuze & Guattari, 1987: 98). In the splitting open of ordinary forms of speech, the breaking up of conversational rules, and the disturbance of narrative closures, through dreams and free association, new possibilities of meaning are formed in which the representation of non-unitary speaking subjects is performed.

BRINGING IT ALL BACK HOME

The case material in the section following this, which describes acts of naming and interpellation, of shaming, othering and being othered, of reaching for recognition and the slow building of an analytic third, begins by giving the reader some bearings on my own subjectivity. The subjectivities of my patients I can guess at, and perhaps know enough of to frame a statement about an intersubjective moment or two, but the ground from which this starts must necessarily be one's own apprehension of self.

As a white South African, as my body enters into analytic space, my skin immediately and irredeemably marks my privilege: I have had access to an excellent education, to a safe and substantial home, to travel, and to quite ordinary calamities of development. None of my relatives were forcibly removed from one location to another, none were tortured or detained or killed. I have been able to enter a profession and climb through the ranks by being good enough at what I do. In so far as I have benefited from my whiteness, I am a perpetrator. I have also been scarred by living in a violent system: I learned as a child to make myself blind to misery daily rehearsed on the streets of the cities in which I grew up, to dismiss as irrelevant to my everyday lifeworld, poverty and illness and starvation. This blindness disconnected me from half the world, and I am a bystander, not a witness, to the society in which I live.

No amount of dissociation, however, prevents messages arriving from the unconscious. What is banished returns; the ejected, projected, comes back to attack me in fearful dreams, deep unease and, most of all, in a lack of a sense of internal safety. My disavowal robs me of innocence and free-ranging reflective capacity (Fonagy & Bateman, 2006).

So I enter the analytic space with fear that I might be confronted with what my disavowal has done, not only to others, but also to myself. If I allow myself curiosity, if I lift the blindfold, what will I see? The attack I expect, and somewhere feel I deserve, will be in the room. I arm myself with further shrouds of denial – my professional knowledge, my liberal values, my conscious good-will, my gradually growing capacity to resonate with suffering, to witness and to participate in grief. The other I encounter – with whom there is no easy moment of meeting – is divided from me by everything I have banished from conscious-ness. She is half of myself, a product of a process in which the dissociative fog has been populated by everything I cannot face about myself. The challenge, therefore, is to discover, own and resonate with my own otherness, incorporate it so that it no longer needs to live outside my own skin.

To enter my humanity fully, I must have a long look at my racist past and acknowledge its many influences on my work. My family was part of a colonial intelligentsia, a group of idealistic 'European' men and women who were very ambivalently placed in the history of the colonial exploitation of Africa. Along with missionaries, doctors and schoolteachers, my parents often found them-selves at odds with successive governments and their policies towards colonised black populations. I grew up in a rural area, with snakes sunning themselves on the back verandah and hippos trampling the nearby mielie fields. I was on a black campus, the only one of my friends who had black neighbours. My friends were horrified that I swam in the same swimming pool as black students. I hated and fought against their racism, but in some ways this overt struggle prevented me from grappling with and understanding the ways in which my family's liberalism in itself perpetuated a process of othering. We might not have been outspokenly racist, but we also did not embrace African ways of life or values, or understand how colonial education was wrenching the heart out of a civilisation that had not asked for our assistance. When white Zimbabweans were at war with black Zimbabweans, fighting for control of their own land, my family and people like us were not forced to confront our racism or die defending it. We excused ourselves as having been in opposition to successive white governments, as 'on the right side'. And we brought class with us, the gap between rich and poor growing with every decade, with whites always middle or upper class, regardless of talent, effort or industry.

Given my history, what is it that constitutes my other? Most primary for me, my other is something about the shame of living between worlds, of not belonging anywhere. I struggled with my interpellation into white Zimbabwean society, and yet understood very little about the lives of the black majority communities with which my family engaged. Shunned by my white peers, I found solace not in friendships with black children, with whom I had little contact, but in books that rehearsed endlessly the idea of Britain as 'home'. I grew up without being surrounded by a 'resonance of alikeness' (Schwaber, 1990: 229), and with this came a deep sense of shame. My encounters with difference therefore confront me with a tangled history of compromised attachments and loneliness framed by daily encounters in which I tried to pass for white, on the one hand and, on the other, to be accepted as benign by the black community my parents worked for, despite the racist policies and deeply paranoid anxiety that kept white and black apart.

Stern (1994) argues that our closest relationships, including those formed in therapeutic dyads, are driven by two forces. One is the compulsion to rehearse past trauma and to reproduce the formative attachment patterns that we acquired in the first years of our lives. The other force is a reaching for a new beginning, for the relationship that will fulfil as yet unmet needs and create opportunities to rewrite old relationship scripts. The traumatic pattern I repeat in the work I have chosen is the resonance of difference that formed my childhood environment: a psychotherapist in a university, my work seldom recognised and sometimes demonised by academic non-clinical peers, and serving a community from which I am separated by class, race and privilege. My capacity to confront this repetition, and to avoid the liberal colonialism of my parents' goodwill and good works, depends on finding a resonance of alikeness, a sense of belonging, a shared project. This must involve the reconstruction of an analytic third, that reflective space through which the therapeutic dyad together observes and constructs meaning and relationship.

INTERPELLATION AND COLLAPSE OF THE THIRD: Two case examples

A young woman, Nosisa, comes to see me. She speaks English with an accent strongly marked by her mother tongue, isiXhosa. She is employed in a large corporate setting. Her experience thus far of her working life has been traumatic. She has been bullied by men senior to her, and has felt excluded from office friendships and social banter. Feedback on her work performance has felt destructive rather than encouraging, and she has become increasingly agitated and depressed. Although she constantly questions her capabilities, and ruminates about her lack of skills and confidence, she nonetheless returns always to the idea of herself as excluded because she is a black woman in a workforce with some diversity but dominated by white men.

As I listen to her history she pours out names of sisters and brothers, cousins and aunts and uncles, names that I pronounce clumsily, forget, fumble with – a world of names that people belong to and I feel excluded from. Sometimes I ask for spellings or laugh at my thick tongue. At this stage, I feel as if I am working blindfolded, weaving my way through a maze, as I try to find the links between her current difficulties and her family history which refuses to stay in my mind, with its many comings and goings, a life scattered through enforced moves, separations, attempts to avoid apartheid schools and 'unrest'. There are too many deaths for me to hold them all, too much loss, too many moments of violent rupture. My shame stops me from asking her to teach me. Gently she teaches me anyway – about township life, the ancestors, a spirituality powerful in her life, a real force against knifings, violence and never having had enough. I am in awe of all she is, has survived, endures. I am appeasing, acquiescent. Every time she says 'in my culture…' my breath stops.

Fittingly, everything comes to a head around names. I spell her name incorrectly and the submission to her medical aid of the account for the sessions ends in queries and delays. She must correct my mistake, which she does with impatience. Between us we have created a near-perfect inversion of her workplace: she has stepped into authority and competence; I am the inefficient, unassertive outsider, struggling to catch up. We have been interpellated as a dyad into a dynamic centuries long, and coming to us through our histories of dominance and submission. The space within this for talking together about what was unfolding between us seemed to evaporate with each collision of worlds unshared. For many weeks there was no possibility of a third space, a reach for recognition.

I meet with a patient, Jacob, who suffers with emphysema. He comments often on his race, the history of race in South Africa, his encounters with shame and shaming in the past because of his racial identity, and his distrust of white people's professed willingness to take responsibility for racial atrocities. He struggles to breathe. A fold of cloth against his skin is too much weight for the bird chest to lift, and he breathes easier standing, towering over me, glistening with sweat, inches from my eyes. He seems to fight me for his breath, as if he thought I'd robbed him of it, coming here to waste it on talk. He tells me he can't do this, coming here, why can't I come to him? I am powerless in the face of this powerful lack of breath. My own lungs cannot move, I watch my breath, and swim in a hum of contested air. Why has he come today in the middle of this attack on the air? He watches me suspiciously for racist attitudes, and I find myself becoming obsequious in gesture, slave to his master. Because I am white and have lungs and because he tells me I am white and have lungs, the power between us never lies still.

REBUILDING THE ANALYTIC THIRD

In either of these cases, when was the right moment to name difference without invoking trauma, and begin building the possibility of a third? How and when did it become possible to substitute a dynamic of submission and domination for one of recognition and mutuality?

Although each of these treatments evolved in ways that made them unique and unalike, there were commonalities in structure, and it is these that need examination. In both there was a period of enactment in which we reproduced a dynamic of domination and submission, interpellated into a discourse of racial trauma and held fretfully in this dyad with no possibility of recognition or a space for an analytic third. My own subjectivity and my acute vulnerability to the dynamic slowly became accessible to me through the enactment.

We kept talking, and as themes repeated themselves, familiar ghosts of my theoretical knowledge appeared as companions, commenting occasionally, making interpretations. We had lived beyond an interpellation into discourses that divided, and reached a point of naming that was no longer traumatic, but the source of agency. So when Nosisa described to me the cruelty of her half-sister, with whom she had lived during her school years, her exclusion from family celebrations, a loveless scene of domestic servitude, I found myself able to think about the connection between this and the ongoing workplace difficulty. I had to give myself permission to float free, to coast in the intersubjective space, to trust my therapeutic skill. Similarly, my sessions with Jacob survived a long period in which his frail body and his prickly sense of discomfort in the presence of what he called my white privilege dominated the space. We came to understand his preoccupation with his body in many ways, through his attachment history and particularly in Oedipal anxiety and fears around his potency. One day, a day on which he again stood over me, struggling for breath, I found myself able to reflect with curiosity on this powerful physicality, my own sense of shrinking into my chair, his view of the top of my head, which made me feel hatless, unprotected. It was the beginning of our analytic third.

The details of these two treatments warrant much more attention. The purpose here, however, is to sketch an architecture – one now sufficiently familiar to me not only from my own therapeutic work, but also from witnessing the work of many others – that describes the shift from interpellation into traumatic discourses to the construction of a working analytic third.

The architecture is underpinned by four grounding principles.

First, I assume that the more I settle with, am aware of, my own gendered and raced history, the less likely I am to dissociate from my own otherness and to project it onto those with whom I work. What our theories teach us is that the unconscious is profoundly other, the repository of difference, an unknowable region. We cannot read it directly; if we could, it would not be unconscious. But if the unconscious remained entirely unknown to us, all would be well. However, it sends messages from the edge, post. It is never 'simply' repressed, silent or absent, just as the other calls constantly in an enigmatic way, challenging us to know her, taunting us with her presence inside ourselves, spilling through the barricades of defence, being one of us. There is no 'real' other: she is a figment of our imagination, an unconscious imagining, too unbearable to be contained in our mind, and so projected outward. The other is half of ourselves, the self we cannot consciously entertain.

Second, I carry with me a knowledge of the ways in which naming might be traumatic, unless I come to terms with the ways in which I am named. I expect names to be shared, but contextualised, like good-enough interpretations, linking their meaning, their history, their affective weight, with their defensiveness and aggression. I guard against the tendency to find being named a form of narcissistic injury.

Third, confronted with difference in subjectivities, I remind myself that my ordinary analytic skills will be adequate if I sit lightly to that difference, being careful not to use it in the service of preoccupation with myself, but rather as a place of play and curiosity.

Finally, through playfulness I assume recognition will be found. I desire a space of carnival in which identity is on display with pride and robustness, not with shame or anger.

REVISITING MEMORY AND DESIRE

Bion suggested that 'every session attended by the psychoanalyst must have no history and no future' (1967: 272). Memory of past sessions and desires about the future, in terms of outcome, curtail a readiness to be fully available in the present. The language that we use contains history within it; we can no more curtail our consciousness of it than we can shed linguistic knowledge. However, for the therapist to meet each session without an agenda involves consciousness of what that agenda might be, and acceptance of agency for its current structure, in all its complex forms. We cannot let go of agendas until we know what they are, and to know psychoanalytically is to bear the burden of history and unconscious desire. This, the fullness of history and a recognition of future dreams, and accountability to both, crafts the possibility of 'innocent' attention. Intersubjectivity instructs us to attend to the co-creation of relationships, and it is precisely the act of accepting memory and desire that gives us as therapists a glimmer of ineffability.

Part of parting with agendas, being agents, not secret agents, is coming to terms with issues of dominance and subordination, deeply embedded in linguistic forms that insist on subject–object splits, that divide us from our actions and provide us with dozens of disguises for our subjectivity. Intersubjective therapy foregrounds mutual recognition and survival of difference and, paradoxically, in this is contained the possibility of negotiation beyond the dynamic of domination, into a shared humanity.

Therapists remember the past and hold hope for the future, but sit lightly to both memory and desire; they must be authentic in their exploration of their own subjectivity but self-effacing in their expression of it; they must own authority but refuse domination; and they must have the capacity to immerse themselves in the experience of their patients but also to recognise the ways in which their own subjectivity has constructed that experience. In doing this, they face hybridity: of theory, of voice; they entertain the possibility of chaos in the carnival of identities to which they offer language.

NOTE

1   An earlier version of this chapter was published in Swartz (2007b).

REFERENCES

Bakhtin, M (1984) *Rabelais and His World* (trans. H Iswolsky). Bloomington IN: Indiana University Press.

Bakhtin, M (1990) *Art and Answerability: Early Philosophical Works by M.M. Bakhtin* (trans. V Liapunov, eds M Holquist & V Liapunov). Austin, Texas: University of Texas Press.

Bakhtin, M (1993) *Toward a Philosophy of the Act* (trans. V Liapunov, eds V Liapunov & M Holquist). Austin, Texas: University of Texas Press.

Benjamin, J (1990) *The Bonds of Love: Psychoanalysis, Feminism and the Problem of Domination*. London: Virago.

Benjamin, J (2009) A relational psychoanalysis perspective on the necessity of acknowledging failure in order to restore the facilitating and containing features of the intersubjective relationship (the shared third). *International Journal of Psychoanalysis*, 90: 441–450.

Bernard-Donals, M (1998) Knowing the subaltern: Bakhtin, carnival and the other voice of the human sciences. In M Mayerfield Bell & M Gardiner (eds) *Bakhtin and the Human Sciences*, pp. 112–127. London: Sage.

Bion, WR (1963) *Elements of Psycho-analysis*. London: William Heinemann Books.

Bion, WR (1967) Notes on memory and desire. *The Psychoanalytic Forum*, 2: 272–273.

Bollas, C (1987) *The Shadow of the Object: Psychoanalysis of the Unthought Known*. New York: Columbia University Press.

Bollas, C (1992) *Being a Character: Psychoanalysis and Self Experience*. London: Routledge.

Butler, J (1997) On linguistic vulnerability. In J Butler *Excitable Speech: A Politics of the Performative*, pp. 1–41. New York & London: Routledge.

Deleuze, G & Guattari, F (1987) *A Thousand Plateaus: Capitalism and Schizophrenia* (trans. B Massumi). Minneapolis: University of Minnesota Press.

Eagle, G (2005) Grasping the thorn: The impact and supervision of traumatic stress therapy in the South African context. *Journal of Psychotherapy in Africa*, 15: 197–207.

Fanon, F (1967) *Black Skin, White Masks*. New York: Grove Weidenfeld.

Fonagy, P & Bateman, A (2006) Mechanisms of change in mentalization-based treatment of borderline personality disorder. *Journal of Clinical Psychology*, 62: 411–430.

Gobodo-Madikizela, P (2003) *A Human Being Died that Night: A South African Story of Forgiveness*. Boston: Houghton Mifflin Co.

Graves, R (2000) *Collected Poems* (eds D Ward & B Graves). London: Penguin.

Guralnik, O & Simeon, D (2010) Depersonalization: Standing in the spaces between recognition and interpellation. *Psychoanalytic Dialogues*, 20: 400–416.

Holquist, M (1990) *Dialogism: Bakhtin and His World*. London: Routledge.

James, W (1981/1890) *The Principles of Psychology*. Cambridge, MA: Harvard University Press.

Jung, HY (1998) Bakhtin's dialogical body politics. In M Mayerfield Bell & M Gardiner (eds) *Bakhtin and the Human Sciences*, pp. 95–111. London: Sage.

Kohut, H (1971) *The Analysis of the Self*. New York: International Universities Press.

Kottler, A (1996) Voices in the winds of change. *Feminism and Psychology*, 6: 61–68.

Kristeva, J (1985) The speaking subject. In M Blonsky (ed.) *On Signs*, pp. 210–221. Baltimore: The Johns Hopkins University Press.

Lazarus, J & Kruger, L-M (2004) Small meetings: Reflections on the application of psychodynamic thought in community work with low-income South African children. *Psychoanalytic Psychotherapy in South Africa*, 12: 48–73.

Ogden, T (1982) *Projective Identification and Psychotherapeutic Technique*. New York: Aronson.

Ogden, T (1994) *Subjects of Analysis*. Northvale, NJ: Aronson.

Sachs, W (1969) *Black Anger*. New York: Grove Press.

Schwaber, E (1990) Interpretation and the therapeutic action of psychoanalysis. *International Journal of Psychoanalysis*, 71: 229–240.

Stern, DN, Sander, LW, Nahum, JP, Harrison, AM, Lyons-Ruth, K, Morgan, AC, Bruschwei-lerstern, N & Tronick, EZ (1998) Non-interpretive mechanisms in psychoanalytic ther-apy: The 'something more' than interpretation. *International Journal of Psycho-Analysis*, 79: 903–921.

Stern, S (1994) Needed relationships and repeated relationships: An integrated relational perspective. *Psychoanalytic Dialogues*, 4: 317–346.

Straker, G (2004) Race for cover: Castrated whiteness, perverse consequences. *Psychoanalytic Dialogues*, 14: 405–422.

Swartz, S (2007a) Reading psychoanalysis in the diaspora: South African psychoanalytic psy-chotherapists' struggle with voice. *Psycho-analytic Psychotherapy in South Africa*, 15: 1–18.

Swartz, S (2007b) Naming and otherness: South African intersubjective psychoanalytic psy-chotherapy and the negotiation of racialised histories. *European Journal of Psychotherapy and Counselling*, 9: 177–190.

Swartz, S & Ismail, F (2001) A motley crowd: The emergence of personality disorder as a diag-nostic category in early twentieth century South African psychiatry. *History of Psychiatry*, 12: 157–176.

Teicholz, J (1999) *Kohut, Loewald, and the Postmoderns*. Hillsdale, NJ: The Analytic Press.

Van der Kalk, BA (1996) Trauma and memory. In B van der Kalk, A McFarlane & L Weisaeth (eds) *Traumatic Stress: The Effects of Overwhelming Experience on Mind, Body and Society*, pp. 279–303. New York: The Guilford Press.

Waumsley, S & Swartz, S (2011) Individual psychotherapy as treatment of choice: Prelimi-nary findings from the UCT Child Guidance Clinic. *South African Journal of Psychology*, 41(3): 279–287.

Winnicott, D (1971) *Playing and Reality*. Harmondsworth: Penguin.

CHAPTER 2

RAISING THE COLOUR BAR: Exploring issues of race, racism and racialised identities in the South African therapeutic context

Yvette Esprey

INTRODUCTION

Positioning myself

This chapter is about race, about the space it takes up and the role it plays in the South African post-apartheid psychotherapy room. My thoughts about this have shimmered somewhere just beneath the surface of my consciousness for many years, prompted to the surface intermittently when an issue in my practice or my teaching forced it to do so, to be hastily banished by avoidant discomfort. For the most part, I have been content to adopt the oft-quoted stance that as a psychodynamically oriented clinical psychologist I maintain a neutral position in my work, and if issues of race, racism or racial identity emerge in the transference, I work with them as I would with any other dynamic. I have been loath to interrogate my own racialised self and how that impacts on the consulting environment I offer, and I have been equally reluctant to acknowledge any traces of my own prejudiced and racist positions or thoughts in my countertransference.

My submerged thoughts were shaken to consciousness when I was afforded the opportunity to participate in a post-graduate clinical social work programme at Smith College in Massachusetts, USA. Smith College has a policy of non-racism which is taken very seriously. As such, discussions about race and racism permeate every classroom interaction. At the outset, I adopted a curious but detached observer's position, wondering what I could learn from Americans about racism; what they referred to as 'the raw nerve of America'. Over the weeks that followed I was struck by the transparency and rawness with which students and faculty of all races engaged around racism, and around its potentially insidious impact on our work as clinicians. I was taken aback by the forcefulness with which students and lecturers invited participation around highly sensitive and emotive issues, and I began to allow myself to engage with an honesty and self-reflectiveness that I had not experienced before. I was aware that as much as the discussions I engaged in were uncomfortable for me, they were still far more comfortable than they would be if I were having them with clinicians and students at home, and therefore far easier to have. I made a decision then that, on returning to South Africa, I would intentionally begin to engage myself and others in these discussions. I am grateful to my Race in Psychotherapy reading group for the transparency and honesty with which we have begun to speak about issues that are deeply personal and uncomfortable, and I am grateful for the opportunities I have been given to discuss with and address colleagues about race in our profession. This chapter chronicles the evolution of my thinking.

It is my objective in this chapter to facilitate reflexivity and discussion around the concept of race as an aspect of identity which, in the person of both the patient and of the therapist, potentially exists as an alive and intrusive dynamic in the intersubjective therapeutic space. It is an aspect of identity which constitutes a complex negotiation both between and within people (Leary, 2000). I am engaging in this discussion from the vantage point afforded me by my particular historical and personal context, as a white, educated, middle-class woman, born in 1970s South Africa, at the height of apartheid. This is not a neutral position; in fact, it is a position which, because of my whiteness, is implicitly one of power and which, as suggested by Suchet (2007), can never be separated from privilege. The need to locate myself as such speaks to the powerful position which race holds as a signifier in South Africa. Positioning myself in terms of my identity and context also corresponds with Benedict's (1943) assertion that 'we must know as much about the eye that sees as about the object seen. The eye that sees is not a mere physical organ but a means of perception conditioned by the tradition in which its possessor was reared' (in Jacobsen, 1998: 10). I am acutely aware that the way in which I write, and the emphases I may choose to give and those I ignore, no matter how thoughtful, are coloured by my particular racial, gender and contextual identity. I am also aware that the fact of my racial identity will shift the way in which this chapter is read, depending on the identity and the contextual origin of the reader's 'eye'.

In writing this, I am aware of the tension within – between interrogating myself and my profession from this perspective, and avoiding doing so. The reasons for such avoidance are complex – this is an avoidance of something that feels complicated and which implicates me, my history, my behaviour and my racialised identity. It is about being afraid: of colluding, of injuring or wounding, of misrepresenting or misunderstanding, of taking a risk and opening up a pathway to a dynamic and an intersubjectively shared unconscious which is murky and threatening. In writing this I am resisting the tension and ignoring the temptation to avoid, because it is my contention that race in the therapeutic dyad has the potential to colour interactions in ways which, if unacknowledged, interrupt the therapeutic endeavour. I suggest further that quite often it does so from a relatively silent position, manifesting in small, sometimes inconceivable and yet palpable shifts in attitudes or behaviour which impact, to greater or lesser degrees, on the integrity and viability of the shared space. As Smith contends, 'it is not so much a matter of when race and racism enter the consulting room, but whether and how we notice it' (2006: 3). In this country, race holds a position in history which has aggressively and violently defined our interactions with one another, and the ways in which we perceive and react to one another. This is a country where self- and other identification on the basis of race happens automatically, almost unconsciously. It is logical then to deduce that it, too, will enter our consulting rooms, whether or not we are consciously aware of it.

Turning a blind eye

In spite of the powerful and pervasive racial flavour which permeates contemporary South African political and media rhetoric, and in the face of the evidence reflected on every street corner of our particular racialised socio-political history and context, discussion of race and racial dynamics evokes tremendous discomfort, and tends to be avoided in ordinary social discourse. Avoidance, even disavowal of the pervasiveness of the impact of our racialised history, is echoed in our clinical contexts. I suggest that the scarcity of discussion of race in therapeutic relationships, clinical supervision, reading groups, scientific meetings, continuing education contexts and in local literature speaks to a deeply entrenched avoidance of the importance of race as it potentially impacts on the clinical dyad.

This avoidance and denial is not unique to the practice of psychoanalytic psychotherapy in South Africa. Rather, it parallels the history of psychoanalytic thinking, where issues of identity – race, gender, sexual orientation – have typically not been the subject of theorising or discussion, and have remained mostly silenced in a discipline dominated by strongly patriarchal, heterosexist and white discourses (Bonovitz, 2005; Suchet, 2004a). Suchet (2004a) comments that the absence of discourse around race in psychoanalytic theory is striking and constitutes a blind spot, considering that psychoanalysis is essentially about the subjective. Over the last two decades this history has begun to be challenged by psychoanalytic theorists emerging from the intersubjective and relational moulds, and contemporary psychoanalytic journals have begun to foreground discussion and debates around the issue of race and racism in the consulting room. This trend has been slow to emerge in the South African literature. Eagle (2005b) notes that while there is an increasing amount of related local research being done in universities by post-graduate students (see Maphosa, 2003; Mbele, 2010), very little of this work is converted into publication and there is a notable lack of published writing which invites scrutiny of the racial dynamics and enactments which occur in therapeutic encounters. Significantly, much of the literature which has been published by South Africans has been done so by white clinicians who are emigrants living abroad (see Straker 2004, 2006; Suchet, 2004a). In thinking about my own experience of living abroad, I would like to suggest that stepping outside of the experience-in-the-moment of living and working in South Africa lends distance which allows for more objective and thoughtful self-reflection. Publishing from abroad may also feel less threatening than publishing from within a professional community in which speaking about race in the therapeutic encounter is distinctly uncomfortable.

While international theorists (see Altman, 1995; Bonovitz, 2005; Eng & Han, 2000; Hamer, 2002; Holmes, 1992; Leary, 2000; Smith, 2006; Suchet, 2007) offer relevant and crucial insights into race and its role in psychotherapy, the particular dynamics which come alive and evolve within the South African psychotherapeutic dynamic are specific to our unique historical, social and political landscape. This is because as much as the concept of race refers to a material reality manifesting in the physicality which becomes our first communication in the world, so too is it a social construction, with meanings which are informed by the cultural and historical milieu (Leary, 1997a). Suchet (2004a) describes race as holding a position within a transitional space between these two positions. In South Africa, the social construction of race is one which is non-static and which morphs continuously in response to shifting social and political trends. It is one which powerfully denotes class, education, geography, culture, language, history and opportunity (Swartz, 2007). As such, there is a growing imperative to build a body of writing and thinking which looks specifically at race and its impact on the practice of psychotherapy in South Africa.

Eagle notes that 'South Africa is a complex place to practice [sic] psychotherapy' (2005b: 199). While deliberate shifts within teaching and training models have been made to incorporate thinking about race as it pertains to psychotherapy, and there is a great deal of academic discussion about race and racism, there remains a notable paucity of experience-near discussion around the concept of race as it transpires in the therapeutic dyad. The use of the word 'race', itself, is laden with complex meaning and connotation, and often reference is made instead to 'culture', which becomes euphemistic for describing difference along racial lines. Eagle (2005b) interrogates the use of the word 'culture' in academic and clinical training contexts, and suggests, for example, that to refer to 'cultural alienation' rather than to being 'black' or 'white' creates less interpersonal tension. She says that ' "race" is the less acceptable sub-text of culture, disguised in this veil in academic circles in order to allow for more "civilized" kinds of dialogue' (Eagle, 2005b: 48). Eagle (2005a) inadvertently substantiates her own point in an article in which she writes about working cross-culturally in South Africa, where the word 'race' does not once appear in the text. Park (2005), in reviewing the use of the word 'culture' in clinical social work literature, suggests that it is used as a signifier of difference, and as a way of maintaining an imbalance of power where the white mainstream is culture-free, and the 'cultured' other is made visible in sharp relief. This observation feels accurate in the history of South African psychotherapy practice and training, and certainly I am aware of my own euphemistic use of the word. This semantic hypersensitivity highlights the complexity of speaking about race in South Africa, and foregrounds the dynamic of avoidance which exists in clinical contexts.

The transition in South Africa from a segregated and silenced society to one in which freedom of speech, social integration and diversity are the optimistic objectives of a new democracy, parallels a contemporary shift in South African psychoanalytic psychology towards embracing an intersubjective paradigm. This implies that the therapist's 'irreducible subjectivity' (Renik, 1993: 561) can no longer be artificially excluded from the consulting room, and increasingly psychoanalytically oriented therapists have the sanction to speak and write transparently from an experience-near perspective about the dynamics which emerge in the encounter. It is against this evolving socio-political and theoretical backdrop that the current chapter has been written.

THERE IS NO SUCH THING AS A PATIENT

To say that psychotherapy is intersubjective is a statement which is no longer debated (Spillius, 2004), just as the classical notion of the analyst as a blank screen has become obsolete in the development of psychoanalytic thinking. That the therapist inevitably brings herself into the consulting room in a way which impacts fundamentally on the encounter is a fact which is widely acknowledged by psychoanalytically oriented theorists, irrespective of where they fall on the classical–relational spectrum. In fact, it is commonly considered that some actualisation of the patient's transference and some unintentional emotional involvement on the part of the therapist are fundamental to therapeutic change (Leary, 2000).

In contrast to the classical psychoanalytic assumption of a one-person psychology, relational theories have shifted to a two-person model. The basic assumption which separates these orientations is the assertion by relationalists that it is the interpersonal relationship, rather than endogenous drives, which provides the foundation for mental life. In classical thinking, the therapist stands outside, observing the interaction, whereas from a relational standpoint the therapist is both an observer of and an inevitable participant in the relationship (Bonovitz, 2005). Interpretation becomes an interpersonal event, and the therapeutic impact of psychoanalytic psychotherapy depends on events which emerge in the interpersonal field (Altman, 1994). In quoting Faulkner in his acceptance speech for the Nobel Prize in Literature in 1950, Zeddies suggests that the analytic task is 'to create something from the human spirit which did not exist before' (2000: 461). This statement underlines the relational assumption that every therapeutic encounter is unique in that it is created by the constellation of a particular therapist and a particular patient. The outcome of each encounter, therefore, is uniquely predicted by the duet formed by each couple.

Core to the intersubjective stance is the notion of thirdness. This concept refers to that which emerges from the space between therapist and patient, and exists beyond the dyad. Green (2000) suggests that the psychoanalytic endeavour is not reducible to that which happens between two people, but that it encompasses something else which is beyond the sphere of observation. Gerson (2004: 73) refers to an 'unseen bridge' between patient and therapist, and Benjamin (2004) posits the existence of a 'third' which arises from within the dyad, and which goes beyond dyadic relating. In invoking Winnicott's assertion that there is no such thing as an infant, Ogden (1994) suggests that there is no analyst, no analysand and no analysis in the absence of the third. While the theoretical stances of each of these theorists unquestionably have significant points of departure, what they all agree on is that something unique emerges from within each encounter, and that this product is greater than the sum of its parts. They agree further that unless this notion of thirdness is thought about and brought into consciousness, the opportunity for therapeutic enactment abounds, and therapeutic action is compromised.

The irrevocable shift towards an intersubjective perspective, and the notion of a shared space which is created uniquely by two subjectivities, makes it impossible not to take into consideration how issues of identity – race, gender, sexual orientation – shape the therapeutic encounter. Both therapist and patient bring into the relationship their unique subjectivities, which include a racialised identity. Benjamin (2004) suggests that constructs such as race and culture are woven into the fabric of the dyad from the outset. Altman (1995) proposes a triadic model to make sense of the analytic space, suggesting that the 'third' is constituted by the numerous social contexts which surround both therapist and patient. Zeddies asserts that there is no such thing as an 'isolated analytic dyad', saying that:

> a full appreciation of the unconscious dimensions of an analytic situation requires seeing it as historically and culturally situated. Meaning and experience are not properties of the isolated minds of radically independent and autonomous agents, nor even of particular intersubjective contexts. People and events are embedded within certain communities and cultures. The larger political, social, moral community contextualizes the dyad. (2000: 483)

This has unassailable pertinence in the South African context. In this country any therapeutic dyad is inescapably nuanced by the individual socio-historical contexts which are brought into the room. Swartz (2007) contends that even in dyads where there is a resonance of racial alikeness between patient and therapist, race as a construct is active in the room.

In therapeutic relationships the colour of our skin is an immediate signifier of similarity or difference and carries with it composite meanings around language, class, education, history and opportunity. I am aware that when starting therapy with a patient who is of another race, I find myself thinking silent questions the answers to which begin to organise the differences which I know exist and create a chasm between us – 'Where were you born and raised?' (I was born and grew up in a segregated white suburb in a comfortable house which had running water and electricity), 'Where did you/could you go to school?' (I went to an all-white, well-resourced government school), 'Who raised you?' (I was raised by my parents, from whom I was not separated during my childhood), 'In which (apartheid) decade were you born?' As these questions form, I am equally aware of the guilt which begins to surface within me as I realise that, whether or not I sought it out, I was and continue to be a beneficiary of apartheid (Straker, 2004). This knowledge and these feelings, along with the conscious and unconscious prejudices which are part of me, accompany me into the room.

Adopting a relational stance allows us to make an assumption that the material reality of, and the social constructions around, our own and our patient's race contribute to creating an environment which is unique. In pondering the transitional nature of race, Leary states that 'race effectively functions as a fact even as it needs to be permitted to vary in each clinical dyad as a narrative possibility with meanings unique to the pair' (1997a: 163). Guided by the evidence in international (Altman, 2000; Leary, 2000; Suchet, 2004a) and local (Kilian 2010; Richards, 2010; Swartz, 2007) literature, and from my own clinical experience and collegial discussions, I assume the stance that racial identity, as a material reality and as a social construct, is an active ingredient in the shaping of therapeutic relationships. Being able to engage constructively with race as an intersubjective variable is contingent on our ability, as clinicians, to acknowledge our own racialised identity and our inability to divorce ourselves from socio-political influences, and to think about how this impacts on thirdness and on our therapeutic task.

PREJUDICED AM I

When Flaubert wrote, 'Madame Bovary, c'est moi,' he succinctly outlined the methodological task for thinking psychoanalytically about racism,

> homophobia, and misogyny. It is only an intimate familiarity – finally un-
> bearable, and therefore transient – with these deadly hatreds that gives us any
> chance to diminish their influence. (Moss, 2001: 1317)

This 'intimate familiarity' refers to the knowledge and experience which we all
have of othering (ourselves and others) on the basis of racial, sexual and gender
identity. Holding prejudices, discriminating against those dissimilar to ourselves,
is a universal human characteristic which both consciously and unconsciously
shapes internally held assumptions and social interactions. Smith (1993) encap-
sulates the undeniable social impact of racial difference in saying that 'theoretically
race is an indefensible category; practically it is an inescapable aspect of social life'
(in Leary, 1997a: 162). Fonagy (2007) and Straker (2006) both suggest that just
as we are blueprinted into our attachment styles and relational patterns through
our early relationships, so too are we blueprinted to take on specific roles and
respond to others in social contexts. Love (2000), a social theorist, contends that
through the process of socialisation we are groomed to take up roles in society.
We act out these roles unconsciously, and unless we intentionally cultivate what
she refers to as a 'liberatory' consciousness (2000: 89), we remain entrenched in
them. If this is so in our social worlds, how can we imagine that these roles are
not enacted too, unconsciously, in therapy? Straker (2006) and Altman (2000)
also speak about the presence of prejudice in all of our interactions, implying that
we classify and respond to ourselves and others along lines forged by identity, be
it gender, race or sexual orientation. This impulse to other and to discriminate
has the potential to interrupt the therapeutic endeavour, where the aim is to find
a resonance of alikeness and therefore a vehicle to empathy. Smith contends that
racial, cultural and ethnic differences are present at every moment of every therapeutic encounter, saying that 'it is around difference and otherness, be it real or
imagined, that our earliest and most primitive defenses gather to split our objects
into them and us, the feared and the safe, the loved and the hated, the privileged
and the excluded, the envied and the denigrated – the different' (2006: 9).

Stern (1991), referring to Gaddamer's assertion that prejudices and prejudgements are essential to being human, suggests that new understanding is only
possible once we have made explicit (to ourselves) the expectations which
govern and limit our formulation of experience and of the other. Similarly,
Moss (2001) and Suchet (2004a) make the point that it is only in owning prejudice as living within ourselves that we are able to begin to think about discrimination in our work.

This is a challenging and vexing notion in post-1994 South Africa. The South African Constitution ranks as a world-first in terms of its assertion of basic human rights and non-discrimination on the basis of race, gender and sexual orientation. White South Africans, in particular, are expected to denounce the racism of the past, and to both embrace and evince non-racism. This imperative, and the shame associated with it, has the potential to shut down honest discussion and the owning of prejudiced feelings. In this way, racially held views and feelings are forced underground, increasing the potential for these attitudes to manifest in unconscious and insidious ways (Hook, 2005). The danger of such enactments exists in the therapeutic context too. Intersubjective and relational models call on us as therapists to engage with the ways in which our subjectivity enters into the consulting room, and how this interacts with our patient's subjectivity, creating a uniquely shared space. This contemporary trend in psychoanalytic psychotherapy has opened up the possibility for the interrogation of therapist-held prejudices.

RACE IN THE 'RAINBOW NATION' CONSULTING ROOM

There are multiple racially linked issues which complicate the practice of psychoanalytic psychotherapy in South Africa, but it is outside the purview of this chapter to interrogate each of them. Included under this umbrella of complicating factors is the fact that prior to 1994, psychotherapy training was dominated by white students, and black[1] students were largely disadvantaged in their attempts to qualify as psychologists (Richards, 2010). This racially skewed scenario will take many years to correct, and is further exacerbated by the image of psychoanalytic psychotherapy as being a discipline of Western origin, alienating potential black students (and patients) who subscribe to alternative or traditional African ways of thinking about the complexity of human beings. In addition to this, therapeutic power dynamics, both in same-race and in mixed-race dyadic configurations, have the potential to mirror and replicate our racialised history (Swartz, 2007). Furthermore, many psychotherapists are unable to conduct therapy in the mother tongue of their patients: when black patients consult with white therapists who typically do not speak an African language well enough to converse in it, the patient has no choice but to communicate in English or Afrikaans, neither of which is their first language. Similarly, it is often the case that black psychotherapists are limited in using their own language in plying their trade – when working with white patients they are required to communicate in a second language, either

English or Afrikaans. Even when working with black patients, black therapists are often required to speak in a second or third African language (Swartz, 2007; Mbele, 2010). Many black therapists, notably, revert to a second language of either English or Afrikaans when working with white patients, or to an African language which is not their mother tongue when working with black patients. In a profession where language and words are the indispensable tools of the trade, this fact has profound implications. It is against this complex and multidimensional backdrop that South African psychotherapists meet their patients.

Unpacking the multiple forms and functions of race and racism in the room is a difficult task. Leary (2000) notes that while examples of racial enactments abound, the development of clinical theory which considers race and racial difference in clinical work is embryonic in its growth. This development can only be facilitated by open and self-reflexive discussions about the manifestation of race in the room. As such, I attempted in this section to speak about some of the ways in which race comes into the room in manifestations which are particular to the South African context. I did this within the framework provided by a relational view of psychoanalytic psychotherapy, holding in mind that both therapist and patient impact indelibly on the colour and texture of the space created between them and, as such, each therapeutic encounter is unique. Suchet's (2004b) suggestion that race occupies a position within a transitional space between being a material reality and a social construction is helpful in thinking about how race presents itself in the South African therapeutic context. Recognising that race can present as both a concrete fact, and as an abstract concept of our own construction, opens up thinking to the myriad ways in which race can emerge in the space between.

Racial enactments 'designate those interactive sequences that embody the actualisation in the clinical situation of cultural attitudes towards race and racial difference' (Leary, 2000: 639). I begin the next section by looking at the racial enactment of relative silence around race in the South African clinical encounter, which I suggest is fed by disavowal and avoidance. I suggest further that silence around race in turn entrenches avoidance and increases the difficulty clinicians have in thinking about and working with racial dynamics as they emerge. The danger is an increase in racially based therapeutic enactments and a greater potential for inviting the presence of what Straker (2006) terms an anti-analytic third. Following a discussion of the anti-analytic third, I look at how racial dynamics and stereotypes have the potential to act as a disguise for the transference, which, if not recognised as such, has the potential to distract therapist and patient from their therapeutic task. I conclude the section by looking at some of the possible enactments which can arise in same- and cross-race dyadic configurations.

Disavowal and avoidance

Through informal discussions with colleagues, across races, where I have invited them to consider whether they are aware of race in the dyad and, if so, whether and how they take it up, I have been struck by a tendency towards either colour blindness or avoidance.

Ridley (in Maphosa, 2003) describes colour blindness as a defence against unintentional racism, reflected in statements which I have heard uttered by colleagues, such as, 'My parents raised me to believe that I am equal to others, so I don't think about whether my patient is Black or White,' or 'Haven't we spoken enough about race in this country? I work with everyone as an individual, not according to their race,' or 'I work dynamically with whatever emerges in the room, why should race be different from any other manifestation of the unconscious?' These anecdotal examples of the denial which exists around the recognition of racial difference in therapeutic contexts is some indication of the difficulty which South African therapists have in talking about race and in acknowledging it as an alive presence in the dyad. Pertinent to this is Hook's (2005) warning about the dangers of the disavowal of racism. He comments on the common paradox of expressing racial tolerance and non-racism which is then coupled with behaviour which is undeniably racist. By disavowing or denying holding racist feelings, racially motivated behaviour is tolerated or excused or rendered invisible (Smith, 2006). In this way racism cannot be challenged. As clinicians, it is tempting for us to hide behind the analytic notion of therapeutic neutrality in saying that we repudiate racism and do not allow it to contaminate the therapeutic space. In doing so we ignore the deeply unconscious workings of prejudice, and run the risk of falling into the trap which Hook (2005) warns us about. I would like to suggest that, in our attempts to avoid the discomfort and pain of working openly with issues of difference, and through the denial of our own deeply embedded prejudiced attitudes and feelings, we unwittingly allow for and perpetuate racist enactments.

Avoidance of working with racial dynamics is a common occurrence in therapeutic encounters. Through conversations with colleagues and in supervisory contexts, both black and white therapists, myself included, acknowledge that bringing up the reality of the difference in the room, or responding to a patient's racially imbued communication, feels painfully difficult and uncomfortable.

In a supervisory interaction between me and a white clinician working with a black patient, the therapist describes a session where her patient, a musician, is talking about the ambivalence he feels about his profession. He has recently been selected to play in an orchestra, and while he is proud of his achievement, he also feels guilty about his chosen career because he thinks of it as being a historically 'white' profession, and he therefore associates it with 'the oppressor' and feels like he is 'sleeping with the enemy'. My supervisee responded to this by making an interpretation based on what she knows about his internal dynamics, about his powerful superego-driven impulses which tend to sabotage or spoil enjoyment of his achievements. When I asked her whether she had linked his allusion to 'sleeping with the enemy' in the form of the white 'oppressor' in any way to the fact of the bi-racial nature of their therapeutic relationship, she visibly cringed. She said that as much as the thought had crossed her mind, she had not known how to bring it into the room, and was aware of her extreme discomfort at the idea of doing so. As such, the issue of race, and of its actualisation in their relationship and in the transference, had not been spoken about. In this example, and in the vignette to follow, the appearance of race in the clinical encounter shuts down on the capacity to think and to reflect on what is happening in the relational field. In these instances, it might be said that the anti-analytic third (Straker, 2006) is in evidence.

Embarking on bi-weekly therapy with me as a newly qualified therapist in the 1990s, Denesh, an Indian patient, had sought therapy to get help in executing his 'life plan'. Although highly successful, Denesh was plagued by insecurities and low self-esteem. He had ambitious plans for himself and hoped to achieve the same measure of financial and professional success as a white friend of his, whom he described as his role model. Denesh described an impoverished childhood growing up in a two-roomed house with his parents, brother and sister. He remembered a pivotal moment which he experienced as a teenager. As a member of his school debating team, he was selected to debate against the top school in the area, a wealthy and highly resourced white boys' school. He recalled arriving at the school and looking up at the ivy-covered walls, knowing he had no place there and feeling envy and anger at his racially based disadvantage. This moment of awakening propelled him to work hard at school and he succeeded in winning a scholarship to a prestigious, traditionally white university. Denesh described the disillusionment he felt when, having gained entrance to the university, he felt no less different. He was treated differently and could not find the courage to flirt with white girls. Dating a white girl became his obsession, and while he did well in his studies, he also worked to increase his self-confidence until he finally succeeded in dating and sleeping with a white student. Throughout our therapy, Denesh repeatedly returned to the same dynamic. As an Indian man he felt inferior and, although married to an Indian woman he had met at university, he continued to pursue extramarital relationships with white women, and experienced intense, but short-lived bursts of self-esteem when he succeeded. Denesh and I were of similar ages and had grown up in the same regional area. This he acknowledged that he knew from having read the number plate on my car, parked in the driveway of my practice. He, however, had lived and schooled in the so-called 'Indian' area, and I in the apartheid-protected white suburbs. While gender-based and racially imbued material entered into the room in multiple forms throughout the therapy, I was paralysed in my inability to address it directly. I recall feeling acutely aware of my historical position of racial power and privilege relative to his, and experiencing overwhelming shame and guilt at the differences in our upbringing, which had been scaffolded by the segregation and discrimination of apartheid. My guilt and related discomfort sabotaged any embryonic thoughts that I had about linking his racially based communication to our relationship in the room, or to his attempts to feel powerful through his triumphing over and devaluing of the women in his life. I was also unable to help him reflect on the racial melancholia (Eng & Han, 2000) which manifested in his desperate attempts to be assimilated into whiteness, and in the disavowal of his own racial identity. Denesh left therapy prematurely after just a year, saying that he felt stuck and tortured and could not see his way through the impasse.

While not easily spoken about or opened up to scrutiny, these clinical scenarios are not uncommon in the South African context. Leary (2000) asserts that unless racial defences and dynamics are recognised and worked with, racial enactments will repeatedly function as detours on the therapeutic journey. Relational theorists suggest that, just as countertransference is not an ill to be eradicated from the analytic context, so too are enactments crucial therapeutic events which, if caught and made sense of, have the potential to contribute constructively to the therapeutic process (Leary, 2000). Relational theorists suggest that enactments do not happen as a matter of course, but constitute special excursions on the clinical roadmap which, through collaboration between patient and therapist, can be made sense of in a way which facilitates therapeutic growth (Leary, 2000). Renik states that enactments are a medium through which therapy progresses, and are 'the required text for the analysis of the transference' (1997: 9). There are, however, instances when an impasse occurs between patient and therapist, where the unconscious content of the enactment is not open to conscious reflection, resulting in stagnant or destructive forms of interaction. In the context of racially constructed enactments, such an impasse could signify the presence of an anti-analytic third.

The anti-analytic third

In outlining her concept of the anti-analytic third, Straker (2006) reflects on the fact that work in the therapeutic dyad is only possible when alpha functioning is present. It is only through the capacity to provide a container for thoughts that the generation of an analytic third (Ogden, 1994) is possible. As described earlier, it is in the space of thirdness that emerges from the dyad that therapeutic action occurs. During the moments of mindlessness which occur as a matter of course in therapy, as therapists we call on pre-given theory to facilitate a return to the reverie which we need to access in order to provide a containing function for our patients. In contrast, the anti-analytic third describes a mindlessness which is generated by a particular set of circumstances, a 'noxious pre-given third' that implicates our social histories as well as our personal ones. These circumstances are typically related to powerful social discourses such as racism or homophobia, and social conditions which pre-date the therapeutic endeavour are produced anew in the particular therapist–patient constellation. Straker (2006) notes that these social conditions map onto a deeply ingrained consciousness of how we see ourselves as subjects in the world, and when this is re-evoked in the therapeutic setting, the therapist is overwhelmed by aversive affects and is unable to think. In these moments we are subject not only to a dynamic unconscious, but also to social discourse.

In retrospect, it makes sense to think about the impasse reached in my therapy with Denesh as resulting from a culmination of multiple moments of mindlessness on my part, potentially attributable to the presence of an anti-analytic third.

In her moving account of a therapeutic encounter, Richards (2010), a 'coloured' South African therapist, reports an experience of the anti-analytic third as it enters her therapy room. She describes the intense countertransference she experiences when memories and thoughts about her and her family's history of forced removal, deprivation and disadvantage as a consequence of apartheid laws are evoked by the communications of her white male patient. She describes how her resentment towards her patient impeded her capacity to think about him, and resulted in moments of countertransferential enactment in the therapy which impacted on the viability of their newly formed relationship. Richards comments that:

I am mindful that the issues that are emerging and occupying me and evoking such strong countertransference could be preventing me from focusing on the therapeutic issues that are pertinent to the case rather than the noise of my own personal responses, in my relationship to myself. I needed to reclaim the capacity to think about this young man in a way that would begin to facilitate the internal work rather than hamper it. (2010: 14)

Race as a road to the unconscious

Leary (2000) contends that racial content is capable of holding multiple meanings simultaneously. Hamer (2002) speaks too about the importance (and difficulty) of holding in mind both the external and psychic realities pertaining to race. Similarly, Bonovitz (2005) suggests that race becomes most relevant in an encounter when an overlap between racial stereotypes and the transference becomes evident. In such instances the racial stereotype is used in the service of the transference.

Such was the case in my therapeutic relationship with a young woman, Angie. She came to therapy hoping to find ways of managing uncontrollable anxiety and depressive episodes. Angie described an extremely chaotic and unsettled childhood. Her father was a physically abusive alcoholic, from whom Angie's mother fled with her children when Angie was six years old. Angie's memories of her relationship with her mother are characterised by her feeling bad and not good enough. There was an absence of physical and verbal affection, and Angie felt frequently denigrated and belittled. She believed that there was something about her which was unlovable, and she longed for her mother's love which felt out of reach. Angie grew up hating herself and presented in therapy with deeply entrenched self-loathing, which manifested as a hatred of her body and physical features. Angie is a black woman. From the beginning of therapy, Angie brought material which was laden with racial meaning, making it possible for me to begin a dialogue around the fact of our bi-racial pairing. Early on, she told me that the fact of my whiteness was material to her having chosen me as a therapist. Whiteness, for her, embodies attractiveness and material success, both of which she aspires to but does not believe is attainable. She described how she hated herself for her blackness, locating all of her self-hatred on the site of her body. It seemed to me that Angie organised her self-hatred around internalised pernicious and destructive racist attributions and projections. For Angie, her blackness also operated as a metaphor for her internal dynamics, which were clustered around devaluation and the affect of shame. As our therapy progressed, it became apparent that in the transference I embodied for Angie her attractive yet unavailable and unreachable mother. I was a mother with whom she could not allow herself to be angry, because she feared the destructiveness of her anger and hatred.

This vignette illustrates Bonovitz's (2005) comment about how race can be used as a communication of the transference. He refers to Akhtar (1999, in Bonovitz, 2005), who asserted that while it is important to validate a patient's experience of racial identity as a material reality in the world, it is also the therapist's responsibility to discern when a focus on race is being used defensively or as a distraction from intrapsychic conflicts. Bonovitz (2005) contends further that by recognising the workings of race, we open up another dimension within which to work therapeutically, and within which to explore intrapsychic conflicts. He contends that mind and society constitute one another, and that our internal world is inextricably linked to and coloured by external reality. In this, the therapeutic relationship becomes a microcosm of the larger socio-cultural context. As South African therapists we cannot escape the influence of our individual experiences of the external world in which we grew up. Equally, we cannot leave these experiences at the consulting room door.

Dyadic configurations

A growing number of theorists suggest that the presence of race and culture in the clinical dyad is a given, and that such is the case irrespective of the racial composition of the therapeutic couple (Altman, 2000; Swartz, 2007). I agree with this position, and contend that because of the particular historical and current racialised milieu in South Africa, and because we all have racialised identities and histories, race is always present across dyadic configurations. As such, discrimination and prejudice are ever-ready to be mobilised and manifested as a learned way of being with another (Straker, 2006). Suchet (2007) comments, however, that much of the current writing and discussion about race in the dyad constitutes an exploration of otherness when a patient of a different racial group enters the room, and that little attention has been given to the manifestations of racial influence in same-race couplings. As we enter for the first time into a therapeutic encounter, race becomes an immediate signifier of sameness or difference which circumscribes ways of being and relating. Even in same-race dyads where there is a 'resonance of alikeness' (Swartz, 2007), the potential for racially based enactments occurs. Mbele (2010) talks about the racially based assumptions which black patients hold about their black therapists and vice versa, and similarly white patients expect a resonance of outlook from their white therapists.

Mbele (2010), Yi (1998) and others contend that minority therapists[2] are more aware of and attuned to the impact of their race on the newly forming relationship, and that white therapists are less so. When seeing white patients, South African black therapists report feeling self-conscious and anxious about the reactions that their being black evokes. Similarly, when seeing black patients, black therapists in this country become aware of intra-black differences which organise around culture, language, social class, education and opportunity. They also have in mind assumptions that black patients may hold and express about them being affiliated to the profession of psychology, which is a traditionally 'white' profession. Similarly, Leary (2000) describes a situation where a black patient questions Leary's 'blackness' when the patient hears that she has decided to train further in psychoanalysis, a traditionally white and Western institution. She says to Leary (2000: 644), 'Are you really Black?'

This hyper-awareness that black therapists have around the fact of their race, and the relative lack of conscious awareness of their race on the part of white therapists, does not make the material reality of whiteness any less significant. It also does not mean that race is not present as a site for enactment in all-white therapeutic dyads. I would go so far as to say that precisely because race in the dyad is not being thought about as consciously by white therapists as it is by black therapists, it becomes a vehicle for unconscious enactments by both patient and therapist. An example of this is seen when race becomes a means of expressing intrapsychic conflicts for victims of trauma (Benn, 2007). The expression of strongly held racist views by patients is often reported by white therapists working with victims of trauma, where, quite often, perpetrators of the incidents are black men. Therapists report feelings of discomfort when trauma victims make racist comments or use racist slurs when referring to black perpetrators, or when they preface racially based comments by saying things like 'you know how *they* are' or '*you* know what I mean'. I suggest that it is precisely because of a resonance of white alikeness, and the shared attitudes and outlook which patients then assume, that they feel able to channel unconscious communication in the guise of racist thoughts and sentiments. This resonance of alikeness creates an intersubjective climate which allows for expression of feeling in a way which would be fundamentally different if the dyad were racially mixed.

White therapists acknowledge that at times when patients make racially based comments, they find themselves resonating with what patients are saying, and they then experience guilt and shame at their own racist attitudes. They describe also feeling torn in the moment, between confronting and working with the racism in the room, and working with it as a vehicle for psychodynamic communication. They acknowledge the extreme discomfort which emerges at the thought of having to name the racism in the room, and open it up to dialogue. It is precisely these moments of mindlessness – when noxious social discourses around race meld with our own personal histories and experiences – which have the potential to interrupt the therapeutic process and create an anti-analytic third (Straker, 2006). At these moments it becomes difficult if not impossible for therapists to think about the unconscious meaning behind what is being communicated. Thinking about ourselves as racialised beings and acknowledging the presence of race in our therapeutic encounters, is the first step to releasing such moments of stuckness which impede us in our therapeutic task.

The elephant in the room

Much of what has been written about race in the encounter has emerged in American literature where the racial dynamics are particular to American history and context. I suggest that the relative absence of published clinical material which details the workings of race in therapeutic interactions in South Africa might be considered to be a racially based enactment on the part of the profession. Leary (2000) asserts that the most common enactment around race is the relative silence about racial issues, both in the therapy room and within the therapeutic community. She describes race as 'one of the most vulnerable of social discourses' and goes on to say that racial experience may be thought about as 'unformulated experience' (Leary, 2000: 640) which is 'experience that is not yet reflected on or linguistically coded but which remains part of our everyday psychic grammar' (Stern, 1997, in Leary, 2000: 641). I suggest that this concept is useful in the South African context where multiculturalism and diversity characterise public rhetoric, but where speaking about issues of race feels precarious and frightening. As clinicians, it is incumbent on us to equip ourselves with an increasingly complex and textured lexicon which will enable us to identify, name and work with the manoeuvrings of race in our consulting rooms. It is also incumbent upon us to begin to dialogue with our colleagues about who we are, and about the impact of race on our profession and collegial relationships.

Race manifests in therapy and in our profession in multiple potential ways. As therapists, developing a sense of our own racialised identity opens the door to attunement around race-bound communication in the room. The task before us is to work collaboratively with our patient in interpreting the role of race in our unique dyad. This process of collaboration begins by acknowledging the presence of the rainbow-coloured elephant in the room, and inviting it to sit down with us.

CONCLUDING THOUGHTS

In this chapter I have attempted to foreground race as an active third (Altman, 1995) in the South African therapeutic encounter. I positioned this within a relational paradigm, which assumes that each member of the clinical dyad brings to the space their unique subjectivity. This subjectivity includes deeply entrenched and developmentally imprinted prejudices and prejudgements, as well as our own particular socio-cultural and racialised histories. It is my hope that opening up a dialogue about race will help to distil the anxiety which local clinicians may have in exposing their work to scrutiny. It is only through accumulating and making sense of clinical material that theory is able to develop (Lemma, 2003), and as such it is important that we resist the urge to remain silent about our enactments around race in our clinical encounters.

Thinking about race and its clinical workings is not a theoretical exercise; it directly implicates the self. Miehls (2001) challenges us to consider the role which racial identity plays in our internal world. He contends that if as therapists we do not examine or articulate our racial identity, we are compromised in our ability to integrate the other when we think about or engage around difference. Swartz (2007), too, calls on clinicians to intentionally scrutinise our racialised histories and selves, in order to minimise the likelihood of dissociation when faced with otherness. If we can come to terms with our own prejudices and limitations, we will more likely be able to be curious and engaged when confronted with difference in the room. Both Miehls (2001) and Swartz (2007) identify empathy as the essential variable which is compromised if we do not work on creating self-awareness and reflexivity around issues of race. Miehls offers an eloquent definition of empathy as he understands it from an intersubjective perspective:

> Empathizing implies that one allows one's own subjectivity to be sufficiently altered so as to allow space for inclusion of the world of the other…one will be sufficiently impacted by the world of the other to allow oneself to be fundamentally reshaped…It is the integration of the other into my sense of self and identity that will substantively change who one is in relation to the other. (2001: 241)

This definition of empathy feels relevant to the work around race and racial difference which awaits us as therapists in South Africa. In working with patients, I am aware of how the space between us opens up and increases in intimacy and depth when we begin to explore the racialised selves which we both bring into the room. This is typically an experience which brings discomfort, but the constructive outcome of sitting with this discomfort becomes evident as the relationship and the work deepen. I have experienced this too in my collegial reading group where, over time, we have begun to trust each other enough to speak with honesty about our experiences of race, both in therapy and in our social worlds. I suggest that such dialogue is essential to the growth of our profession in this country. As I conclude this chapter I am aware that I am challenging myself and my colleagues to begin to speak and write about an issue which has always been present, but which we have been more comfortable hiding. In so doing, I invoke Robert Frost's invitation to 'take the road less travelled', believing that, in doing so, it will make all the difference.

NOTES

1   I use 'black' to refer to South Africans who were previously disadvantaged. When applicable in the text, I use specific racial categories such as 'Indian' or 'coloured' to refer to particular racial groups.
2   While in South Africa, black people constitute the numerical majority, minority in this context relates to that which deviates from the standard of whiteness which universally denotes being racially majoritarian (Krog, 2010).

REFERENCES

Altman, N (1994) A perspective on child psychoanalysis 1994: The recognition of relational theory and technique in child treatment. *Psychoanalytic Psychology*, 11: 383–395.

Altman, N (1995) *The Analyst in the Inner City: Race, Class, and Culture through a Psychoanalytic Lens.* Hillsdale, NJ: The Analytic Press.

Altman, N (2000) Black and white thinking: A psychoanalyst reconsiders race. *Psychoanalytic Dialogues*, 10: 589–605.

Benjamin, J (2004) Beyond doer and done to: An intersubjective view of thirdness. *Psychoanalytic Quarterly*, 73: 5–46.

Benn, M (2007) Perceived alterations in racial perceptions of victims of violent crime. Unpublished research report. Department of Psychology, University of the Witwatersrand.

Bonovitz, C (2005) Locating culture in the psychic field: Transference and countertransference. *Contemporary Psychoanalysis*, 41: 55–76.

Eagle, G (2005a) Therapy at the cultural interface: Implications of African cosmology for traumatic stress intervention. *Psychology in Society*, 30: 1–22.

Eagle, G (2005b) 'Cultured clinicians': The rhetoric of culture in clinical psychology training. *Psychology in Society*, 32: 41–64.

Eng, DL & Han, S (2000) A dialogue on racial melancholia. *Psychoanalytic Dialogues*, 10: 667–700.

Fonagy, P (2007) The development of prejudice: An attachment theory hypothesis explaining its ubiquity (with A Higgitt). In H Parens, A Mahfouz, S Twemlow & D Scharff (eds) *The Future of Prejudice: Psychoanalysis and the Prevention of Prejudice*, pp 63–79. Lanham/Boulder/New York/Toronto/Plymouth: Rowman & Littlefield Publishers.

Gerson, S (2004) The relational unconscious: A core element of intersubjectivity, thirdness, and clinical process. *Psychoanalytic Quarterly*, 73: 63–98.

Green, A (2000) The intrapsychic and intersubjective in psychoanalysis. *Psychoanalytic Quarterly*, 69: 1–39.

Hamer, FM (2002) Guards at the gate: Race, resistance, and psychic reality. *Journal of the American Psychoanalytic Association*, 50: 1219–1237.

Holmes, DE (1992) Race and transference in psychoanalysis and psychotherapy. *International Journal of Psychoanalysis*, 73: 1–11.

Hook, D (2005) The racial stereotype, colonial discourse, fetishism, and racism. *The Psychoanalytic Review*, 92: 701–734.

Jacobsen, MF (1998) Introduction: The fabrication of race. In MF Jacobsen *Whiteness of a Different Color*, pp. 1–12. Cambridge, MA: Harvard University Press.

Kilian, D (2010) Contextual twinship: Race in my post-apartheid therapy room. *International Journal of Psychoanalytic Self Psychology*, 5: 483–487.

Krog, A (2010) *Begging to be Black*. Cape Town: Random House Struik.

Leary, K (1997a) Race in psychoanalytic space. *Gender and Psychoanalysis*, 2: 157–172.

Leary, K (1997b) Race, self-disclosure, and 'forbidden talk': Race and ethnicity in contemporary clinical practice. *Psychoanalytic Quarterly*, 66: 163–189.

Leary, K (2000) Racial enactments in dynamic treatment. *Psychoanalytic Dialogues*, 10: 639–653.

Lemma, A (2003) *Introduction to the Practice of Psychoanalytic Psychotherapy*. Chichester: Wiley.

Love, BJ (2000) Developing a liberatory consciousness. In M Adams, WJ Blumenfeld, R Sastaneda, HW Hackman, ML Peters & X Zunigo (eds) *Readings for Diversity and Social Justice: An Anthology on Racism, Anti-Semitism, Sexism, Heterosexism, Abelism and Classism*, pp. 470–474. New York: Routledge.

Maphosa, MJ (2003) Black clients' personal experiences of therapy having been in therapy with a white female therapist or counselor. Unpublished research report. University of the Witwatersrand, Johannesburg.

Mbele, Z (2010) *Black Clinical Psychologists' Experiences of Race in Psychodynamic Psychotherapy*. MA research report, Department of Psychology, University of the Witwatersrand, Johannesburg. Accessed from http://wiredspace.wits.ac.za/jspui/bitstream/10539/11305/1/Black%20clinical%20psychologists%20experiences%20of%20race%20in%20psycho-dynamic%20psychotherapy%202011b.pdf on 31 October 2012.

Miehls, D (2001) The interface of racial identity development with identity complexity in clinical social work student practitioners. *Clinical Social Work Journal*, 29(3): 229–244.

Moss, D (2001) On hating in the first person plural: Thinking psychoanalytically about racism, homophobia and misogyny. *Journal of the American Psychoanalytic Association*, 49: 1315–1334.

Ogden, T (1994) The analytic third: Working with intersubjective psychological facts. *International Journal of Psycho-analysis*, 75: 3–19.

Park, Y (2005) Culture as deficit: A critical discourse analysis of the concept of culture in contemporary social work discourse. *Journal of Sociology and Social Welfare*, 32(3): 11–33.

Renik, O (1993) Analytic interaction: Conceptualizing technique in light of the analyst's irreducible subjectivity. *Psychoanalytic Quarterly*, 62: 553–571.

Renik, O (1997) Conscious and unconscious use of the self. *Psychoanalytic Inquiry*, 17: 5–12.

Richards, C (2010) When race gets in the way: Transference, counter-transference and the challenge of keeping personal issues to a whisper. Paper presented at the South African Psychoanalytic Conference, Solms-Delta Farm, Franschhoek, February.

Smith, D (1993) Let our people go. *Black Scholar*, 23(3/4): 74–76.

Smith, HF (2006) Invisible racism. *Psychoanalytic Quarterly*, 75: 3–19.

Spillius, EB (2004) Comments on Owen Renik. *International Journal of Psycho-analysis*, 85: 1057–1061.

Stern, DB (1991) A philosophy for the embedded analyst: Gadamer's hermeneutics and the social paradigm of psychoanalysis. *Contemporary Psychoanalysis*, 27: 51–80.

Straker, G (2004) Race for cover: Castrated whiteness, perverse consequences. *Psychoanalytic Dialogues*, 14: 405–422.

Straker, G (2006) The anti-analytic third. *Psychoanalytic Review*, 93: 729–753.

Suchet, M (2004a) A relational encounter with race. *Psychoanalytic Dialogues*, 14: 423–438.

Suchet, M (2004b) Whiteness revisited: Reply to commentary. *Psychoanalytic Dialogues*, 14: 453–456.

Suchet, M (2007) Unraveling whiteness. *Psychoanalytic Dialogues*, 17: 867–886.

Swartz, S (2007) The power to name: South African intersubjective psychoanalytic psychotherapy and the negotiation of racialized histories. *European Journal of Psychotherapy and Counselling*, 9(2): 177–190.

Yi, KY (1998) Transference and race: An intersubjective conceptualization. *Psychoanalytic Psychology*, 15: 245–261.

Zeddies, TJ (2000) Within, outside, and in between: The relational unconscious. *Psychoanalytic Psychology*, 17: 467–487.

CHAPTER 3

SUBJECTIVITY AND IDENTITY IN SOUTH AFRICA TODAY

Glenys Lobban

In this chapter South African subjectivities and identities will be explored. Mama defines subjectivity as 'the conscious and unconscious thoughts and emotions of the individual, her sense of herself and her ways of understanding her relation to the world' (1995: 2). She argues that subjectivity is constructed through the 'constant resonance between psychodynamics and social experience' (1995: 133). Historically, psychologists have tended to address identity and subjectivity at the micro level, focusing on a particular individual patient and how she[1] sees herself at both the conscious and the unconscious levels, how her subjectivity developed and the interventions which could be used to help her to expand and transform her sense of identity. This approach has been critiqued in recent years and a new crop of analytic theorists have argued that we cannot understand the individual separate from her social milieu and that individual and social factors are inter-implicated in the development of subjectivity and identity (see Dimen, 2011).

Questions about how identity should be defined are especially evocative in the South African context. In apartheid South Africa the state played a particularly obtrusive role in the constitution of subjectivities, which made it patently obvious that identity was not simply an individual choice. Under apartheid, the government 'went to macabre lengths to distinguish groups by race' (Orkin & Jowell, 2006: 284) and racial identity was externally imposed on all individuals, who were defined as either 'white' or 'non-white' (Africans, Indians, Asians, coloureds). Ethnicity/race was elevated as the superordinate category for defining identity in the apartheid state, which also 'denied a sense of "South Africanness" to the majority of citizens' (Grossberg et al., 2006: 72). The government 'enforced social and spatial segregation between ethnic groups both to satisfy the dominant ideology and to ensure differential access to resources and power' (Orkin & Jowell, 2006: 284). The doctrine of white supremacy had a profoundly negative impact on individuals who were classified as not 'white', an impact that affected both their material circumstances and their psyche and self-evaluations (Biko, 1970, 1971). Those classified as 'white' under apartheid reaped material benefits, but their sense of identity was also racialised and circumscribed.

In 1994 apartheid was replaced by a non-racial, majority-rule liberal democracy. One of the new government's goals was to facilitate liberation from these apartheid, colonial, race-based identities. This raised the question of how South Africans should define their sense of identity, what categories would replace the old apartheid taxonomy. Since 1994, politicians and academics have debated the 'question of how to build a common sense of belonging to the South African nation' (Roefs, 2006: 77) among the diverse groups that make up the South African 'rainbow nation'. The 2003 South African Social Attitudes Survey, a national survey of approximately 2 500 South Africans, investigated whether these attempts to change the form of South African identity had been successful. Some interesting trends emerged regarding people's conscious ideas about their social identities. The individuals surveyed felt a strong sense of identification with South Africa: 83% of respondents said they would rather be a citizen of South Africa than any other country, and 93% were proud of being South African (Grossberg et al., 2006: 58). There was evidence that 'a national identity is in the process of formation' and that many South Africans had 'dual identities' (Roefs, 2006: 94), where they combined a strong national identity as a South African with a strong race, class or language identity. Also, 'identity markers' were shown to have broadened beyond race. When individuals were asked to choose their primary identity marker, family was first choice of identity (29%), followed by race or ethnic background (22%), occupation (17%), gender (10%) and nationality (8%). There was a larger variety of identity markers when compared with 1998, when 40% of South Africans chose race as their primary identity (Grossberg et al., 2006: 67).

Like individuals everywhere else in the world (see Bromberg, 1998), these South African subjects proved to be multifaceted; they had developed multiple lenses through which they viewed themselves: family, gender, ethnicity, class, peers, sexual orientation, religion, tribe, workplace, language, nation. Their subjectivity was made up of a melange of conscious thoughts and ideas about their various identities or selves, interwoven with unconscious judgements and feelings about these selves. I believe that some of the broad political questions about how to build a South African identity could be better addressed if psychologists developed more specific theories and data regarding the development of subjectivity in South African subjects. In service of such specificity, in this chapter I interrogate the development of racialised subjectivity in an individual case – the 'patient' is a South African born in apartheid South Africa in 1949. It is my hope that my discussion will have relevance beyond the psyche under apartheid, and that it will help to explain the development of racialised subjectivity, and subjectivity in general. I describe the work of two prominent theorists on the self and subjectivity, namely Philip Bromberg and Amina Mama, and use their ideas to illuminate the case. I conclude with a discussion of some broader questions related to psychotherapy and identity in South Africa today.

THE WORK OF BROMBERG AND MAMA ON SUBJECTIVITY

Psychoanalytic theories enhance our understanding of how an individual's self and identity develop within the context of her nuclear family, but they have certain defects when we try to use them to understand how identity and subjectivity develop. Firstly, psychoanalytic theories often tend to define 'identity' as unitary, assuming that each individual has one 'self' or 'personality' that is invariant across different roles and situations. Philip Bromberg (1998) has tried to correct this emphasis and I will briefly describe his work on multiplicity. A second problem with psychoanalytic theories is that they do not focus sufficiently on how culture shapes subjectivity, how 'the construction of personal identity is a complex continuing affair in which we are inscribed in culture in a myriad of contradictory ways' (Rivera, 1989: 28). I outline some of Amina Mama's (1995) ideas about how the subject is socially constructed.

Bromberg argues that personal identity, the 'sense of me-ness' (1998: 273), is constituted by multiple different subjectivities. He views the mind as 'a loose configuration of multiple self-states' (1998: 12). Our sense of 'being a self' (1998: 181), of possessing a 'unitary self', is a 'necessary illusion' (1998: 12), which 'depends on the presence of an ongoing dialectic between the separateness and unity of one's self-states, allowing each to function optimally without foreclosing communication and negotiation between them' (1998: 272). The 'ability to stand in the spaces between realities without losing any of them' (1998: 273) is what constitutes psychological health. (Occasional moments of dissociation do occur in the healthy individual but they are fleeting and easily reversed.) Bromberg argues that each individual has 'a set of discrete, more or less overlapping schemata of who he [sic] is' (1998:181). Each of these is 'organized around a particular self-other configuration which is held together by a uniquely powerful affective state' (1998:181). Over time, these self–other configurations become more coherent and this 'comes to be experienced as a cohesive sense of personal identity – an overarching feeling of being a self' (1998: 181). Some individuals cannot 'stand in the spaces', their self-states do not all fit under 'the umbrella of me-ness' (1998: 273). The sense of personal identity of these people is predicated on 'the dissociative unlinking of self-states' and is tightly located 'within whichever self-state has access to consciousness and cognition at a given moment' (1998: 12).

Bromberg does not specifically address the way in which culture impacts the formation of a person's individual self-states, or the way in which culture might shape how the sum of the self-states is organised. He references culture obliquely via his references to the 'other'. In his theory, each self-state has a particular set of powerful affects that adheres to it. Self-states develop out of interactions between the self and the other. Bromberg does not specify whether he thinks these 'others' are acting as the representatives of the culture or simply as individuals. He also does not consider whether social factors impact on how an individual groups and organises her selves, whether she can experience her set of selves in a flexible way and 'stand in the spaces', or whether she has to resort to dissociation and foreclose her identity. In a recent paper (Lobban, in press), I suggested that the culture's response to the individual affects the ways in which she configures her self. I investigated the subjectivity of immigrants to North America and found that an immigrant who feels accepted and positively evaluated by American culture will see her various selves positively, and will be able to experience her multiplicity and 'stand in the spaces'. However, an immigrant who is relentlessly interpellated as 'the second class other' by the culture (for example, a poor immigrant of colour, who speaks little English), will be particularly susceptible to defining herself in negative terms. She might try to protect her self esteem by dissociating her 'foreign' selves as 'not-me' and defining only a narrow band of 'American' self-states as acceptable, as 'me'. (Lobban, in press)

The work of Mama (1995) explicitly addresses how a person's subjectivity, her experience and evaluation of herself, is formed in interaction with her social milieu. Mama argues that subjectivity is 'both individual and socio-historical at the same time' (1995: 62). The individual's subjectivity is constructed through the 'constant resonance between psychodynamics and social experience' (1995: 133), through the dialectical relationship between discourse (which resonates with and echoes 'the institutionalized and formal knowledges, assumptions and ideologies of a given social order') and psychological factors (1995: 98.). Mama argues that 'both discourses (theorized as conveyors of history, culture and social meaning) and individual subjects are produced in a continuous dialectic, out of reverberations between historical-cultural and psychological conditions' (1995: 133). Every individual occupies 'a variety of subject positions' (1995: 117) at any one time and racialised subjectivity is but one dimension of subjectivity. Mama offers a critique of western psychologists who define being black solely as a lack of 'whiteness', and therefore identify 'white racism as the sole factor in Black identity' (1995: 52). She argues that identity among black Africans is influenced by many factors beyond white prejudice and racism, and that 'the cultural reservoirs of thousands of years of history make colonial racial attitudes more marginal' (1995: 105) in their impact on self-esteem and subjectivity than they are in certain other areas, such as the Caribbean. Racialised subjectivity is just 'one dimension of subjective processes which involve constant negotiations and change in the course of social relations' (Mama, 1995: 142). Mama says that people are 'not simply either black or white but rather complex, multilayered beings, with a capacity to move between positions, create new ones, and constantly negotiate and re-negotiate their identities as they struggle to make sense of a world in which fixed categories are constantly subverted and changed' (1995: 142). Mama offers a methodology for interrogating a person's subjectivity and inscription by culture; she describes a case study of a group of black women in the United Kingdom where she was the participant observer. She gathered information from these women about how they constructed their own subjectivities; how they experienced themselves via the lenses of race and gender, and the particular discourses that influenced them (Mama, 1995).

A CASE STUDY: The development of racialised subjectivity

The work of Bromberg and Mama offers a framework with which to conceptualise the case I wish to investigate. My case study deals with one family and is a vivid illustration of the impact of cultural categories on subjectivity. There is one unusual thing about my case: I am the subject of the case study; it is my subjectivity I will interrogate. I am able to put my own subjectivity under the microscope because an unexpected event occurred in my life which made me feel turned totally inside out. My mother Margaret, who had stage four breast cancer, revealed a family secret at a family braai in Cape Town in 2004, which totally surprised us all. She told our assembled extended family that my maternal grandmother Nellie was actually coloured, but had 'passed' as white her whole life. I felt like a bolt of lightning had smashed into me, and all I could do was hope that my identity was shatterproof. I had my mitochondrial DNA tested in South Africa in 2006, after my mother died. The test showed that I am not 'white' genetically; I am 'Eurasian', mixed race, a mixture of European and Asian. My closest current genetic matches are individuals in India, Sri Lanka and the Maldive islands. (The laboratory director expects to find South African matches for me once their database gets larger.) These events set off a cascade of reactions within me, and gave me a front row seat from which to observe my own racialised subjectivity and how I had been inscribed by apartheid.

Before I describe what I discovered about my subjectivity, I will give a brief family history and introduce my maternal grandmother, Eleanor Marie Browne, who was always called Nellie. (Some of this history is factual – it is based on documents and photographs in my family's possession – but a lot of it is less objective and is based on my conjectures, and the questions that occurred to me as I assimilated the information my mother had so dramatically revealed.) My mother was deeply attached to her mother, Nellie, so Nellie's personality and values infused my childhood even though she died when I was just eight months old. My maternal grandmother's family was a uniquely South African melange. Alfred, Nellie's 'white' English father, arrived in Cape Town after a long sea voyage in 1890. South Africa was the land of opportunity for white colonials like Alfred. He was an electrician who came to seek his fortune in South Africa, accompanied by his two sisters. In Cape Town he met Adinah, my maternal grandmother, and they got married. Adinah was an educated young woman from a relatively successful coloured family. It is likely that she lived in a mixed working-class neighbourhood like District Six when they met. (In the 1890s, segregation by race existed in the Cape but it was not enforced by law [Magubane, 2010]. Some mobility based on class was thus possible for some coloureds.)

Lured by the glint of gold, Alfred and Adinah set off in an ox wagon for Johannesburg, 1 000 miles away. We have a faded sepia photograph of Adinah and her sisters-in-law, attired in long Victorian skirts and English hats, sitting in their ox wagon en route to the goldfields. Nellie was born in Johannesburg in 1894. Alfred got a job as an electrician on a gold mine. The Brownes lived as a white family in Johannesburg, thrived financially and became middle class and Nellie and her sister went to white schools and churches. After Nellie had finished high school, she began training for a career as an operatic soprano. Her mother Adinah died of influenza when Nellie was 18 years old. We have no information about what went on at the psychological level in any of our cast of characters. How did Alfred feel about the fact that Adina was coloured? Did they inform their daughters that they were bi-racial? How was it decided that the children and Adinah should 'pass' as white?

When she was in her twenties Nellie fell in love with Edward, yet another English immigrant seeking his fortune in South Africa. Edward got a job as a mining engineer in modern-day Namibia, 2 000 miles away. The couple settled down in Windhoek and had two children in rapid succession (my mother, Margaret, was the younger child), but then tragedy struck and Edward died of Hodgkin's disease. Nellie returned to Johannesburg and tried to figure out how to support her two children. The family was extremely poor. In the early years Nellie worked as a live-in housekeeper in private homes, stipulating to her employers that her children had to accompany her. After many years of hardship, she rented her own home in Johannesburg and opened a typing school for young women. Nellie was a devout Episcopalian and she sang in the church choir every Sunday morning. She was also a medium with second sight, so on Sunday nights she and her children were regulars at the séances that were held at a local spiritualist community. We do not know whether Nellie shared the fact that she was bi-racial with her husband Edward or whether she stood guard over her secret all through her life, a lonely sentinel. I like to think that Edward, a romantic and a poet, knew her secret and didn't give two hoots about it. Despite many offers, Nellie refused to remarry, claiming religious reasons – that God assigns everyone only one true partner – but I now wonder whether she avoided remarriage because she feared that the fact that she was passing as white would be revealed.

Nellie never admitted to my mother that she was bi-racial or that Adinah was coloured. My mother explained to me that she had figured out the family secret by the time she was 10 years old, from hints her mother had let slip. Her mother often told her: 'There is only one thing about myself that I regret and really wish I could change,' but she would not reveal what that thing was. Once my mother was alerted to the existence of a 'secret', she kept trying to piece stray bits of information together and puzzle out what it was. She said: 'I finally figured it out, I realised my mother was coloured, that when she said she wished she could change one thing she meant she wished she could change her race and be all white.' (I have a different association to my grandmother's lament; I believe that the thing my grandmother wished she could change or end was her 'passing' – she wished she could stop 'passing' and relax all the vigilance that 'passing' must have necessitated.) Until she revealed all at the family braai when she was 80, my mother never discussed the 'secret' with anyone, including her own brother. He remained in denial even after the family braai, saying, 'That's just like Margaret; she always tries to find a way to be centre stage whenever our family gets together.' My mother was in a loving marriage with my father for more than 30 years, but she never told him her 'secret'. My father Archie adored my beautiful, brilliant mother and offered his support and unconditional acceptance to her as a salve for her bottomless insecurity. I wonder what my father would have made of my mother's secret. He was a South African, with that paternalistic brand of racism found in many English-speaking whites. How would he have contained the contradictions between his abiding love for my mother and his prejudicess about coloureds? Did he perhaps have suspicions about Margaret's coloured roots which he chose not to air for some reason?

I asked my mother why she finally decided in 2004 to reveal the family secret. Her answer was:

> Now we are in the new South Africa and apartheid is really dead, it is safe for me to tell you about Nellie and her mother. If other people find out, nobody can report us to the police, or throw us out of our house or school and move us to a coloured area.

Her words parted a stage curtain for me, and suddenly the drama of a life spent 'passing for white' came alive in front of me. Now I had insight into the origins of my mother's relentless self-doubt. She was smart, vivacious and very beautiful, but she was riddled with concerns about being good enough, about how other people evaluated her. As a child I formulated a class-based interpretation of my mother's brittleness; I saw it as the fallout from her impoverished childhood. Now I suddenly saw that her fragile self-esteem was a side effect of her 'passing': my mother lived in fear of being unmasked as a fraud, her 'white' life snatched away, punishment meted out by the authorities. In addition, she had internalised the apartheid government's adulation of 'whiteness' (Suchet, 2007) and this coloured her self-image and her image of her mother, whom she also adored. My mother was happy and productive during much of her life, presumably because she managed to dissociate her self-states that were derived from her coloured origins. Now that I have laid out the bare bones of my family story, I will try to analyse my subjective experience as I lived inside that story. Let me rapidly make a disclaimer and give a testimonial about my politics, because I am about to enter the uncomfortable underbelly of racism. I have always been a passionate advocate of social justice. In my youth I fought against apartheid and left South Africa to escape my automatic white privilege.

My mother's revelation had a profound impact on me, even though it did not change my actual life circumstances in any way. Initially, before my DNA test, I was very excited about being genetically Eurasian; I began to feel more a part of the new 'rainbow nation', more of an 'us' than a 'them'. White South African friends joked that I could trade in my 'white guilt' (Straker, 2007). An unexpected chain of events occurred after the laboratory director phoned me in New York to tell me my DNA results. He explained that a call was standard practice when the laboratory had sensitive information which disconfirmed the client's current ethnic label. I felt that he called because he had bad news to impart (the way it is the doctor, not the nurse, who calls if the biopsy turned up cancer). I did not set eyes on him, but I imbued him with medical authority and assumed from his accent that he was a white South African. He told me that I was not white in genetic terms, I was 'Eurasian'. I was 'interpellated'. Dimen defines interpellation as 'the process by which subjectivity is hailed into being' by the state (2011: 6). The laboratory director hailed me as 'Eurasian' and I felt as if he was branding me with a negative label, as if being 'Eurasian', being not pure white, was something to be ashamed of. Suddenly my excitement about my new status dissolved. 'I found out that I was not all White, but I felt that I was not White at all' (Lobban, 2011a: 84). I unconsciously applied to myself the one-drop rule (Broyard, 2007) which was used in apartheid South Africa to define race. I concluded that even one drop of coloured blood dissolved all my 'whiteness'. I lost my subjective experience of myself as white. The next thing I experienced was a dramatic drop in my self-esteem. I felt a sense of malaise and emptiness. This is how I described it in my journal:

> I look at myself and find fault with everything about me, my smile, my voice, my body. I have a sense of not fitting into my skin right, like my skin shrunk in the dryer, and I am trying desperately to get it on. I am not who I seem to be, I am wearing a mantle I do not deserve to wear.

My 'whiteness' had cushioned me and bolstered my self-esteem, confidence and entitlement. Now I felt like a decrepit old car that was not firing on all cylinders, and was leaking self-esteem.

I visited the Iziko Slave Lodge Museum in Cape Town, where I learned more about the history of the coloureds. South African coloureds are descended from the 63 000 slaves that the Dutch East India Company brought to the Cape between 1658 and 1795. Most of them came from around the Indian Ocean: Mozambique, Madagascar, India, Sri Lanka and the Indonesian islands. I was extremely upset about some of the information I gleaned about the conditions of slaves at the Cape in the 18th century, particularly the problems experienced by the female slaves. (I learned, for example, that the doors to the Slave Lodge were left unlocked when the Dutch East India Company ships were in Cape Town harbour, so that the sailors could have free access to sex with women slaves of their choosing.) In 1836 all slaves at the Cape were freed. Adinah was born in about 1860, after emancipation, but we have no further information about her family's circumstances.

Once I labelled myself as 'Eurasian' I began viewing myself through a new lens, a lens tinted by racist stereotypes which I did not even know I possessed and am not proud of. Apparently, these stereotypes had been waiting in the wings, like ambitious understudies, and they surged onstage as soon as they saw an opening. They were all predicated on the notion that 'whiteness' is the yardstick of value, status and privilege. The stereotypes included: slaves as powerless beasts of burden who are subject to physical and sexual abuse; Indian women as passive, downtrodden, without rights; coloured women as alone, discarded, desperately poor and living hand to mouth, rootless. I began to experience myself, and think and feel about myself, via these stereotypes. My subjectivity was altered, I experienced myself as an old, unattractive woman, as 'careworn, invisible, powerless, a downtrodden beast of burden…good only for cooking and serving men'

(Lobban, 2011a: 85). I also felt that I needed to come clean, to confess, warn others that I was not who I appeared to be.

I was haunted by vivid disturbing dreams. In one dream, I was therapist to Suzanne, my best friend from childhood, who was going through a dramatic, traumatic life event. We were discussing whether I could be her therapist; did she feel that she and I were too close? As we talked, a storm erupted from her face and lightning and thunder came out of her right cheek, then that cheek went back to normal and her left cheek sent out bolts of lightning. We just kept chatting as if nothing unusual was happening. My interpretation: Suzanne was me, possessed by a wild internal storm that kept erupting. In another dream, I was in South Africa all alone and I discovered my childhood dog, a white Maltese terrier, lying on the grass. The dog had been injured and was all in pieces. I knew I had to try to save her, to put her back together. The interpretation here seemed crystal clear to me: I was trying to mend my white self. But there was an addendum: my actual childhood dog was run over by a car; I tried to save her life but was unsuccessful. Perhaps I was sending myself a message to cease trying to resuscitate my old white self?

'WHITENESS'

Eng and Han (2000) describe racialised subjectivity in North America. They argue that 'whiteness' in the United States is not a neutral label; it is an 'ideal' and a 'set of dominant norms and ideals' that a citizen of North America has to possess in order to emerge from the melting pot as a fully assimilated American (2000: 670) (see also Altman [1995, 2000] and Harris [2007, 2009]). Suchet (2004, 2007) and Straker (2004, 2007) discuss the issue of 'whiteness' as it applies within the South African context. In apartheid South Africa, 'whiteness' was also the gold standard, but there was no corresponding South African dream seducing blacks with promises of assimilation. 'Whiteness' and the power and privilege that went with it were blatantly reserved for those people in South Africa who were classified as all white. Clearly, during the 22 years of my life which were spent in South Africa, I absorbed the message that you needed to feel all white to bathe in 'whiteness' and soak in the self-esteem, confidence and entitlement that it promises.

It was astounding to me that I was using a 'whiteness' prism to scrutinise myself and I was frustrated because I couldn't just switch lenses. I was having my own mini version of 'double consciousness', a term coined by WEB Du Bois (1903) to describe how African American subjectivity was inflected by the racist views of the white majority. He defined it as the 'sense of always looking at one's self through the eyes of others, of measuring one's soul by the tape of a world that looks on in amused contempt and pity' (Du Bois, 1903: 2). What was particularly odd was that this was an internal conflict invisible to others. I was looking at myself through a 'whiteness' prism but nobody in the outside world identified me as coloured or treated me as such; they still read me as white and continued to assign me the privilege and power of 'whiteness'. Desperate to shift the terms of the debate, I asked myself how I would address a similar problem if it were presented by one of my patients. I tried mentalising, articulating my feelings to myself, and I talked to friends and colleagues, but to not much avail. Eventually I decided I had to write myself out of my bind. (I wished that I was a painter or poet; it was hard to use prose to plumb the depths of all the intense, rippling feelings with which I was struggling.) Eventually I wrote two short pieces on the subterranean dive my subjectivity had taken (Lobban, 2011a, b). The writing helped me to access my therapist self, to start viewing myself through an analytic lens and come to a self-diagnosis. I decided that I was immersed in my own version of the 'racial melancholia' that Eng and Han (2000) describe; I had lost my sense of myself as someone with a white self who was entitled to claim 'whiteness'. Even as all this drama was unfolding, and I was reeling from my personal lightning bolt, my sense of identity did not shatter, my subjectivity did not shrivel up or get totally taken over. I turned out to have a multiplicity of selves and subjectivities. My other selves, my mother self, my therapist self, my teacher self, my sister self and so on were all present and functioning, and this helped to replenish the self-esteem that I lost when my white self evaporated.

RESIGNIFICATION

Once I had articulated my problem, I could start down the road to what Judith Butler (1997) terms 'resignification'. She uses the term to describe the process whereby a person who is interpellated can free herself and her subjectivity from the stranglehold of an interpellation. The person 'elects to own the essentialist caricatures abjecting her and thereby re-empowers herself' (Dimen, 2011: 81). As a person inhabits and reinterprets the social category to which she is assigned, she redefines it. As I interrogated and redefined 'the labels "Eurasian" and "not

White", stripping off their racist patina, to paint them in rainbow hues' (Lobban, 2011b: 157), I discarded many of my stereotypes and constructed my own new image of slave women. I began to feel tremendous pride that I hailed from such hardy, resilient stock. I kept thinking about the courage, fortitude and intelligence of those women, traits which enabled them to survive the ships that transported slaves to the Cape and the horrendous conditions at the Slave Lodge. I began to read life histories of slaves in South Africa and North America and I also searched out African American artists – such as Kara Walker – who explored the psychic impact of enslavement. Als comments: 'In Walker's work slavery is a nightmare from which no American has yet awakened: bondage, ownership, the selling of bodies for power and cash have made twisted figures of blacks and whites alike, leaving us all scarred, hateful, hated and diminished' (2007: 70). As I eagerly read fact and fiction about impressive bi-racial individuals, my feelings about being 'Eurasian' gradually became more positive and I began to feel attractive and vital once more.

My subjectivity was altered during this resignification process. The changes were subtle and very difficult to render in words but I will make my best attempt. Now my feelings about race and ethnicity loom large, while they were previously more intellectual and less salient. I bunched a number of different selves together before – they were all covered with the same veneer, 'whitewashed' by my sense of my own 'whiteness'. Now that veneer has been stripped off and those selves don't hold together in the same way. Instead, I have to register each self separately and try to figure out a new way to group them. Should I leave them disconnected or should I try to 'rainbow-wash' them or do I need to find some entirely different self configurations? I am much more attuned to the racial register in conversations and interactions now; the ways in which a person's ethnicity is subtly alluded to or denigrated or erased during an interaction, and the degree to which the perpetrator and victim are aware of the transaction. I keep getting preferential treatment because others read me as white. These moments still elicit an initial entitled subjective response from me, but now that sense of entitlement is troubled by my knowledge that I am not all white. I am acutely aware of the store of self-confidence and assurance that I accumulated in my many years of membership in the 'whiteness' club. I took it for granted before, but now those feelings are very noticeable and obtrusive and I cannot seamlessly integrate my sense of self-assurance within my subjectivity, as I did before. My 'white guilt' (Straker, 2007) has not lessened since I learned the family secret; instead, it has increased, because I now have a deeper understanding of the ways in which racism can ravage the self. Sometimes I feel guilty about possessing my white entitlement, as if I am holding stolen goods.

What tools can psychoanalytic theory offer that would help us understand the seismic shifts I experienced in my subjectivity after I learned my family secret and tried to understand how subjectivity is constituted from the vantage point of the participant observer? Mama and Bromberg argue that we have multiple selves and this is borne out by my experience. I had access to many other selves while my crisis about being 'Eurasian' was playing out, and this multiplicity helped me to weather the storm that raged on my racial subjectivity front. Mama highlights the role of discourse, of historical–cultural factors in the construction of subjectivity. These factors played a very important role in my racialised subjectivity. I reproduced apartheid stereotypes and assumptions about white superiority which played out in my conscious and unconscious experience. Discourse also had an impact on how I organised and grouped my selves. Various of my selves were 'white-washed', bunched together under the rubric of 'whiteness', and this contributed significantly to my sense of self-cohesion. I am not clear precisely how discourse took its psychic hold on me. Bromberg argues that intense affect is attached to each of our self-states and that we may dissociate those self-states with intense negative affective loading. I wonder if negative affect was the glue that calcified and bound some of my racialised self-states. Most of my childhood interactions with my parents were relatively calm and benign, but I vividly recall my mother's occasional intense, angry outbursts at me when she thought I was behaving in a 'lower class' way. (The word she used to describe such behaviour was 'Jaap' or 'Jaapie', a derogatory term pertaining to members of the white Afrikaans group in South Africa.) My hypothesis now is that this term was my mother's coded way of referring to behaviours she saw as 'coloured'; that she felt angry, ashamed and scared when she thought that my behaviour read as 'coloured'. These moments were laden with my mother's own racism and shame and her fear about being unmasked as 'passing' for white, which had been passed down through the generations. Were such interactions, which were amplified by negative emotions, the domestic moments when apartheid discourse took its hold on my psyche? Were they the crucible of my racialised subjectivity?

I think often about how my mother, my grandmother and my great-grandmother must have felt as they each precariously balanced on their 'passing' tightrope. I wonder how each of them kept their secret coloured selves hidden, and how much they felt defined by those selves. Did they succeed in dissociating or banishing their coloured selves, or did they wake up each day with a sinking feeling, conscious that they had a dangerous secret that had to be protected lest they be labelled as the 'other'? And what did being 'other' mean to them? How did they feel about being coloured? How much did they imbibe the racist attitudes of their time and view themselves through that lens? How often did they feel terror about being unmasked and forced out of their neighbourhood? I think most about my great-grandmother Adinah, about whom I know the least. I wonder what happened to her family left behind in Cape Town and how she felt about being separated from them. Was she the first person in her family to 'pass'? Did she have to jettison her family in the Cape, and many of her cultural traditions, in order to make her 'passing' foolproof? Did she sometimes wish she could just call the whole thing off, cease playing a role and go home to District Six? Each of these women occupied a variety of other subject positions in addition to 'coloured, passing as white'. I hope that their successes in these other areas replenished the self-esteem which was leached away by their secret.

ON BEING COLOUR-BLIND

I register the ethnic and racial issues which are at play in the clinical arena more acutely since I discovered our family's coloured roots. My journey down 'Resignification Road' (Lobban 2011b) has had a positive impact on my work with my patients. I have also become more courageous about addressing these issues directly with my patients, when I deem that appropriate. I was working with a number of bi-racial patients at the time I started down my road to resignification and this caused me to look at these cases with a fresh eye. Leary argues that the 'most common enactment in the field of psychoanalysis' in North America is 'our relative silence about racial issues' (2000: 647). Swartz (2007) discusses how the disavowal of difference can impact on interracial therapeutic dyads in South Africa. My work with one bi-racial patient, whom I will call Martha, helped me register my own capacity to be 'colour-blind' (Lobban 2011b: 160). Martha is a 30-year-old American bi-racial patient with a white, North American father who is a lawyer, and a Latina mother from the Dominican Republic, who is a teacher. Martha entered psychotherapy to try to figure out the direction in which she wanted to go in life, both professionally and romantically. As Martha was growing up in North America, she witnessed many moments when people behaved in a racist fashion to her mother, treating her as if she was less smart or valuable because she was Latina and not white. Martha's mother spoke excellent, but accented, English and Martha was fiercely protective of her. Martha also felt guilty about her comfortable middle-class life because her mother's family was poor and her childhood had been deprived. Martha avoided competing with her mother and outdoing her, and she felt guilty about her attachment to her white father. Martha felt that she could never put her mother second; she had to constantly keep her love of her mother and her father in balance in order to compensate for the wounds that her mother received from the society's racism.

I was sympathetic to Martha's dilemma because I also felt protective of my mother, who had grown up very poor, began working at the age of 16 and never attended university. After I learned about my 'Eurasian' status, I had a sudden revelation about Martha. It is usual for my patients in New York to mention the ethnicity of the cast of characters they describe to me, and this occurs particularly when the person they are describing is of a different ethnicity from theirs. So, for example, a patient will report: 'I have a new boss, he is white (or Asian, etc.), not black like me.' What I realised was that I had failed to notice that Martha did not specify the ethnic origins of anyone in her cast of characters, no matter whether they were a friend or a lover or a co-worker. When I asked Martha about the cultural background of her new lover, it opened up the therapy dramatically. It turned out that the lover was white and that Martha felt her mother disapproved, that she needed Martha to be involved with a person who was Latina. I began to understand that Martha had developed her own personal strategy to cope with her conflicting loyalties in her interracial family. She acted as if she was 'colour-blind' and tried 'to erase race' (Lobban, 2011b: 160). When I asked myself why I had failed to notice that Martha was acting 'colour-blind', I decided that the most potent explanation was that I had developed a similar strategy of acting 'colour-blind' in my family, which enabled me to deny the many clues that my mother's family had coloured roots. Here is an example: I did not wonder why my mother was the only mother in our sleek, white, Johannesburg suburb who believed in fate, astrology and spirits, or why my grandmother chose to become a medium and take her children to séances every week. There was also no other house on our street where the dead grandmother paid visits in times of family crisis. (We did not see my grandmother but my mother sensed her mother's presence near her at these times, and was grateful that her mother had come to keep her company.) I labelled my mother's behaviours and beliefs 'eccentric', following my pragmatic, Presbyterian father's lead. Once I knew about the 'secret', I realised that my mother's ideas about ancestors, spirits and fate were quite common among some coloured and black South Africans. This was not individual eccentricity. A better hypothesis is that Nellie learned these beliefs from Adinah, that they were part of the folklore passed down by our coloured ancestors.

After I wrote a paper about my therapeutic relationship with Martha and my discovery that both us acted as if we were 'colour-blind' (Lobban, 2011b), I asked Martha to read it in order to obtain her consent for publication. I realise in retrospect that I also hoped that reading the paper would help Martha to break beyond her erasure of colour, that she would have an 'aha!' moment about her 'colour blindness' that matched mine. This was not Martha's reaction; instead, she critiqued my thesis about the salience of race in the formation of her subjectivity. Martha said she felt that I had made too much of the racial differences between her parents in my paper. She said:

> Maybe it's a generational thing, but I talked to quite a few friends my age, black, white and Latina, and they agreed with me that none of us really register colour or factor it in when we choose friends and companions. I know from reading the newspaper that some people still act and think in racist ways in America and have stupid stereotypes about different groups, but this is not true of my peers.

I did not argue with Martha about our contrasting views or try convince her of the rectitude of my thesis and she showed no interest in returning to the issue of race and 'colour blindness'. In fact, we never came back to this issue because Martha got a job abroad shortly thereafter and chose to use her remaining time in therapy to focus on her feelings about moving.

It is interesting to speculate about the relative merits of my position on race and Martha's response. Is there, as Martha suggests, a generational divide where younger Americans are more comfortable with interracial interaction and less prone to stereotype the 'other'? The alternative possibility is that Martha possessed certain unconscious feelings about race which she could not allow herself to access, because she feared they might undo the delicate balance she maintained in her triangular relationship with her parents. Perhaps there is a grain of truth in both my position and Martha's position. The use of racial/ethnic markers to define identity may be on the decrease in young North Americans, and yet the mystique of 'whiteness' still has power at an unconscious level and shaded Martha's relationships with her white father and her Latina mother in different ways.

CONCLUSIONS

The 'new' South Africa allows us to contrast the psychic effects of both the government's new open-ended approach to the definition of identity, and the old rigid race-based definition of identity. In post-1994 South Africa, 'social integration is advancing steadily, even if economic inequality and spatial integration are proving more intractable' (Orkin & Jowell, 2006: 292). It is possible that there is an age divide in South Africa, where young people who have lived most of their lives post-apartheid see the landscape differently and would not automatically choose race as their identity marker. It is also possible that the old apartheid dogma of white supremacy lives on in the unconscious of black and white South Africans in some form, that the power of the 'white gaze' (Chipkin, 2010: 17) persists in the unconscious. Fanon (1963, 1967) was one of the first authors to delineate the ways in which colonial prejudices are internalised by the colonised. Biko suggested that South African blacks could fight their subjection through 'Black Consciousness' where they identified their own 'complicity in the crime of allowing [themselves] to be misused' (Biko, 1970: 29). Many white South Africans also want to liberate themselves from the old colonial categories (Krog, 2010). Since 1994 politicians and academics have grappled with the question of how to undo the damage which apartheid wrought on the psyches of the oppressed. Chipkin argues that 'third world and SA nationalism is an attempt to liberate ourselves from the categories which colonialism or apartheid trapped us in', and produces 'a collection of individuals able to express their individuality in a myriad multiple manners' (2010: 16, 17). The question for South African psychologists to ponder is how psychoanalytically inflected therapy could further this liberation. Judith Butler's (1997) work on 'resignification' (see earlier) is particularly relevant for this issue. If therapists were educated in a climate that allowed them to acknowledge and grapple with the ways in which they had been shaped by discourse, then they could resignify the identities they had interpellated and in turn help their patients towards their own resignifications.

More clinical data on the formation of identity and subjectivity in South Africa are needed, so that we can delineate how South Africans see and evaluate their racial identities today and the mechanisms whereby 'culture saturates subjective experience' (Dimen, 2011: 4). I hope that my description of my racialised subjectivity helps to explain how we are interpellated by culture, and how we internalise discourse, often in ways that are outside of our awareness and remain unconscious. I make no claims that the precise striations which were etched onto my psyche by the culture I encountered (the apartheid-era dogma of white supremacy) have any universality. These striations were particular to my subjectivity, but I hope that the processes at work in my case will prove to be more generally applicable, and that my outline of these processes expands our understanding of how subjectivity gets constituted. If we can deconstruct racialised subjectivity and become more specific about how it is constituted, perhaps that will allow us to figure out how to really move beyond identity politics towards multiplicity. In Gordimer's short story 'Beethoven was one-sixteenth black', she says 'once there were Blacks wanting to be White. Now there are Whites, wanting to be Black. It's the same secret' (2007: 3). She concludes that 'our kind, humankind doesn't need any distinctions of blood percentage tincture. That fucked things up enough in the past' (2007: 15).) Psychologists in South Africa could play an important role in helping their patients to move beyond those 'distinctions of blood percentage tincture' if they were taught about the power of discourse and how to facilitate resignification.

NOTE

1   In this chapter I use 'she/her/hers' as universal pronouns that subsume 'he/him/his'.

REFERENCES

Als, H (2007) The shadow act. *The New Yorker*, 8 October, pp. 70–79.
Altman, N (1995) *The Analyst in the Inner City: Race, Class and Culture through a Psychoanalytic Lens*. Hillsdale, NJ: The Analytic Press.
Altman, N (2000) Black and white thinking: A psychoanalyst reconsiders race. *Psychoanalytic Dialogues*, 4: 589–605.
Biko, S (1970) Black souls in white skins? In S Biko *I Write What I Like*, pp. 19–26. San Francisco: Harper Collins.
Biko, S (1971) White racism and black consciousness. In S Biko *I Write What I Like*, pp. 61–72. San Francisco: Harper Collins.
Bromberg, P (1998) *Standing in the Spaces: Essays on Clinical Process, Trauma and Dissociation*. Hillsdale, NJ: The Analytic Press.
Broyard, B (2007) *One Drop*. New York: Little, Brown and Company.
Butler, J (1997) *The Psychic life of Power: Theories in Subjection*. Stanford, CA: Stanford University Press.
Chipkin, I (2010) Panel – Identity: Are there any South Africans? *Helen Suzman Foundation Series*, 14th issue, March: 15–17.

Dimen M (2011) Introduction. In M Dimen (ed.) *With Culture in Mind: Psychoanalytic Stories*, pp. 1–7. New York: Routledge.

Du Bois, WEB (1903) *The Souls Black Folks*. New York: Dover Publications.

Eng, DL & Han, S (2000) A dialogue on racial melancholia. *Psychoanalytic Dialogues*, 10: 667–700.

Fanon, F (1963) *The Wretched of the Earth*. New York: Grove Press.

Fanon, F (1967) *Black Skin, White Masks*. New York: Grove Press.

Gordimer, N (2007) *Beethoven was One-sixteenth Black*. New York: Farrar, Straus, Girar.

Grossberg, A, Struwig, J & Pillay, U (2006) Multicultural national identity and pride. In U Pillay, B Roberts & S Rule (eds) *South African Social Attitudes*, pp. 54–76. Cape Town: HSRC Press.

Harris, A (2007) The house of difference: Enactment, a play in three scenes. In M Suchet, A Harris & L Aron (eds) *Relational Psychoanalysis, Volume 3: New Voices*, pp. 81–95. Mahwah, NJ: Routledge.

Harris, A (2009) The socio-political recruitment of identities. *Psychoanalytic Dialogues*, 19: 138–147.

Krog, A (2010) *Begging to be Black*. Cape Town: Random House-Struik.

Leary, K (2000) On the face of it: Difference and sameness in psychoanalysis. *Contemporary Psychoanalysis*, 43: 469–473.

Lobban, G (2011a) Glenys: White or not. In M Dimen (ed.) *With Culture in Mind: Psycho-analytic Stories*, pp. 81–86. New York: Routledge.

Lobban, G (2011b) Martha: Resignification Road. In M Dimen (ed.) *With Culture in Mind: Psychoanalytic Stories*, pp. 155–161. New York: Routledge.

Lobban, G (in press) The immigrant analyst: A journey from double consciousness towards hybridity. *Psychoanalytic Dialogues*.

Magubane, BM (2010) From union to a democratic South Africa: Change and continuity. *The Journal of the Helen Suzman Foundation*, 57: 5–8.

Mama, A (1995) *Beyond the Masks: Race, Gender and Subjectivity*. New York: Routledge.

Orkin, M & Jowell, R (2006) Ten years into democracy: How South Africans view their world and themselves. In U Pillay, B Roberts & S Rule (eds) *South African Social Attitudes*, pp. 279–295. Cape Town: HSRC Press.

Rivera, M (1989) Linking the psychological and the social: Feminism, post-structuralism and multiple personality. *Dissociation*, 2: 24–30.

Roefs, M (2006) Identity and race relations. In U Pillay, B Roberts & S Rule (eds) *South African Social Attitudes*, pp. 77–97. Cape Town: HSRC Press.

Straker, G (2004) Race for cover: Castrated whiteness, perverse consequences. *Psychoanalytic Dialogues*, 14: 405–422.

Straker, G (2007) The crisis in the subjectivity of the analyst: The trauma of morality. *Psycho-analytic Dialogues*, 17: 153–164.

Suchet, M (2004) A relational encounter with race. *Psychoanalytic Dialogues*, 14: 423–438.

Suchet, M (2007) Unraveling whiteness. *Psychoanalytic Dialogues*, 17: 867–886.

Swartz, S (2007) The power to name: South African intersubjective psychoanalytic psycho-therapy and the negotiation of racialized histories. *European Journal of Psychotherapy and Counselling*, 9(2): 170–190.

PSYCHODYNAMIC PSYCHOTHERAPY

SECTION

TRAUMATIC
STRESS

PSYCHOTHERAPY AND DISRUPTED ATTACHMENT IN THE AFTERMATH OF APARTHEID SOUTH AFRICA

Cora Smith

INTRODUCTION

While there are a few trained psychoanalysts in the country who practise in pockets of privileged socio-economic communities, a purist pursuit of psycho-analysis is beyond the reach of most South Africans. This chapter is based on four clinical cases chosen because they are representative of the ways in which psychoanalytic concepts and ideas are applied in child psychotherapy undertaken in state hospitals and community clinics in the South African context. Because of the restrictions in terms of resources, trained staff, and the disadvantage of patients with limited funds and time available, the work by its very nature is short term, disrupted and often incomplete. Nevertheless, it is argued that an understanding of the implications of disrupted attachment and the use of psycho-analytic ideas and concepts can help patients to be thoughtful and reflective in relation to their own affects, traumas, motivations and behaviours. Additionally, it is apparent that psychotherapists also benefit from psychoanalytic thinking, concepts and techniques in understanding the powerful transferences and projections that result from working in traumatised communities, and which assist in limiting the ubiquitous burnout that so often occurs among colleagues who work in these conditions for any length of time. These four cases were chosen because they are representative of the difficulties faced in post-apartheid South Africa where apartheid still casts a long shadow over its citizens, who continue to struggle with disrupted family constellations, violence and trauma, competing cultural practices and diverse epistemologies of meaning. The use of psychoanalytically informed psychotherapy in assisting patients and therapists to deal with their painful legacies will be demonstrated. It is hoped that the value of psychoanalytically informed psychotherapy can be considered in other contexts faced with limited resources and short-term applications. These cases not only challenge notions of idealised psychoanalytic practice in the South African context, but also bring into focus contemporary global debates about theoretical purism versus theoretical plurality, as well as the general financial pressure to produce shorter-term interventions (Chessick, 2001; Green, 2005; Kernberg, 1993, 2007; Wallerstein, 2005a, b).

BACKGROUND

The consequences of South Africa's previous apartheid policies, specifically the Group Areas Act (No. 41 of 1950), the pass system and the migrant labour system, have been both long reaching and devastating for many South African families. These laws separated families from each other, disrupted parental partnerships and deprived children of secure relationships with their parents. Many children were sent to grandparents or aunts in the 'homelands', where they were often reared in poverty. Despite the advent of a new political dispensation in 1994, the pattern of parcelling children around between families continues today, albeit for different reasons. For many this pattern of rearing has become familiar and normative. Children are sent to live with families in different provinces and often face a change in language and subculture as well. For others, the fracture of family structure is exacerbated by the pandemic of HIV/AIDS, resulting in large groups of AIDS orphans being cared for by older siblings, overburdened and aging grandparents or remote extended family members. The results have been tragic. Children have lost their childhoods, many have become parents prematurely and all have had their family characterised by disruption and loss. Many of the caregivers are reluctant parent figures, communicating their ambivalences, resentments and anger openly or unwittingly. Others are simply overwhelmed.

These disrupted family structures have impacted negatively on the quality of attachment in early childhood. Many of these children are developing severe insecure attachments or what is often termed 'reactive attachment disorders' (APA, 2000). They have difficulty forming lasting relationships, they struggle to establish trust in relationships and many go on to develop personality difficulties. As these individuals grow into adolescence and adulthood, many abort their education, have unwanted pregnancies, choose unsuitable partners and begin to repeat the same cycle of dispatching their children to other families. Some engage in high-risk sexual practices and find themselves HIV/AIDS positive. Others transmit HIV/AIDS to their children.

From a psychodynamic point of view, the lack of secure attachments has implications for the development of the self-structure, the internalisation of the parental objects, and the maturity of their defences. These building blocks of object relations are often eroded at the very outset of development, leaving individuals with very few ego resources to cope with extraordinary demands, stressors or traumas. Based on 28 years of clinical experience in a large state academic hospital and in several community clinics, I argue in this chapter that psychoanalytically informed psychotherapy is helpful in understanding the repetitive self-defeating cycles that are witnessed in the lives of so many from disrupted and dismantled family backgrounds. It is also helpful in assisting psychotherapists working in under-resourced settings with disadvantaged families to manage their countertransference responses of hopelessness and secondary traumatisation. The use of psychoanalytic ideas and concepts has been beneficial to patients who have been able to use these ideas to come to terms with their traumatic losses, and unacceptable feelings or attitudes toward their overwhelming duties and often unwelcome responsibilities. Drawing on case material, the chapter will illustrate the development of impaired attachment and the subsequent internalisation of neglectful or persecutory parental objects. The lack of ego strengths and the use of primitive defence mechanisms leading to maladaptive coping and impaired relationships will be traced.

THE 'RAINBOW NATION': AFTER 1994

After the promise of the first South African post-apartheid democratic election in 1994, expectations for change and immediate transformation of fortune for many disadvantaged South Africans were unrealistically, perhaps even dangerously, high. Expectations of access to health and welfare services, improved schooling and basic human rights resulted in a deluge of demand and the poorly planned and limited resources previously available to the privileged few were hopelessly overwhelmed. In addition, there are an estimated 8 million illegal immigrants or unofficial refugees from neighbouring states living in South Africa that add a further burden on state health services (Solomon, 2005). Subsequently, ideal-istic policy planning, leadership and management based on political patronage rather than skill or training, spiralling corruption and the failure to prioritise appropriately according to national and provincial budgets have resulted in a disillusioning failure of delivery of essential services in many parts of the country. The result has been a complete lack of confidence in the education system in South Africa, where the matriculation pass rate is at an all-time low, the number of public school matriculants has dropped and the number of school dropouts has increased since 2005 (Dugmore, 2011). In addition, South Africa has been ranked as having one of the highest murder and robbery rates globally (Altbeker, 2007). In effect, hundreds of South African families are deeply traumatised by the violent assault and death of loved ones (Kaminer & Eagle, 2010). In the health sector, unnecessary deaths occur due to the failure to repair and maintain basic hospital equipment, incompetent budgeting and dysfunctional adminis-tration (Bateman, 2011). Sadly, infant and child mortality rates have increased since 2007 (UNICEF, 2010). Added to these woes was the government's initial failure to provide timeous medication to contain the HIV/AIDS pandemic (Heywood, 2010), which resulted in the death of many adults and parents in the prime of their lives, leaving ruptured family structures and countless AIDS orphans to fend for themselves (Smith & Albertyn, 2011). While AIDS is now recognised as a chronic global disease and is being successfully treated in many Western countries, only 28% of HIV/AIDS-infected people in Africa, mostly in sub-Saharan Africa, are receiving antiretroviral drugs (Earls et al., 2008). It is noted that while there is one disease there are two distinct epidemics: one char-acterised by epidemiological characteristics and the other by access to treatment (Sepkowitz, 2006). As the incidence of HIV/AIDS has spread in South Africa, the incidence of death in adults and children caused by secondary infection, such as pneumococcal pneumonia as well as associated tuberculosis infection, has increased steadily (Gray & Zar, 2010). Finally, the exodus of professionally skilled colleagues as they emigrate out of fear, disillusionment or both has deprived the country of desperately needed resources.

In the face of limited resources, long waiting lists and overwhelming need in South Africa, the role of psychoanalytic psychotherapy, theory and ideas needs careful elucidation. Does psychoanalysis have anything to offer the South African context? If so, what kind of psychoanalytic paradigm would be appropriate to the South African context? Is there a uniform psychoanalytic paradigm? Is psychoanalysis not pre-paradigmatic? What would inform the choice of an appropriate psychoanalytic approach? And what would the clinical practice of such psychoanalytic thinking look like?

THEORETICAL CONSIDERATIONS

The issue of allegiance to a particular psychoanalytic theoretical orientation is of particular importance as psychoanalysis faces a global crisis of relevance and survival in the harsh economic environment of managed healthcare and a digital age of instant gratification and quick results (Fonagy interviewed by Jurist, 2010; Silver, 2003; Stepansky, 2009; Wallerstein, 2005a, b). The question of whether there should be adherence to a purist approach embodying a single psychoanalytic theoretical approach is relevant because this then impacts on the practice of such an approach and its debated suitability to the South African context. In addition, the question of whether psychoanalysis is pre-paradigmatic (Kuhn, 1996), a dominant narrative (Green, 2005), theoretically pluralist (Wallerstein, 2005a) or should enter the scientific mainstream (Kernberg, 2012a; Stepansky, 2009) has significant implications when considering the future of psychoanalytic practice, not only in under-resourced countries such as South Africa but also in the global economy of managed healthcare and the demand for short-term, evidence-based interventions. Psychotherapy in general may be considered pre-paradigmatic as the clashing epistemologies of humanism, cognitive behavioural therapy, psychoanalysis and the eco-systemic approach compete for legitimacy. Psychoanalysis itself may be considered pre-paradigmatic as it is without a dominant paradigm, being characterised by many competing schools of thought: drive theory, ego psychology, object relations theory, self-psychology, relational psychoanalysis, constructivist and intersubjective approaches.

By contrast, the argument for theoretical pluralism is evident in the influence of postmodernism on contemporary psychoanalysis. Postmodernism would regard notions of a unified paradigm as a relic of the dominant narrative of modernism. Intersubjective and relational psychoanalytic thinking as refracted through a postmodern lens embraces an epistemological pluralism (Altman, 1995; Aron, 1996; Benjamin, 1998; Davies, 1996; Hoffman, 1998; Mitchell, 1997; Renik, 1993, 1996; Stern, 1997). As knowledge is regarded to be contextual, it would be argued that psychoanalytic concepts and interventions can only be understood within the linguistic, theoretical and ideological frameworks in which they are embedded. Patients are challenged to construct their personal meanings based on their unique developmental experiences and the matrix of social, linguistic and cultural influences in which they live. The appeal of postmodernist influence on psychoanalytic thought has been that the dominant narratives of race, gender and sexual orientation, which have historically marginalised minority groups, have been challenged. The relevance of such an approach is obvious in the South African context. Hence, more appropriate psychoanalytic theories may be those that do not privilege internal experiences and fantasy life at the cost of external impingements that require acknowledgment or overt challenge by virtue of their unjustness.

A further consideration in the choice of theory and approach in the South African context regards the roots of psychoanalytic thinking. Walls (2004) has argued that because psychoanalysis is the cultural product of 19th century Western Enlightenment, its emphasis on liberal individualism has limited its applicability across races, classes and cultures. He argues that the contemporary shift away from the universalising of a Eurocentric perspective, brought about by the advent of globalisation, has called for the reorienting of traditional psychoanalytic assumptions about human nature towards those that are more appropriate to the recognition of a culturally pluralistic world. By this argument, relational psychoanalytic theories have the capacity to interrogate socially constructed dimensions of the analytic dyad, including race, class, gender, culture, ethnicity and sexual orientation, and hence offer pertinent theoretical and clinical possibilities lacking in traditional psychoanalysis (Altman, 1995). These possibilities offer the promise and hope for psychoanalytic psychotherapy to address some of the important political and cultural sources of psychological suffering. Within relational psychoanalysis, the unconscious as manifest in everyday life and in the transference and countertransference of psychoanalytic therapy is restructured to include social, political and cultural differences.

THEORETICAL LIMITATIONS AND CONTRADICTIONS

Notwithstanding the opportunities offered by relational psychoanalysis, the value of drive theory, ego psychology, object relations, attachment theory and self-psychology in contributing to meaningful psychoanalytic thinking and understanding cannot be discarded. In addition, although relational psychoanalysis has much to offer, it is not without its limitations and contradictions (Mills, 2005, 2012). While postmodern psychoanalysis argues for a plurality of views, it paradoxically privileges its own view over others. Concepts that are widely disputed within psychoanalysis currently include: concepts such as drive theory, and the death instinct in particular, being supplanted by object relations theory; the ego's replacement by the self to provide a global all-encompassing entity; the assertion that psychic life begins with factual reality based on infant observation; the relegation of castration anxiety below separation anxiety; the role of attachment theory that replaces infantile sexuality; the conceptions of memory based on neuroscientific findings rather than repression; and, finally, the use of self-disclosure where enactments versus therapeutic neutrality are debated (Green, 2005). Attempts at rapprochement range from appeals for tolerance of psychoanalytic pluralism (Wallerstein, 2005a, b) to ambitious attempts at comprehensive psychoanalytic integration (Fonagy, 2001; Fonagy & Target, 2007), often compromised by glaring epistemological and ontological contradictions. Interestingly, Green (2005) points to a paradoxical 'enigma' that despite the practice of psychoanalysis applying different techniques based on theoretical assumptions that are often incompatible, they each nevertheless obtain some positive results.

It is with this enigma and awareness of contradictions and paradoxes that one engages a psychoanalytic approach appropriate for state hospitals and community clinics in South Africa, offering shorter-term interventions and a capacity to accommodate the impingements of context. In my focus on four clinical cases in this chapter, I argue that the use of psychoanalytic ideas in developing countries must include theoretical flexibility and significant changes in methodological application. Psychoanalytically oriented psychotherapy, rather than idealised classical psychoanalysis, is by necessity a given. Psychotherapy is often disrupted and sessions are often missed due to difficulties with transport or financial limitations. Breaks occur without adequate preparation, which impacts significantly on transference phenomena and undermines the therapist's sense of efficacy and purpose. Due to time constraints, the focus of the therapy must selectively neglect certain psychodynamics, and the decisions about what to prioritise and what to exclude are based on trial and error as much as on clinical experience. Where significant trauma has occurred, as is often the case, certain defences need to remain intact and ego strengths fortified. Other defences, which may be impeding psychic function, need to be interpreted and unconscious dynamics worked through.

THE HEALING POWERS OF MUTILATION

The first case study to be presented is one that challenged my cherished beliefs about attachment, trauma, ethics and comfortable middle-class values. Nokuthula (isiXhosa female name meaning 'quiet person'), a nine-year-old AIDS orphan, came to the local community clinic with symptoms of enuresis, encopresis and stealing. Her mother had died when she was five years old and she had been parcelled round to various extended family members until she was finally placed with her grandmother, who was depressed, overburdened and resentful. Her father died shortly after her birth, apparently due to an 'unknown illness', a local euphemism for AIDS. Prior to her death, her mother had been very ill and unavailable to Nokuthula for lengthy periods. Nokuthula was emotionally deprived and appeared depressed, angry and miserable. On first meeting, she was wary and simply looked at the various toys without engaging in any meaningful or symbolic play. She made little eye contact but occasionally stared vigilantly at me. After several sessions she developed a pattern of playing with various small animals in the sandpit. The outcome was always the same in that the baby animals were left out of the enclosures to fend for themselves and the adults seemed to be self-involved and unaware. At times she played with the dolls and, similarly, the babies would be left out of the home at the end of an outing or ignored at the family meal. It was clear that Nokuthula was repeatedly playing out her sense of abandonment and that she had a deep sense of feeling overlooked, unseen and disregarded. I commented on her feelings of being invisible and overlooked and how sad this made her. She seemed surprised at my attention to her play and continued to play as though I did not exist. I interpreted that she ignored my existence in the playroom much as she felt ignored and overlooked by her maternal objects. This was usually rewarded with a cold glare and further dismissal, leaving me feeling that I was a nuisance and spoiled her game. Such 'looks that kill the capacity for thought' (Wheely, 1992) were effective in shutting down any reflective function I was hoping to achieve.

After a while her babies began to be scolded for being naughty and a nuisance. Her feelings of anger at her neglectful, abandoning objects were slow to emerge. While it was apparent that Nokuthula was insecurely attached, her disengaged style appeared to reflect her feeling of being discarded and unseen in the play-room. She evoked a feeling of remoteness in me and I suggested that she expected me to find her small, insignificant and a nuisance too, in the way she felt when her mother was ill and when her *gogo* (isiZulu term for 'granny' used by many South Africans) was tired. Over time, Nokuthula spoke of her sense that she was 'not a good girl' when her mother was ill and that her wishes for attention were naughty and she felt a nuisance. I also commented that now she felt she was not a good grandchild and that she felt ungrateful for her *gogo*'s efforts and had spoilt her life. She nodded in agreement and solemnly continued her game.

Over time, it was clear that she felt heard and seen in the therapy and that her grandmother, who was seeing her own therapist, was working through her anger and resentment at the loss of her daughter and the added burden of a young grandchild to rear in her old age. Nokuthula's stealing had stopped, she was no longer encopretic and she was making friends at school. Her enuresis, however, remained obstinate and she felt extremely ashamed about this. She felt humiliated and likened herself to a naughty, lazy baby that needed nappies and deserved a hiding.

After bringing Nokuthula to play therapy for 11 sessions (these were inter-mittent due to taxi strikes and transport costs), her grandmother announced that she would be taking Nokuthula to her late parents' home province, where she would undergo various traditional rituals that had been neglected by the family. One aspect included the removal of the last digit of the left small finger as a symbol of clan membership. This ritual, referred to as *ukungqumla ingqithi*, is practised by some Xhosa and Zulu people as a way of welcoming an indi-vidual into the membership of a particular ethnic clan (Hammond-Tooke, 1989; Ngubane, 1977; Swartz, 1998). I was highly ambivalent about this practice and felt it would be both traumatic and harmful to Nokuthula to undergo this form of mutilation. As her attachment was insecure and we were attempting to consol-idate *gogo* as her primary attachment figure and her secure attachment base, it seemed unwise for this maternal figure to preside over a traumatic mutilating procedure. In addition, she was responding well to the play therapy. An object relations theoretical frame inclusive of attachment concepts was incorporated into this psychotherapy, as so many of the child cases seen in local clinics have severe attachment ruptures in their lives. Contextually, an increase in rates of disorganised attachment among children from poor, disadvantaged communities in South Africa has been reported (Tomlinson et al., 2005). In agreement with Robbins (2007), relational psychoanalysis has more recently considered attachment theory to be the developmental basis for deeper psychological structures, with a more sophisticated approach to the implications for the development and functioning of the internal world.

Nokuthula was duly sent off to undergo her traditional clan membership ritual and have her fingertip removed without any form of anaesthetic. When she returned to the clinic some two months later, her grandmother announced proudly that Nokuthula had not wet her bed since her ritual. Nokuthula beamed and showed her raw, bulbous wound to the entire clinic with obvious pride. The wound was purple, ugly and disfiguring.

In her play therapy that day, Nokuthula played out the welcoming ceremony she remembered and made food for all the guests she invited to her ritual, including myself. She told me with great feeling that she now had a family. I remember thinking – but did not comment – that she had not met this family before and would not see them regularly or consistently so they could not become meaningful attachment figures. I felt anxious that this honeymoon feeling of elation would finally fade as she realised over time that her newly found attachment figures would not materialise into meaningful relationships. This concern of mine did not appear to perturb Nokuthula in the least. At the end of the session when Nokuthula got up to leave, I looked down at her sandpit scene and noted that for the first time all the baby animals were placed together with their families. After several more sessions Nokuthula ended therapy as her grandmother was satisfied that her final symptom of enuresis had finally resolved. At a six-month follow up Nokuthula remained dry and appeared confident and happy.

The outcome of this case was disconcerting for several reasons.

First, mutilation is usually considered painful and disfiguring and therefore associated with trauma. Fears that the traumatic, abusive and oppressive effects of this mutilation could lead to a worsening of her psychological symptoms and further regression, as some psychodynamic theorists would suggest (Garland, 1998; Herman, 1992), were not supported. Furthermore, Nokuthula's own family, who could be expected to protect her from such additional trauma, inflicted this mutilation upon her. Failure to protect Nokuthula from such trauma would challenge the notion of parental figures providing a secure attachment base as a prerequisite for establishing reflective function and thereby the capacity to be aware of self and others as independent psychological and emotional beings. All these assumptions would be further coloured by the lens of a dominant Western, middle-class narrative where such rituals are considered primitive and uncivilised. In traditional African belief systems, misfortune – including bodily symptoms – is attributed to ecological imbalance, pollution (e.g. state of impurity due to menstruation, miscarriage, abortion or contact with death), impaired social relationships or bewitchment. In African ancestor worship the spirits of the deceased are believed to look after the interests of their descendants, but they can also send illness and misfortune if moved to wrath (Niehaus, 2005). The relationship of the ancestors to their living relatives is somewhat ambivalent, as both punitive and benevolent responses may manifest. Ancestral benevolence is assured through observance of ritual and sacrifice. The usual reasons for ancestral interference in the affairs of the living are failure to accord due respect to seniors or neglect of necessary rituals that should be performed at pivotal points in the life cycle – birth, initiation, marriage and death.

It could be argued that compliance with traditional ritual in the case of Nokuthula alleviated considerable anxiety and ambivalence in her grandmother and that this anxiety would have been communicated to Nokuthula both consciously and unconsciously. This could have occurred by a process of projective identification. As *gogo*'s sense of being unclean and disrespectful of her ancestors was projected onto Nokuthula, her granddaughter internalised this projection, manifesting with encopresis, enuresis and stealing, all considered unclean and disrespectful behaviours which were then punished and rejected through *gogo*'s experience of Nokuthula as disrespectful and ungrateful. Parental projective identification has a profound impact on a child, who is under great pressure to comply with the parent's need for her to act as repository for the parent's intolerable emotions and states of mind. The child therefore enacts the role she has been assigned. Children are vulnerable to this kind of pressure because they need to be loved by the parent, even if the price is the development of a distorted sense of self as a result of parental projections. The uncleanliness could no longer be located in Nokuthula when *gogo* dealt with her own anger and resentment in her therapy and acknowledged her contribution to her misfortune by accepting responsibility for not completing the required traditional rituals.

Notably, the work on Nokuthula's anger at the abandonment by her parental figures had not really developed in this therapy. I felt that Nokuthula had been severely traumatised and had suffered multiple compounded losses, as is often the case in child trauma where the loss of parents invariably results in a move to a different home, a change of school and a new town. Familiar places, friends, support structures are all lost at once (Smith & Holford, 1993). In considering the impact of her multiple losses, the psychotherapy was focused on establishing ego resources and not undermining defences that retain coping resources in the face of real trauma (Kaminer & Eagle, 2010; Straker, 1994). Prematurely confronting Nokuthula's defences regarding her anger at her parents' abandonment through death would have undermined her trust and heightened her resistance to the therapy. Additionally, it was thought that because Nokuthula's attachment to her granny was insecure, the interpretation of her anger at her internal maternal object would have overwhelmed her coping resources. In accordance with Fairbairn's (1943) theory of repression of bad objects, it seemed psychologically essential to preserve the perception of the parent as benign and protective, as it would have been intolerable to consciously acknowledge internal bad object relationships. Fairbairn (1943) indicated that traumatic experiences with a parent are often felt to be particularly shameful, and because self and object representations are always linked, the child unconsciously believes herself to be involved in her parents' badness. As a result the external object, although in this case deceased, is protected and the badness is internalised by the child.

The idea was to establish a secure attachment relationship in the therapy through an experience of felt security. Once established, the therapeutic relationship becomes a developmental crucible within which to help the patient deconstruct attachment patterns of the past and construct new ones in the present. The concepts of parental attributions, including attachment patterns, and projective identifications derive from very different paradigmatic assumptions and indicate two different levels of psychic experience (Silverman & Lieberman, 1999). Parental attributions and their associated attachment behaviours are observable within clinical material and are understood to represent the more conscious manifestations of experience. Alternatively, projective identification incorporates an unconscious, fantasy-level process. The intention was to address both these processes in the therapy once Nokuthula had developed the ego resources to tolerate disavowed or dissociated thoughts and feelings associated with the premature death of her mother. This was not to be, due to the early removal of Nokuthula from her therapy by her grandmother. Despite this lack of resolution of repression of internal bad object relationships that would seem essential to her mourning process, Nokuthula had done rather well.

Finally, the issue of a dominant Western, middle-class narrative which gives ontological priority to individual needs over societal and cultural requirements

(Walls, 2004) requires discussion. A crucial distinction between the traditional African worldview of an individual and that of Western thought is that in the African view, it is the community that defines the person and not his/her individualistic qualities (Gumede, 1990; Menkiti, 1984; Mkhize, 2004; Taylor, 1994). As a result, the requirements of the community take precedence over individual need. Many African people within South Africa currently adopt a hybridised explanatory system that allows the incorporation of both Western and traditional beliefs (Eagle, 2005). The notion of a communal or collectivist self is ontologically diverse from that offered in psychoanalytic thinking (Altman, 2005), and with such fundamental differences in how identity is situated contextually within different cultural or religious belief systems psychoanalytically oriented psychotherapists require considerable adaptations to their thinking and practice. In clinical practice it is often the case that patients find psychoanalytically informed interpretations regarding ambivalent affects in relation to their parental figures disrespectful. As a result, such links need to be made with caution and great sensitivity. Finally, while in principle it is regarded as politically correct to respect the different practices of varying cultures or religious groups in the spirit of respecting a plurality of cultural views, it becomes less defendable when particular practices are destructive or oppressive of vulnerable groups, such as disempowered women or children. In addition, it is possible to regard a particular tradition within a culture as harmful without disrespecting the entire culture (Dhai & McQuoid-Mason, 2011; Macklin, 1999). It is also noted that culture is not static and that all cultures change over time (Gyekye, 1997). Where cultural or religious practices reinforce the subordinate position of woman in families, the position of cultural relativism becomes ethically indefensible (Bowman, 2003). Eagle (2005) has pointed out that the dilemma facing the therapist is to reconcile her psychoanalytic assumptions and clinical practice while empathically engaging the patient's frame of reference with regard to what a culturally embedded sense of cure or meaning is. In the case of minors, this becomes all the more complex, as they do not choose a particular cultural practice from any position of independent adult autonomy. The outcome of this case challenges many psychoanalytic theoretical assumptions about trauma, loss and healthy psychic function. Far from feeling discarded, abandoned and further traumatised by her mutilation, or oppressed and disempowered, Nokuthula felt incorporated, affirmed and identified with her family clan, which afforded her a sense of secure attachment and an integrated sense of self.

THE DEATH OF FATHER CHRISTMAS

There is a complex debate within the psychoanalytic literature regarding the process of mourning and the transformation of internal objects. Freud (1917/1957) took the view that the mourner suffers due to his or her internal attachment to the deceased and that the aim of mourning is to detach those feelings and attachments from the lost object. The ego, then freed from its former attachments, is available to attach to a new living person. Baker (2001) contests this view, suggesting that a continuing internal relationship with the lost object is found in many bereaved individuals. Recently Kernberg (2010) voiced similar concerns, questioning whether grief and mourning are indeed a time-limited experience completed with the process of identification with the lost object, as suggested by Freud (1917/1957). He also challenges whether mourning is completed with the reworking of the depressive position and the reinstatement of the good internal object, as mentioned by Klein (1940). As a result of a profound personal loss, Kernberg (2010) subsequently proposed a review of 'normal' mourning. He suggests that mourning may bring about a permanent alteration of psychological structures that affect various aspects of a bereaved individual. These structural consequences of mourning comprise the establishment of a persistent internalised object relationship with the lost object that affects both ego and superego functions. Furthermore, Kernberg (2010) suggests that the persistent internalised object relationship develops in parallel to the identification with the lost object, and the superego modification includes the internalisation of the value system of the lost object.

When working with extreme trauma and loss in children, the debate regarding mourning becomes more complex with the recognition that children still have an immature cognitive apparatus, are psychologically developing and their primary objects continue to play an active role in their lives (Sugarman, 2009). The child's cognitive immaturity influences how they present material and how the psychotherapist responds. In the case of pre-schoolers this task is all the more challenging. In keeping a psychoanalytic frame for thinking and mindfulness, the aim is that underlying painful feelings can be understood and given words and meaning.

Garland (1998) describes the response to trauma as comprising two stages. First, the nature of the trauma re-evokes infantile persecutory anxieties as the trauma can be experienced as a loss of both internal and external good objects. This leaves the individual with an internal world peopled by only bad objects.

The second stage involves the mind responding to trauma by trying to make sense of it in terms of earlier experiences, thus linking affects, transference phenomena and defences with a difficult relationship in the past. In the case of a small child, trauma need not necessarily re-evoke earlier persecutory anxieties as these anxieties may be developmentally current and ongoing. However, trauma can also confirm and perpetuate developmental anxieties, leaving the child with a distorted sense of intrinsic badness.

Some years ago on the morning of Christmas Eve, I received an emergency referral while at the Child and Family Unit. The child concerned was four-year-old Dora, whose mother had been brutally murdered by robbers on the weekend. Robbers had entered the home and, when disturbed by the parents, they bludgeoned the mother to death and severely injured the father, who subsequently survived. The father, Dora and her younger brother of nine months, who was being breast fed by his mother at the time, were locked in a cupboard for approximately five hours while the robbers ransacked the house. During this time Dora had witnessed the murder of her mother and the assault on her father. Her father later reported that while locked in the cupboard he was unable to comfort his nine-month-old infant son, who screamed throughout this period. He was also bleeding profusely from his head wound and could not see clearly as his eye had been damaged. In an effort to contain Dora, he had told her to open her Christmas presents that had been stored in the cupboard. As the father was still in hospital recovering from his injuries, a close family friend had brought Dora to the clinic. Dora was reported to be tearful, bewildered, struggling to sleep and having bad dreams. On meeting, Dora was an attractive child who appeared sombre and somewhat stilted.

In the playroom I explained that I knew some very bad things had happened to her and her family and that I was someone who spoke to children about their feelings and worries. Dora did not respond and instead wandered around the room looking at the toys. She finally sat at a small table and proceeded to draw a simple house. The first house that she drew had a door, some windows and a large roof. I asked her to tell me about her drawings. Dora said, 'The baddies came, they climbed in through the roof and they hurt the mommy and daddy.' I commented that some 'baddies' had climbed into her house and hurt her mommy and daddy too. She nodded. I said that she must have been very frightened when that happened. She nodded and said that Father Christmas was dead and that her daddy had been crying in the cupboard. I added that all the nice things about Christmas had been spoiled and that it felt like Father Christmas was dead, too. I also said that it was so bad even her daddy had been crying. I commented that she must have been feeling sad and sore and very scared. She agreed and said that she was scared that the 'baddies' would come back and hurt her daddy again. I commented that she was afraid that Father Christmas had been killed and that the baddies would kill her daddy too. She nodded again. I commented that she had not mentioned her mommy and that perhaps she felt too frightened to talk about her mother. She ignored me and continued to draw. She drew a second house that was attached to the first but which had no windows or doors. I suggested that perhaps if her house did not have windows and doors, she might have been safe from the 'baddies' and they would not have been able to hurt her mommy and daddy. She nodded in agreement and proceeded to draw a third house. I asked her to tell me about the third house. She said this house was 'far away' and that she would have to go and 'live there now'. I said that she felt all alone now and that she felt she was far away from the people she loved. She nodded dolefully and stared at her drawing. I was left with the feeling that something vital had died that day and indeed carried that feeling for many Christmas's after.

As is often the case in child trauma, Dora's losses were compounded by subsequent moves to various caretakers within the extended family while her father recovered and struggled to cope as a single parent. These changes included the loss of her home, her nursery school and all the familiar places and people she knew.

In addition, the family lived far from the clinic and the father could only manage to bring her for weekly play therapy for a six-month period. I was very aware of 'making a little go a long way', as is often the case with state hospital patients (Pollet, 2010). When faced with a limited time frame in which to work, it is best to negotiate a realistic commitment from the parent that he/she is able to meet rather than allow a drawn-out pattern of missed appointments and failed commitments unrealistically accepted under pressure. In this way, the psychotherapist can avoid adding themselves to the list of 'abandoning adults' (Hunter-Smallbone, 2009).

During this time Dora asked for the toys she had at her previous home, specifically her teddy 'Edward' and her pram. As the therapy progressed, Dora played out the 'baddies' robbing houses, mommy figures getting sick and dying and daddy figures who were busy, sad and depressed. She never mentioned her sibling. She often wished to set fire to the crooks who had hurt her mommy. She became withdrawn at nursery school and complained that she had no best friend. Dora said that she wished her mommy would come back and that no one would steal cars. She also described a very realistic recurring dream: 'In my dream I am in bed sleeping but the others are watching TV and the crooks came through my bedroom window and they kill my whole family with a knife. And they tell me to stand still while they kill my family. Then they go away.' The dilemma in interpreting this dream is that although it is typical of the sort of nightmare reported by children who have experienced extreme trauma, it is not only a re-experiencing of the trauma as a feature of Post-traumatic Stress Disorder but also an expression of her internal world. Trauma is usually not repeated or enacted literally; there is an internal response to that traumatic event. It is accepted practice to respect the child's defences in the case of trauma to facilitate coping resources and recovery. Support for the patient's ego, which has been overwhelmed by the trauma, may facilitate the opportunity for later analysis of conscious and unconscious fantasies connected with the traumatic experience (Blum, 2003). However, it is noted that Dora 'stood by passively' as her family were murdered in her dream and that she had very ambivalent feelings about this passivity. This could be attributed to her terror and to being immobilised by her anxiety, or it could be interpreted as evidence of her ambivalent attachment to her bad internal maternal object that had abandoned her and displaced her with a sibling. In the case of mourning, it is common practice to deal with ambivalent feelings by elucidating the nature of the hostility to the lost object.

On termination, Dora had settled in her new nursery school and had made a best friend. Her nightmares had stopped and her sleep difficulties had ended. She remained afraid that robbers would harm her father and she often thought of her mother and wished she would 'come home again'.

The father remarried some two years later to a close family friend who the children knew well and the family made sporadic contact with the clinic as various family issues arose. Soon after the marriage, Dora's stepmother fell pregnant and I received a most surprising call from Dora herself, now seven years old, who navigated the cumbersome labyrinth of the hospital switchboard and requested an 'appointment'. Her stepmother was a sensitive and insightful woman who had been attending her own psychotherapy in an effort to manage her newly reconstituted family as she also had two children from a previous marriage. She reported that Dora had recently become oppositional and difficult to manage. Dora then announced her wish to see me.

I had not seen Dora since her initial bout of play therapy. She had grown into a tall, striking, latency-age child. We returned to her old playroom where Dora proved to be quite verbal and played creatively. She said that she loved her stepmother very much but that she loved her daddy best. She said that it was hard to share with all her new siblings and she hoped her stepmother would have a little boy, as there were too many girls in the family. She then began to paint. She painted her 'family', which comprised herself, her father and a very large and obviously pregnant mommy. I asked her to tell me about her painting and she became annoyed and began to paint over it. I commented that it seemed she wished that she was the only child in the family and that her stepmother's new baby would spoil that wish. I added that she must have some very mixed, sad and cross feelings. I suggested that she might be worrying that she would lose her stepmother when she had her new baby just as she had lost her own mommy after her baby brother was born. Also that it might feel as though she had to share her mommy with her brother and that this must have made her feel sore and angry and that when her mommy was murdered she must have felt very bad. Dora stopped painting over her initial picture. She said that she still thought of her dead mommy but did not miss her as much and then, surprisingly, said that she had missed me. She also said that she still worried robbers would hurt her daddy and new mommy. Hence, Dora appeared to associate her stepmother's pregnancy with the traumatic loss of her mother and this pregnancy had re-evoked her feelings of sibling rivalry and ambivalence at her maternal object for being displaced. It also evoked her fears of the associated trauma and hence her renewed anxieties about her parents' security.

While there are many aspects that could be discussed with regard to this case, I wish to focus on only a few. First, it is interesting to note that Dora referred to the death of her mother as the death of Father Christmas, indicating a very simple but powerful understanding that her mother's death would be a profound, pervasive and permanent loss of something very precious. This is despite the fact that at the age of four years, Dora's cognitive understanding that death is finite had not yet fully developed. Instead, children at this age tend to have a very concrete understanding of the death of a parent as having gone to be with God or to be in heaven, much as one goes to the shops or visits granny. The eventual comprehension of permanent loss tends to be experiential as the child realises day after day that the deceased parent does not return. Parents are often distressed that their pre-schoolers, having been told of a grandparent's death, start enquiring when they will return after a few days or weeks. Dora was not only aware that a terrible loss had occurred, but she was also unable to name the devastating fact that her mother had been murdered. Children, in particular, avoid internal phenomena such as affect when it is too frightening or too painful to bear (Sugarman, 2009).

Naming such fears and helping the child express them is essential. Most very young children are capable of insight in so far as they are able to reflect on their own minds and understand their behaviours, affects and fantasies. Small children do have limited affect tolerance and in the case of trauma are able to distinguish reality from fantasy.

The second point I wish to raise is the role of repression. In a contemporary psychoanalytic model (Fonagy, 2001; Fonagy & Target, 2007; Wallin, 2007), repression is thought of as the intentional keeping out of consciousness of the meaning of a memory rather than the memory itself (Knox, 2003). By this argument, uncovering repression during psychotherapy is therefore not the recovery of a previously unavailable memory but rather a change in the understanding and processing of feeling in relation to the repressed material. It was evident to me that Dora was avoiding the feeling associated with the murder of her mother in her own limited but effective little way, but she was perfectly conscious of the fact that her mother had been murdered.

The third point is that even during a very simple interaction with a small child of limited verbal ability, the communication of her intolerable, unspeakable and unthinkable feelings was very powerfully projected onto me, leaving me with a profound feeling of death, loss and mourning. The task of the psychotherapist in these circumstances is to receive and listen to such feelings and hopefully process and make sense of them for the child (Lanyado, 2009). These processes are quite clearly evident in the trauma work with a very small child and effective even when working in a short-term model.

The fourth point is that while it is clear that her stepmother's pregnancy re-evoked unresolved feelings of ambivalence with regard to Dora's displacement and her mother's untimely death, the very fact that she continued to remember, think of and carry her maternal object is evidence of an internal representation of the deceased parent signifying adaptive bereavement (Baker, 2001; Silverman & Worden, 1992). A Kleinian view would conceive of mourning as a process of reparation in which the destructive fantasies unleashed by the loss are contained and a positive internal relationship with the lost object is re-established. It can be argued that Dora's unconscious wish for reparation with the internal maternal object is evident in her constant concerns regarding the safety and security of her surviving parent and her new stepmother. Indeed, she returned to therapy, as she needed help to name and process her anxiety and ambivalence with regard to her pending displacement and associated feelings of destructiveness and badness. Nevertheless, it is difficult to assess the extent to which Dora's fear of additional or further trauma to her external objects was based on reality and to what extent it was a function of her wish for reparation.

THE JOYS OF REVENGE

The theme of revenge, despite its prominence in mythology, literature, history and politics, is surprisingly neglected in the field of psychoanalysis (Beattie, 2005; Rosen, 2007). Despite this, revenge is very popular, as evidenced recently in the public address by the United States president, Barack Obama, when announcing the death of Osama Bin Laden. He said, 'We can say to those families who have lost loved ones to al-Qaeda's terror, justice has been done' (Obama, 2011). Thousands of Americans were televised around the world celebrating this death while simultaneously thanking their God and asking for blessings. This is despite the fact that 76% of American citizens identify themselves with Christianity (Kosman & Keysar, 2009), a religion with basic tenets that embrace forgiveness and oppose murder. Enactments of revenge are accompanied by regressive use of defences such as denial and splitting. By focusing on the righteousness and justified nature of the claim and entitlement to retribution, the avenger may render his or her sadism egosyntonic (Rosen, 2007).

In general, the wish for revenge serves a number of psychic functions. Of particular significance is the understanding of revenge as a defence against feelings of shame, loss, guilt, powerlessness and mourning. Where revenge is a prime motivator for psychic survival in the face of devastating loss or betrayal, it may serve a positive function for the avenger. This paradoxical state of affairs raises a disturbing feeling of disquiet, as described in the following case.

Fikile was nine years old when she accompanied her brother to the clinic together with her mother. Her brother had been attending the clinic for some time and her mother was attending parent counselling as part of his intervention. Her mother mentioned in passing that Fikile was a very good child despite the terrible thing that had happened to her. It transpired that Fikile and a friend had been part of a lift scheme, where a taxi driver would fetch them from home and take them to school. Her mother paid monthly for this service. Some months previously, the taxi driver had dropped off all his passengers and insisted on taking Fikile to his house, where he raped her before returning her home. Fikile immediately told her mother of the rape when she returned from work. Her mother had Fikile examined and found that her daughter had indeed been raped.

She was enraged by the betrayal of the taxi driver with whom she had entrusted her child. However, she did not report the matter to the authorities and instead mobilised her adult sons and nephews, who lay in wait for the taxi driver one morning and, with Fikile present, proceeded to beat him senseless until her mother was satisfied that 'justice had been done'.

Fikile was subsequently referred to me for trauma counselling. Fikile recounted her story authentically and was animated and engaged. She was able to reflect on her feelings and had no features of post-traumatic stress at all. She said that she felt better as the taxi driver 'got what he deserved' and that her family had 'taught him a lesson'. She felt that he would never try to hurt her or any other little girl ever again. Fikile was doing well at school, was integrating with her friends, slept well, did not have any nightmares and did not worry about being unsafe. Her play was creative and although she recounted the rape experience as very painful and scary, she felt that she had survived the trauma and put it behind her as the perpetrator had been punished. She also felt supported and affirmed.

To succumb to revenge enactments is to resort to primitive defences such as denial, splitting and projective identification (Rosen, 2007). While it is clear that the child's mother in this case undertook the revenge enactment, the 'benefits' were that Fikile felt supported and vindicated by her family's actions. This did indeed help her defend against feelings of helplessness and shame that often serve to compound trauma. As the regressive defensive behaviours were located in her mother, one could speculate as to whether such sadistic gratification in the maternal object would be harmful to Fikile as a role model. It must be noted that her mother did not present a pattern of regressive or sadistic behaviours, so that outside of this enactment of revenge, the mother was an ordinary, law-abiding citizen whose actions were 'justified' by her belief that the criminal justice system would not be effective in prosecuting the perpetrator and bringing him to justice. This opinion would be supported by the very poor conviction rate of child sex offenders in South Africa (Conradie, 2003).

Notwithstanding a certain empathy for the mother's position, it remains obvious that if private citizens were to take the law into their own hands and undermine the basic principles of a just, democratic and civilised society, it would be a very dangerous development. It is likely that revenge in this instance was an attempt to restore a narcissistic injury within the mother. While revenge may serve to restore a narcissistic wound, it is nevertheless considered a primitive attempt at righting a wrong or undoing a hurt, by whatever means (Kohut, 1977). In the case of the mother, her psychic functioning reveals defensive splitting which may have been part of general paranoid-schizoid functioning in Kleinian terms or the result of regressive functioning (Herman, 1992) as a consequence of her own trauma in dealing with the rape of her child. While rage and vengeful acts may appear primitive, Poland (2006) argues that lust for revenge need not reflect a primitive way of relating. Vindictiveness need not imply an incapacity for empathy but rather a lack of sympathy for another. It is possible to retain a capacity for empathy or attuned sensitivity despite vengeful feelings. It is also possible that Fikile's mother was an empathic and sensitively attuned maternal object, given Poland's (2006) argument.

However, given that the feelings of revenge were enacted, certain moral concerns arise. The ethics and morality of her revenge enactment suggest a pre-conventional stage of moral development embracing an obedience–punishment orientation (Kohlberg, 1977), which would be developmentally consonant with Fikile's formulation of moral dilemmas. Thus, the punitive consequences for the perpetrator resulting from her mother's act of revenge would have resonated with her developmental understanding of moral justice. Poland (2006) argues that adaptation and revenge are of the same family and considers them conceptual cousins. While it is difficult to speculate on the internal world of the mother, this revenge enactment was indeed adaptive for Fikile, albeit that the act offends many sensibilities.

TAINTED BY AN INTERNAL BROTHEL

The following case is an example of the difficulties of working in a psychoanalytically informed manner with children who are mismanaged by the social services that are purported to be their guardians. After the 1994 elections and the demise of the apartheid government, social services were dismally under-resourced and under-prepared to cope with the demand for integrated child services for all South African children. The situation worsened with the HIV/AIDS pandemic and the government's initial failure to make antiretroviral treatment available to patients. As a result of HIV/AIDS denialism (Chigwedere et al., 2008), a legacy of orphaned children was left at the mercy of inadequate social services. Subsequently, some of the most vulnerable children, already with unprocessed trauma, were subjected to further trauma from repeated separations and failed foster placements within the social service system. As a consequence, these children have less opportunity to develop an internal world populated by more benign figures to help support them against intrusive and persecutory experiences in either internal or external worlds.

The difficulties in offering a consistent therapeutic alliance and creating basic trust to assist the child in establishing a sense of containment over their inner turmoil and chaos become apparent in the next case. Apart from the external barriers to receiving assistance, these children offer considerable internal resistance as they are often mistrusting, angry and destructive, making efforts at therapeutic engagement difficult.

Benita was four years old when I first met her. It was late on a Friday afternoon when her mother walked into the waiting room of the clinic and announced that she had come to give her daughter up to 'the welfare' as she was 'possessed by the devil'. I indicated that the clinic was not a welfare organisation and did not have any statutory powers or placement facilities and that her request was somewhat unusual and required some explanation. Following a lengthy interview with the biological mother, during which time Benita played with the doll's house in the corner, her mother explained that Benita had been 'caught having sex' with a temporary lodger in her apartment and that she was now soiled and contaminated. As Benita was considered complicitous in this act of obvious sexual abuse, her mother regarded Benita as 'possessed by the devil' and would no longer have her in her home. Her mother promptly left Benita in the clinic and did not bother to wait for the arrival of social services. After social services had fetched Benita, it was noted that she had turned the doll's house into a very explicit brothel. Benita was subsequently placed in a children's home and brought to play therapy weekly. Her social worker reported that her father was unknown and her mother was a well-known prostitute who lived in a single-room apartment; she partitioned off a section of this room with a curtain when she serviced clients. Benita was fully aware of her activities and, as it later transpired, would often peek through the curtain and observe her mother's sexual activities. Benita played out her internal badness repeatedly with various expressions of a highly idealised mother in her psychotherapy. She felt that if she had not been so bad and naughty her mother might have loved and kept her. Bonita was placed in over seven different foster placements. Each time she would alarm and provoke her foster parents by sexually interfering with their children and, having ruptured her foster placement, she would be returned to the children's home. Despite considerable efforts to prevent her from repeated foster placement breakdowns and repeated rejections, Benita would be placed with yet another unsuspecting family. Throughout this time, her biological mother would emerge for two or three annual visits and promise to fetch Benita and take her home. This never materialised and Benita would make excuses for her mother's failure to keep her word. This tragic attempt to protect the external mother from criticism is an example of Fairbairn's (1943) moral defence against bad objects, where the child's denial or repression of any memories of a frustrating object serve to retain the hope of future fulfilment.

Finally, when placed with the eighth foster family, who had no children in the home, Benita was 12 years old. This foster placement lasted for two years and was the longest she had ever stayed in a family. Unfortunately, at this time Benita became ill with an acute kidney infection and when she was admitted to hospital it was discovered that her second kidney was defunct and had to be removed. Social services decided to contact her biological mother and inform her of this decision. Her mother arrived at the hospital and with great dramatic flair promised to support Benita through her surgery and then take her home. Benita rejected her foster mother immediately and refused to see her. After the surgery, she returned to the children's home where she stayed until she completed school and found a job. Her mother never came to fetch her.

It appeared that Benita ruptured every one of her foster placements in an attempt to retain an attachment to a needed parent by viewing her rejection as deserved and thereby keeping the rejecting parent 'good'. Benita solved the fundamental problem of staying attached to a frustrating and alluring (exciting) internal object (Fairbairn, 1944) that promises but frustrates delivery of care and nurturance by internalising the bad object and confirming her badness by engaging in behaviours that resulted in repeated rejections from her foster families. Another consideration might be that through Benita repressing her painful affects of rejection, she was able to identify with the betrayer and aggressor and thereby repeat such experiences of rejection (Fraiberg et al., 1975). Lanyado (2009) notes that there are two extreme defence mechanisms which help the individual survive, namely dissociation and identification with the aggressor. The danger is that these survival mechanisms can continue long past their usefulness and become part of a defensive structure that avoids unpleasant and painful realities.

Benita attended play therapy throughout her childhood but this was peppered with breaks as some of her foster families could not bring her to therapy and there were two periods in her adolescence when she terminated the therapy herself. This occurred once at the age of 14 years when she returned to the children's home after her surgery and again when she was 16. Children in foster care or placement in children's homes are often abandoned by a living parent who repeatedly reconnects and re-abandons the child (Hunter-Smallbone, 2009). The grief process at the loss of such a parent remains both complex and incomplete and is characterised by anger, guilt, self-blame, fear and helplessness. The relationship with the abandoning parent is likely to have been ambivalent and characterised by insecure attachment, leaving the child feeling unlovable and intrinsically bad. It is also important to distinguish the task of psychotherapy from the maternal role, which is to establish a secure attachment. The therapeutic relationship, apart from providing a secure working alliance, also evokes transference feelings, which contribute to the revival of insecure attachment. Psychotherapy is not an alternative form of parenting. The psychotherapist's focus on unconscious material and defences against painful feelings evokes anxiety and ambivalence toward the therapy. Benita terminated psychotherapy herself shortly after her surgery and her mother's final betrayal, as she could not bear to think that her mother would never take her home and that the reunion fantasy would never be. My own fury at her mother for her destructive and dishonest promises while visiting Benita in the hospital had led me to interpret Benita's disappointment and rage at her mother's final betrayal too soon in the process. I revived an insecure attachment and the associated ambivalent affects in the therapy and Benita, overwhelmed by these feelings, fired her psychotherapist for several months.

When Benita returned to psychotherapy aged 16 years, she was tense, drawn and traumatised, which was unusual as she tended to be quite easy-going, vocal and upbeat. It transpired that she had spent the weekend with her mother and had asked her mother why she had given her up to a children's home. Her mother had explained that Benita was a very evil child and that she was unable to cope with her. She told Benita that she (Benita) had locked a small child in a disused stove when she was approximately six years old and that as a result the child had died. Benita was horrified and had come to 'see her file' because she did not recall the event and was sure that I would have remembered this and noted it in her file, as I 'knew everything about her'. Benita continued to experience herself as bad due to the internalised badness of her frustrating object, which she attempted to retain as a pristine object. However, in this instance, although she doubted her own memory and experience, Benita returned to the therapy to validate her confusion and did not entirely accept her mother's destructive projections.

Benita terminated her psychotherapy after leaving the children's home. Over the next few years I received an annual call from Benita informing me of her life circumstances and her whereabouts, but she refused to come in and see me. She would always phone and, without identifying herself, assume that I knew who she was. Fortunately I always did recognise her voice. She had an extremely high turnover of jobs and relationships. Finally, in her early twenties, Benita called and requested an appointment. Again, she simply assumed that I would still be at the clinic.

Benita walked into my office and resumed her psychotherapy as though there had been no break. She recounted how she had been very promiscuous and that she had now finally settled down. She had married a very stable young man from a 'nice' family and despite loving him very much, she was currently having an affair with a very exciting but irresponsible young man. She knew this was unwise but she could not help herself and anyway, her husband was rather 'boring'. She felt that as I 'knew everything about her' I would be the best person to help her. I suggested that she was re-enacting an internal sense of badness and that she would repeat an experience of rejection with this affair. I also commented on her sense of emptiness and tendency to get bored in relation-ships and that she was something of an 'intensity junkie', which helped defend against the emotional void. Benita was very taken with the notion of being an 'intensity junkie' and felt that this resonated with her internal experience and her tendency to seek out novelty at the cost of long-term mature relationships. Benita phoned again almost a year later to report that she had left her husband and become pregnant by her then unsuitable lover, who had predictably become 'boring'. She had returned to her husband and was hoping that he would accept the child as his. She wanted me to know that she really was an intensity junkie and that she hoped she would not repeat her own experiences of abandonment and reconnection with her unborn child.

Benita had certainly repeated a pattern of promiscuity in alignment with her mother's rejection of her as a bad object soiled by sex. She also repeated a pattern of rejection and reconnection that was the experience of her childhood. She was able to reflect on her own internal state of emptiness and self-destruc-tiveness, albeit for fleeting moments. Despite not returning to psychotherapy, she continued to use the internalised therapist as her emotional memory and reflective compass at difficult times in her life.

CONCLUDING REMARKS

The four cases presented describe the value of psychoanalytic concepts and ideas in psychoanalytic psychotherapy in the South African context, despite restrictions of time and resources. Each case challenged psychoanalytic theoretical epistemologies, concepts, practices, cultural belief systems or issues of ethical relativism. It is also clear that the practice of psychoanalytically oriented psychotherapy in the context of disadvantage and limited resources cannot be characterised by rigid theoretical loyalties and that technique, practice and certain conceptualisations often come from epistemologically diverse theories. This is evident in the chapter, with the application of concepts from attachment theory and drive theory, each of which holds contrasting epistemologies of primary motivation. Despite these theoretical contradictions, the 'enigma' of positive effects nevertheless occurred in each case (Green, 2005). Rather than fearing the theoretical differences within the psychoanalytic paradigm, the insights offered by these diverse theories and applications should be embraced and integrated as they ultimately contribute to effective and meaningful psychotherapy outcomes. Technical pluralism need not imply theoretical confusion, as the tension between clinical practice and theoretical purism within the field of psychoanalysis is well recognised.

Finally, a psychoanalytic approach that privileges context and accommodates a diversity of cultural beliefs and practices is necessary for social relevance in the South African context. It is here that the most difficult ontological, epistemological, methodological and moral issues often arise. The very conceptualisation of the self differs within psychoanalytic thinking as a rather egocentric concept when compared to the African concept of self, which is considered communal or collectivist. Working with issues such as agency and boundaries often directly challenges deeply held cultural beliefs and practices. Issues of personal responsibility and the role of defences against painful separation and autonomy assume a different hue in this context. Certain interpretations can therefore be experienced as persecutory and/or alienating. Decisions have to be made to consider neglecting certain themes and defences within psychotherapy, and accepting that such practice of psychodynamic psychotherapy is 'incomplete' when compared to the idealistic practice of classical psychoanalysis. Perhaps we should consider the notion that, rather than being superior to local hybrid applications, Western applications of psychoanalysis may be inappropriate to the South African context (Swartz, 2007). The very notion of 'criticising' parental figures, albeit through the interpretation of internalised fantasy of negative parental objects or actual failed attunements, strikes at the very heart of the required cultural respect for elders and ancestral figures. As most black South Africans adhere to a mix of traditional beliefs, Christian religion and modern healthcare practices, an acceptance of these contradictions to the psychoanalytic frame is essential for the psychotherapist.

Ethical dilemmas are raised when adopting a position of cultural relativism. Cultural practices that include mutilation, subservient roles of women, racism between different ethnic and language groups, prejudice against individuals of homosexual orientation, and punitive practices in child rearing that condone child abuse are difficult to bear in the very personal psychotherapeutic context. Sensitivity and tolerance are not always possible and, in some cases, not desirable or morally defensible. These issues are brought into stark relief when minor children infected with HIV are taken off antiretroviral therapy and treated by traditional healers instead, with certain death as the outcome. While an acceptance of cultural relativism is often encouraged in clinical practice, the bleed into ethical relativism is often difficult to gauge and at times painful to witness. Ironically, while the practice of parcelling out infants to multiple caretakers is often referred to by contemporary parents as part of their 'culture', it is in fact a consequence of the Group Areas Act under apartheid legislation, where mothers working as domestic helpers in 'white' areas were not permitted to keep their infants with them and were forced to send these infants to relatives in the 'homelands'. This practice has become both familiar and normative for many contemporary parents, who unknowingly regard it as a 'cultural' practice worth defending despite its roots in apartheid ideology.

The inherent contradictions in applying psychoanalytic thinking in a context with disparate worldviews, belief systems and understandings of trauma and psychic suffering inevitably lead to psychoanalytic pluralism in practice that is both ontologically and epistemologically diverse. For theoretical purists, this is an unpalatable compromise; for theoretical pluralists, this enriches debate. When practising psychoanalytically oriented psychotherapy in a developing country such as South Africa, it is often assumed that the compromises and adaptations made by psychotherapists are unique to the South African context. It is worth noting that with globalisation, the preference for behaviouristic interventions by managed healthcare, the contemporary expectation for instant results and the exorbitant cost of long-term psychoanalysis have placed the practice of classical analysis in jeopardy even in developed, first world countries (Fonagy, 2006; Jurist, 2010; Kernberg, 2012a, b; Silver, 2003; Stepansky, 2009; Wallerstein, 2005a, 2012). It may be that the future of the practice and training of psychoanalysis depends on its adaptation to a contemporary, digital-age, 21st century society for its survival. The pressure to adapt and seek effective psychoanalytic interventions that are flexible, socially relevant and short term is not only a South African dilemma but a global one as well.

REFERENCES

Altbeker, A (2007) *A Country at War with Itself: South Africa's Crisis of Crime.* Johannesburg: Jonathan Ball.

Altman, N (1995) *The Analyst in the Inner City: Race, Class and Culture through a Psychoanalytic Lens.* Hillsdale, NJ: The Analytic Press.

Altman, N (2005) Manic society: Towards the depressive position. *Psychoanalytic Dialogues,* 15(3): 321–346.

APA (American Psychiatric Association) (2000) *Diagnostic and Statistical Manual of Mental Disorders (DSM-IV-TR).* Washington, DC: APA.

Aron, L (1996) *A Meeting of Minds: Mutuality in Psychoanalysis.* Hillside, NJ: The Analytic Press.

Baker, JE (2001) Mourning and the transformation of object relationships: Evidence for the persistence of internal attachments. *International Journal of Psychoanalysis,* 18: 55–73.

Bateman, C (2011) Fix the damn system: Johannesburg's tertiary hospital doctors. *South African Medical Journal,* 101(3): 154–155.

Beattie, HJ (2005) Panel report: Revenge. *Journal of the American Psychoanalytic Association,* 53: 513–524.

Benjamin, J (1998) *The Shadow of the Other: Inter-subjectivity and Gender in Psychoanalysis.* New York: Routledge.

Blum, HP (2003) Psychic trauma and traumatic object loss. *Journal of the American Psychoanalytic Association,* 51: 415–431.

Bowman, P (2003) Interrogating cultural studies. In P Bowman *Interrogating Cultural Studies: Theory, Politics and Practice,* pp. 1–18. London: Pluto.

Chessick, RD (2001) The contemporary failure of nerve and the crisis of psychoanalysis. *Journal of the Academy of Psychoanalysis,* 29: 659–678.

Chigwedere, P, Seage, GR, Gruskin, S, Lee, TH & Essex, M (2008) Estimating the lost benefits of antiretroviral drug use in South Africa. *Journal of Acquired Immune Deficiency Syndromes,* 49(4): 410.

Conradie, H (2003) Are we failing to deliver the best interest of the child? *Crime Research in South Africa,* 5(1): 8–32.

Davies, JM (1996) Linking the 'pre-analytic' with the postclassical: Integration, dissociation and the multiplicity of unconscious process. *Contemporary Psychoanalysis,* 32: 553–576.

Dhai, A & McQuoid-Mason, D (2011) *Bioethics, Human Rights and Health Law.* Cape Town: Juta & Company.

Dugmore, H (2011) A is for apple, R is for results. *WITS Review,* April, 16: 18–23.

Eagle, G (2005) Therapy at the cultural interface: Implications of African cosmology for traumatic stress intervention. *Journal of Contemporary Psychology,* 35(2): 201–211.

Earls, F, Raviola, GJ & Carlson, M (2008) Promoting child and adolescent mental health in the context of the HIV/AIDS pandemic with the focus on sub-Saharan Africa. *Journal of Child Psychology and Psychiatry,* 49(3): 295–312.

Fairbairn, WRD (1943) The repression and the return of bad objects (with special reference to the war neurosis). *British Journal of Medical Psychology,* 19: 327–341.

Fairbairn, WRD (1944) Endopsychic structure considered in terms of object relationships. *International Journal of Psychoanalysis,* 27: 30–37.

Fonagy, P (2001) *Attachment Theory and Psychoanalysis.* New York: Other Press.

Fonagy, P (2006) Evidence based psychodynamic psychotherapies. In PDM Task Force *Psychodynamic Diagnostic Manual*. Silver Spring, MD: Alliance of psychoanalytic organizations.

Fonagy, P & Target, M (2007) The rooting of the mind in the body: New links between attachment theory and psychoanalytic thought. *Journal of the American Psychoanalytic Association*, 55(2): 411–456.

Fraiberg, S, Adelson, E & Shapiro, V (1975) Ghosts in the nursery. A psychoanalytic approach to the problems of impaired infant–mother relationships. *Journal of the American Academy of Child Psychiatry*, 14(2): 387–421.

Freud, S (1917/1957) Mourning and melancholia. In J Strachey (ed. and trans., with A Freud) *Standard Edition of the Complete Psychological Works of Sigmund Freud, Volume 14*, pp. 243–258. London: Hogarth Press.

Garland, C (1998) Thinking about trauma. In C Garland (ed.) *Understanding Trauma: A Psychoanalytical Approach*, pp. 9–31. London: Duckworth.

Gray, D & Zar, HJ (2010) Community acquired pneumonia in HIV-infected children: A global perspective. *Current Opinion in Pulmonary Medicine*, 16(3): 208–216.

Green, A (2005) The illusion of common ground and mythical pluralism. *International Journal of Psychoanalysis*, 86: 627–632.

Gumede, M (1990) *Traditional Healers*. Johannesburg: Skotaville.

Gyekye, K (1997) *Tradition and Modernity: Philosophical Reflections on the African Experience*. New York: Oxford University Press.

Hammond-Tooke, D (1989) *Rituals and Medicine*. Johannesburg: Donker Press.

Herman, J (1992) *Trauma and Recovery: From Domestic Abuse to Political Terror*. London: Pandora.

Heywood, M (2010) Civil society and uncivil government: The Treatment Action Campaign (TAC) versus Thabo Mbeki, 1998–2008. In D Glaser (ed.) *Mbeki and After: Reflections of the Legacy of Thabo Mbeki*, pp. 128–162. Johannesburg: Wits University Press.

Hoffman, IZ (1998) *Ritual and Spontaneity in the Psychoanalytic Process: A Dialectical-constructivist View*. Hillside, NJ: The Analytic Press.

Hunter-Smallbone, M (2009) Child psychotherapy with children looked after by local authorities. In M Lanyado & A Horne (eds) *The Handbook of Child and Adolescent Psychotherapy: Psychoanalytic Approaches*, pp. 316–327. London/New York: Routledge/Taylor Francis Group.

Jurist, E (2010) Elliot Jurist interviews Peter Fonagy. *Psychoanalytic Psychology*, 27(10): 2–7.

Kaminer, D & Eagle, G (2010) *Traumatic Stress in South Africa*. Johannesburg: Wits University Press.

Kernberg, OF (1993) The current status of psychoanalysis. *Journal of the American Psychoanalytic Association*, 41: 45–62.

Kernberg, OF (2007) The coming changes in psychoanalytic education: Part II. *The International Journal of Psychoanalysis*, 88(1): 183–202.

Kernberg, O (2010) Some observations on the process of mourning. *The International Journal of Psychoanalysis*, 91: 601–619.

Kernberg, OF (2012a) Psychoanalysis and the university: A difficult relationship. In OF Kernberg *The Inseparable Nature of Love and Aggression: Clinical and Theoretical Perspectives*. Washington, DC: American Psychiatric Publishing.

Kernberg, OF (2012b) 'Dissidence' in psychoanalysis: A psychoanalytic reflection. In OF Kernberg *The Inseparable Nature of Love and Aggression: Clinical and Theoretical Perspectives*. Washington, DC: American Psychiatric Publishing.

Klein, M (1940) Mourning and its relation to manic depressive states. In M Klein *Love, Guilt and Reparation: And Other Works 1921–1945*, pp. 344–369. London: Hogarth Press.

Knox, J (2003) Trauma and defences: Their roots in relationship. An overview. *Journal of Analytical Psychoanalysis*, 48: 207–233.

Kohlberg, L (1977) Moral development: A review of the theory. *Theory into Practice*, 16(2): 53–59.

Kohut, H (1977) *The Restoration of the Self.* New York: International Universities Press.

Kosman, BA & Keysar, A (2009) *American Religious Identification Survey (ARIS): Summary Report.* Hartford, Connecticut: Trinity College.

Kuhn, T (1996) *The Structure of Scientific Revolutions* (third edition). Chicago & London: University of Chicago Press.

Lanyado, M (2009) Psychotherapy with severely traumatised children and adolescents: 'Far beyond words'. In M Lanyado & A Horne (eds) *The Handbook of Child and Adolescent Psychotherapy: Psychoanalytic Approaches*, pp. 300–315. London/New York: Routledge/ Taylor Francis Group.

Macklin, R (1999) *Against Relativism: Cultural Diversity and the Search for Ethical Universals in Medicine.* New York: Oxford University Press.

Menkiti, IA (1984) Person and community in African thought. In RA Wright (ed.) *African Philosophy: An Introduction*, pp. 51–91. Lanham, MD: University Press of America.

Mills, J (2005) A critique of relational psychoanalysis. *Psychoanalytic Psychology*, 22(2): 155–188.

Mills, J (2012) *Conundrums: A Critique of Contemporary Psychoanalysis.* New York: Routledge.

Mitchell, S (1997) *Influence and Autonomy in Psychoanalysis.* Hillside, NJ: The Analytic Press.

Mkhize, DL (2004) Psychology: An African perspective. In N Duncan, K Tatele, D Hook, N Mkhize, P Kiguwa & A Collins (eds) *Self, Community and Psychology*, pp 4.1–4.29. Cape Town: David Philip.

Ngubane, H (1977) *Body and Mind in Zulu Medicine.* London: Academic Press.

Niehaus, I (2005) Witches and zombies of the South African lowveld: Discourse, accusations and subjective reality. *Journal of the Royal Anthropological Institute*, 11(2): 191–115.

Obama, B (2011) Presidential address. Special report: The end of Bin Laden. *Time*, 177(20): 14–31. New York: Time Inc.

Poland, WS (2006) Revenge. *American Imago*, 63(3): 355–357.

Pollet, S (2010) Making a little go a long way: Early intervention. In MB Heller & S Pollet (eds) *The Work of Psychoanalysts in the Public Health Sector*, pp. 13–22. New York: Routledge & Taylor Francis Group.

Renik, O (1993) Analytic interaction: Conceptualizing technique in light of the analyst's irreducible subjectivity. *Psychoanalytic Quarterly*, 62: 553–571.

Renik, O (1996) The perils of neutrality. *Psychoanalytic Quarterly*, 65: 495–517.

Robbins, T (2007) Contextualizing Bowlby: Commentary on Fonagy and Target. *Journal of the American Psychoanalytic Association*, 55: 469–478.

Rosen, IC (2007) Revenge – the hate that dare not speak its name: A psychoanalytic perspective. *Journal of the American Psychoanalytic Association*, 55: 595–619.

Sepkowitz, K (2006) One disease, two epidemics: AIDS at 25. *New England Journal of Medicine*, 345: 2411–2414.

Silver, CB (2003) A survey of clinicians' views about change in psychoanalytic practice and theoretical orientation. *Psychoanalytic Review*, 90: 193–224.

Silverman, RC & Leiberman, AF (1999) Negative maternal attributions, projective identification, and the intergenerational transmission of violent relational patterns. *Psychoanalytic Dialogues*, 9: 161–186.

Silverman, P & Worden, JW (1992) Children's reactions to death of a parent in the early months after the death. *American Journal of Orthopsychiatry*, 62: 428–441.

Smith, C & Albertyn, L (2011) Child and adolescent psychiatry: Challenges and opportunities in Africa. In DM Ndetei & CP Szabo (eds) *Contemporary Psychiatry in Africa: A Review of Theory, Practice and Research*, pp. 315–331. Kenya: Arcodile Publishing Limited.

Smith, C & Holford, LE (1993) Post-traumatic stress disorder in South Africa's children and adolescents. *Southern African Journal of Child and Adolescent Mental Health*, 5: 57–69.

Solomon, H (2005) Turning back the tide: Illegal immigration into South Africa. *Mediterranean Quarterly*, 16(4): 90–111.

Stepansky, PE (2009) *Psychoanalysis at the Margins*. New York: The Other Press.

Stern, DB (1997) *Unformulated Experience: From Dissociation to Imagination in Psychoanalysis*. Hillside, NJ: The Analytic Press.

Straker, G (1994) Integrating African and Western healing practices in South Africa. *American Journal of Psychotherapy*, 48(3): 455–467.

Sugarman, A (2009) Child versus adult psychoanalysis: Two processes or one? *International Journal of Psychoanalysis*, 90: 1255–1276.

Swartz, L (1998) *Culture and Mental Health: A Southern African View*. Cape Town: Oxford University Press.

Swartz, S (2007) Reading psychoanalysis in the diaspora: South African psychoanalytic psychotherapists' struggle with voice. *Psychoanalytic Psychotherapy in South Africa*, 15: 1–18.

Taylor, C (1994) The politics of recognition. In C Taylor & A Gutman (eds) *Multiculturalism: Examining the Politics of Recognition*, pp. 25–74. Princeton: Princeton University Press.

Tomlinson, M, Cooper, P & Murray, L (2005) The mother–infant relationship and infant attachment in a South African peri-urban settlement. *Child Development*, 76(5): 1044–1054.

UNICEF (2010) *Levels and Trends in Child Mortality, Report 2010*. Estimates developed by the UN Inter-agency Group for Child Mortality Estimation, UNICEF, WHO, The World Bank, United Nations DESA/Population Division. Accessed from http://www.childmortality.org/files_v9/download/Levels%20and%20Trends%20in%20Child%20Mortality%20Report%202010.pdf on 1 November 2012.

Wallerstein, RS (2005a) Will psychoanalytic pluralism be an enduring state of our discipline? *International Journal of Psychoanalysis*, 86: 623–626.

Wallerstein, RS (2005b) Dialogue or illusion? How do we go from here? Response to Andre Green. *International Journal of Psychoanalysis*, 86: 633–638.

Wallerstein, RS (2012) Will psychoanalysis fulfil its promise? *International Journal of Psychoanalysis*, 93: 377–399.

Wallin, DJ (2007) *Attachment in Psychotherapy*. New York, NY: Guilford Press.

Walls, GB (2004) Toward a critical global psychoanalysis. *Psychoanalytic Dialogues*, 14(5): 605–643.

Wheely, S (1992) Looks that kill the capacity for thought. *Journal of Analytic Psychology*, 37(2): 187–210.

CHAPTER 5

TRAUMATIC STRESS, INTERNAL AND EXTERNAL: What do psychodynamic perspectives have to contribute?

Gill Eagle

Working in the traumatic stress field for the past 25 years in South Africa as therapist, trainer, clinical supervisor, consultant and researcher – with populations as diverse as rape and torture survivors; political detainees; accident, crime and domestic violence victims; combat veterans; refugees and the traumatically bereaved – I have found it of great value to draw upon aspects of psychodynamic thinking and practice, as will be elaborated in this chapter. During these 25 years the landscape of trauma and trauma intervention has changed markedly. My earliest exposure to trauma intervention was through involvement in the feminist-influenced, rape crisis organisations that grew up around the country in the 1970s. The counselling offered by these organisations was located within a crisis counselling model influenced by insights from feminism about understanding the causes and effects of sexual violence. Later, in the 1980s, like many other progressive professionals in the country, I became involved in an anti-apartheid group, the Organisation for Appropriate Social Services in South Africa (OASSSA), which aimed to address mental health issues relating to oppression and political repression, including trauma-related issues. Two central projects of OASSSA were, firstly, to offer counselling services to ex-detainees, many of whom had been tortured or abused during their time in detention, and secondly, to run crisis counselling workshops for community groups. The latter often entailed conducting some trauma intervention for the trainees themselves, many of whom had been damaged in a variety of ways within the political system. During this time few of us explicitly understood our work within the framework of traumatic stress, a diagnostic and conceptual category that really only gained purchase in South Africa in the early 1990s, although it is now widely employed by a range of practitioners and theorists across the country. Pioneers of trauma work in South Africa tended to become involved in such work in large part out of a political commitment to victims and survivors, given that traumatised populations often represent groups that have been oppressed in some way. In contemporary South Africa there is a much broader spectrum of people involved in trauma work dealing with a wide range of victims, much of this work being undertaken in workplace employee assistance programmes. The field of traumatic stress studies has grown exponentially internationally over the last two decades and local practitioners have been exposed to a number of different conceptual models for treating and understanding traumatic stress. While there has been training in technique-focused approaches such as Traumatic Incident Reduction (TIR) and Eye Movement Desensitisation and Reprocessing (EMDR) (Kaminer & Eagle, 2010), there has perhaps been less emphasis on the contributions that psychodynamic theory can make to such work, except within specifically psychoanalytic forums. This chapter will elaborate and discuss some of these contributions for a wider audience.

CONTEXTUALISING TRAUMATIC STRESS CONDITIONS IN SOUTH AFRICA

Thinking and writing about traumatic stress in post-apartheid South Africa is a rather daunting task, in large measure because it is difficult to do justice to the range and complexity of issues that might be encompassed under this topic. It seemed to me that it would be important to begin by sketching out some of the historical and contemporary contexts in order to understand the kinds of traumatic events and experiences that trauma interventionists in South Africa have found/find they were/are required to deal with.

A history of violation

As the introduction to the book discusses, South Africa has been characterised by a violent and oppressive past that saw colonial exploitation extended into the more modern apartheid state in which the vast majority of the population were denied basic human rights on the basis of a complex system of racial categorisation and capitalist relations. In order to maintain this unjust political dispensation, the state employed considerable repressive force of both an ideological and physical/ structural nature. The history of conflict between those fighting either to maintain or to overthrow the apartheid state has left its mark in the form of remembered violations such as the detention, torture and assassination of actual and suspected political activists; participation in the military conflicts on the border of the country; and violent confrontations between rival political party members, and between activists and those suspected of collaborating with the government of the time. Many of the gross human rights violations perpetrated prior to 1994 were exposed during the hearings of the national Truth and Reconciliation Commission (TRC, 1998) that took place in the years soon after the African National Congress was elected into power during the first truly democratic elections the country had seen. It was evident during the TRC hearings that the violence committed during the apartheid period had left many traumatised at both individual and collective levels and it was often almost unbearable to come to know and engage with the cruelty and suffering that was laid bare during the hearings. While there has been considerable criticism of the TRC process from a range of different quarters (see for example, Jolly, 2010; Posel, 2006; Van der Walt et al., 2003), it was evident that the spirit within which it was undertaken, under the leadership of Archbishop Desmond Tutu, was designed to bring about some sort of political, spiritual and psychological healing through a process of catharsis, confession, bearing witness and, in many instances, the anticipation of forgiveness and reconciliation (Gobodo-Madikizela, 2008). Individual stories told during the public hearings were intentionally chosen so as to represent collective forms of traumatisation and there was a hope that the unearthing of material that had been denied and repressed at a political level would bring about both relief on the part of victims and their families and remorse on the part of the perpetrators and those who had supported them. Although not overtly couched in these terms, it could be argued that in addition to serving an overtly political function in relation to justice and retribution, the TRC process was designed to facilitate what broadly might be understood psychodynamically as exploration of that which had been repressed (in many different senses), emotional catharsis, working through, reparation and mourning. Rather than burying the past, it needed to remain active in people's minds if they were to move forward into a new dispensation in a reconciliatory spirit sensitive to past damage and committed to the non-repetition of abuses of power. A powerful strand then in trauma work in South Africa is the ongoing need to hold in mind a past that brutalised many and continues to stimulate resentment, bitterness, guilt and defensiveness despite the TRC hearings, although the TRC may well have served to help many to metabolise some of this traumatic past to a greater or lesser extent.

In addition to the gross human rights violations highlighted by the TRC, it has been observed that apartheid had more pervasive and insidious effects. These included racial segregation, discriminatory laws and practices, forced removals of people, migratory labour, lack of access to schooling and basic services, and the devaluation and humiliation of individuals based on skin colour and racial differentiation (Kometsi, 2008). The Apartheid Archive Project,[1] launched in 2009, aims to document what has been termed the more quotidian or everyday impact of the apartheid system. Based on personal testimonies, the project has begun to explore some of the psychological features of people's lives, related to experiences of racism in particular. For example, researchers have focused on the role of domestic workers and the suffering entailed in separating from their young children in order to maintain employment, on the violations entailed in being ostracised and excluded from public spaces, and on the confusion, shame and anger evoked in witnessing parents demeaned and treated with disrespect and contempt. Beneficiaries and perpetrators of racism have also evinced feelings of alienation, shame and guilt. These historical relations and associated memories also continue to infuse current-day interactions (and perhaps more particularly those of a traumatic nature).

In engaging in trauma-related work in post-apartheid South Africa, it is incumbent upon interventionists to hold this history in mind and to recognise not only the direct intergenerational transmission of traumatic material but also the manner in which violence, suffering and misfortune in the present may carry residues of this collective past. Similar to the manner in which psychodynamic theorists argue for the appreciation of developmental history in understanding the significance of contemporary traumatic events for the individual (Garland,

1998a), so too, in some respects, does the socio-political history of the country colour the interpretation of traumatic events in the present in important ways.

Contemporary social problems contributing to traumatisation

Having pointed to the violence of apartheid both at the level of state repression and everyday practices, and having proposed that the present is still very much influenced by this past, it is also important to outline some of the other more contemporary features of South African society that render large numbers of people vulnerable to traumatic kinds of stresses. Without going into detail about all of these features, it should be noted that statistics demonstrate that motor vehicle accident rates are very high, many of these involving serious injury and loss of life; violence against women and female children is extraordinarily pervasive, with partner abuse widespread and reported rape figures among the highest in the world; and gang violence and homicide among young adult men is also of significant proportions (Kaminer & Eagle, 2010). In the recently conducted South African Stress and Health (SASH) study, researchers found that nearly 75% of interviewees reported having experienced at least one traumatic event in their lifetime (Williams et al., 2007: 850). The study included both direct exposure and exposure related to personal loss and witnessing traumatic events. Both nationally and internationally, life in South Africa has become associated with vulnerability to crime and it has become rare to encounter individuals who have not been either directly or indirectly exposed to some form of crime in their work or home environment, or indeed to multiple such events. In the SASH study it appeared to be the norm rather than the exception for those surveyed to report exposure to more than one traumatic event, with close to 10% of the sample reporting exposure to six or more traumatic events (Williams et al., 2007: 849). As summarised in Altbeker's 2007 review of violent crime, 'South Africa ranks at the very top of the world's league tables for violent crime' (quoted in Kaminer & Eagle, 2010: 13). In the 2007 National Crime Victims Survey, some 22.3% of respondents interviewed (more than one in five individuals) reported direct exposure to crime in the preceding 12 months (Pharoah, 2008: 7). If one considers that the families, acquaintances and work colleagues of this somewhat over 20% of the population may well have also been affected by the survey victim's exposure to a crime, it is apparent that a large proportion of South Africans are likely to carry some awareness of vulnerability to crime and associated affects. South African Police Service statistics for 2009/2010[2] reflect the following patterns per 100 000 of the population: 34.1 murders, 35.3 attempted murders, 416.2 serious assaults, 138.5 sexual offences, and 129.4 robberies, reflecting disturbingly high levels of interpersonally driven attacks, in addition to burglaries, muggings and thefts. It is also commonly accepted that many crimes go unreported, particularly those of a sexual nature. It cannot be disputed that crime is a serious social problem and it is evident that concerns about vulnerability to crime are pervasive among the South African population, creating a sense of background stress to everyday living. One of the ways in which this manifests is in 'Fear of Crime', 'the emotional response to potential victimization' (Adams & Serpe, 2000: 607), levels of which increased steadily from 1998 to 2008 (Pharoah, 2008). Fear of crime often translates into behavioural and interpersonal constriction (such as fear of travelling outside of one's immediate neighbourhood and fear of strangers). In this respect high levels of crime, and particularly of violent interpersonal crime, have multiple effects beyond those of severely traumatising direct victims. It is also evident that rather than subsiding over time with the introduction of the new political dispensation, crime levels and perceptions of vulnerability to crime have increased, suggesting that many citizens feel uncontained by the present government in this respect, and this contributes to disillusionment, anger, anxiety and fear. The SASH study also confirmed that with exposure to increased numbers of events, there was evidence of increased psychological distress or mental health difficulty as measured by a global distress scale, with 'those with the most traumas (six or more)…5 times more likely to be highly distressed than those with no trauma' (Williams et al., 2007: 853).

A further significant stressor in post-apartheid South Africa is the AIDS epidemic, discussed at some length elsewhere in the book. There has been considerable debate about the links between HIV contraction risk, AIDS and vulnerability to traumatic stress (Nightingale et al., 2010), given that the life threat implied by exposure to the virus is often not immediate and that terminal illness may be staved off by antiretroviral treatment. However, it has been demonstrated in a variety of studies that the diagnosis of life-threatening or terminal illnesses may well lead to traumatic stress-related conditions (Kaminer & Eagle, 2010). AIDS-related deaths are also clearly implicated in traumatic bereavements, often compounded by the stigma and consequent secrecy still attached to the condition. In a study into the mental health of 60 AIDS-orphaned children in Cape Town, it was found that 73% scored above the cut-off point for Post-traumatic Stress Disorder (PTSD) (Barbarin et al., 2001: 22). The researchers speculate that the traumatic stress-related responses may have stemmed not only from the loss related to final death, but also from the horror of witnessing the ongoing deterioration and disability of parents prior to this. Given the prevalence of AIDS in South Africa, it is evident that large numbers of individuals and families have been, and will continue to be, exposed to the ravages of the illnesses associated with compromised immune functioning, and to premature AIDS-related bereavements, often of a multiple nature within extended families. Again, what is evident is a rupture to the social fabric that creates a sense of widespread contamination and the possibility of loss.

A final aspect of South African society that warrants mention in relation to traumatic stress is the influx of many thousands of economic and political migrants, asylum seekers and refugees from other African countries. Among these refugees, a significant proportion has been subject to torture, abuse, imprisonment, genocide, rape, sexual and other assaults, and the destruction of homes and family, implying vulnerability to classic traumatic stress symptoms and conditions. Their trauma-related suffering is further compounded by their displacement and need to expend resources in adjusting to an unfamiliar environment (Grootenhuis, 2007). Beyond these adjustment difficulties, there is also widespread exposure to xenophobia, abuse and exploitation in this current environment, some of which is cynically perpetrated by precisely those entrusted with the welfare of refugees within South African state systems. The possibility of xenophobic violence, which came to a head with the disturbing attacks and murders of 2008, continues to threaten the social fabric and points to ongoing scapegoating and intergroup conflict. Allegations of 'foreigner's' involvement in the commission of crime are often used to justify discrimination, but many attacks on refugees appear to be driven by envy, projection, displacement of aggression, and sadistic exploitation of those who are most vulnerable. The maltreatment of refugees by significant proportions of the population suggests a disquieting underbelly of resentment and intolerance that belies the assertion of values of *ubuntu* and the upholding of human rights and dignity.

PSYCHODYNAMIC CONTRIBUTIONS TO UNDERSTANDING HISTORICAL, COLLECTIVE AND PERVASIVE TRAUMATISATION

It is apparent, then, that people living in South Africa are vulnerable to traumatisation of a variety of kinds, leading to the suggestion that the society as a whole is a damaged and 'traumatised' one, whatever this implies at a psychic and a social level. While there are problems with the direct and sometimes oversimplistic extrapolation of psychodynamic constructs from the clinical consulting room to social formations, there are ways in which psychodynamic thinking is helpful in attempting to understand some of the likely consequences of the kinds of contextual difficulties outlined thus far. In the first instance, psychodynamic theory allows us to entertain notions of unconscious and preconscious forces at play in psychic functioning. This awareness assists us to appreciate the way in which the interpretation of present events is inevitably shaped by personal and social history. Danieli (1985), Laub (1998) and others have written about how experiences of Holocaust survivors come to be unconsciously represented in the lives of their offspring and even in successive generations, manifesting in dreams, enactments and traumatic repetitions. This intergenerational transmission of traumatic life experiences cannot be explained purely in terms of exposure to the recounting of events or caretaking by 'damaged' parents, but involves the internalisation or even introjection of such content at more primitive, unconscious levels, in part through complicated object relating during early childhood or infancy. There has been considerable speculation that similar unconscious transmission of painful, abject, fearful, paranoid and aggressive states of mind may have taken place across generations in South Africa, although it has proved difficult to research such relations. Perhaps because the atrocities committed by the apartheid state are more recent and exist in living memory for many more people, it is important to entertain the possibility of conscious, preconscious *and* unconscious associations to life under apartheid. The awareness that the past may manifest in the present in unexpected, indirect and unconscious ways may help clinicians to appreciate the affective intensity and traumatic associations that particular events carry for individuals. I would maintain that an awareness of the possible aliveness of this history in the present is potentially invaluable in the knowledge and skills repertoire of post-apartheid trauma practitioners.

Alongside the awareness that current events may be infused with past meanings of particular kinds related to the socio-political history of South Africa, it is also worth bearing in mind the strong pull towards repression and forgetting that psychodynamic theorists have observed as characteristic of responses to traumatic stimuli. Freud and Breuer's early work on hysteria and conversion disorders was predicated on the notion that events experienced as too traumatic to be consciously symbolised became repressed and manifested indirectly in symptom formation. Laub and Auerhahn have written more recently on the relationship between exposure to massive psychic trauma and 'knowing and not knowing', maintaining that it 'is the nature of trauma to elude our knowledge because of both defence and deficit' (1993: 289). They argue that because knowing trauma can be 'a momentous, threatening, cognitive and affective task', it may be defended against by being rendered unconscious, and that, at the level of deficit, 'trauma also overwhelms and defeats our capacity to organize it' (1993: 289). Trauma-related memories may thus be more or less accessible to consciousness and communication depending upon the nature and severity of the experience, the capacity of the ego to bind anxiety, and the proximity of the individual to the event. Remembering and integrating traumatic contents is dependent upon the capacity to mobilise an 'observing ego' and upon interpersonal (such as in the form of a therapist) and cultural supports. The TRC was designed to produce a context in which those giving testimony were to some extent witnesses to their own histories and were offered both psychological and institutional support, even if this was not always borne out in practice. However, it has been observed that some 10 years on, there has been considerable contestation over the remembering and forgetting of apartheid, with a strong cultural pull towards 'moving on' and 'letting bygones be bygones'. Thus there are ideological forces abetting a form of social repression of this past. Young adult South Africans may well find themselves conflicted in wishing to establish an identity independent of struggle and oppression, yet simultaneously seeking to honour the sacrifices of their parents or, alternatively, to distance themselves from their parents' past collusion with the state. In this respect there is still considerable turmoil at a social and perhaps intrapsychic level as South Africans attempt to integrate the past without becoming overwhelmed or paralysed by this knowledge (Gobodo-Madikizela, 2008).

In addition to helping interventionists to think about the importance of the past in the present, psychodynamic theory also offers some useful ways of thinking about the likely impact of living in a contemporary environment characterised by high levels of crime, loss, risk and danger. In Freud's (1920/1948) seminal paper on many of the mechanisms at play in traumatic stress conditions and responses, 'Beyond the pleasure principle', he makes reference to the fact that trauma, by definition, involves a breach of the psychic boundary or protective shield of the self. In the normal course of events the ego is designed to protect the individual against potential sources of distress.

> In order to deal with aversive stimuli, the psyche, and more particularly the ego, becomes attuned to anxiety provoking cues in the environment, so as to anticipate, and therefore prepare for, exposure to such anxiety. With this

> signal anxiety the psyche protects itself from becoming overwhelmed by anxi-
> ety/displeasure by optimizing psychical resources available to deal with stress
> prior to the encounter. (Eagle & Watts, 2002: 9)

The sudden, overwhelming and transgressive nature of traumatic events is such as to preclude the binding of anxiety, and the individual is left psychologically compromised in various ways, many of these now detailed in the symptom patterns described under the diagnostic categories of Acute Stress Disorder and PTSD (APA, 2000). One of the consequences of direct exposure to trauma is that the distinction between signal and automatic anxiety is lost (Garland, 1998b), rendering trauma survivors vulnerable to constant and powerful anxiety, particularly in situations that bear any resemblance to the traumatic event. In South Africa, with its pervasive risks of traumatisation, it may well be the case that the population in general struggles to realistically appraise threat levels in the environment and that, even if at less intense levels than manifested in direct victims, there is increased anxiety-proneness related to difficulties in appropri-ately attending to signal anxiety. This may manifest in hyper-vigilance, suspi-cion in interpersonal interactions, avoidance of certain places and people, and increased irritability and propensity for aggression. When it is apparent that the world may not be a benign, meaningful and predictable place, assumptions argued to be constructive to mental health (Janoff-Bulman cited in Kaminer & Eagle, 2010), it may prove difficult to devote psychic energy to creativity and to constructive loving and working. Awareness of risk may produce both height-ened anxiety and a kind of psychic constriction. Kirschner draws upon the work of a range of psychodynamic theorists (including Ferenczi, Klein, Winnicott and Lacan) in proposing that 'every society recognizes the parents' (or surrogates') duty to provide a reliable second skin around the child, a transitional zone in Winnicottian terms, within which the child can safely assimilate the rules of the socius…', and that complementing this is 'an equally vital requirement for a kind of third layer of protection and sustenance of the community's symbolic, linguistic structure, which encompasses systems of meaning, belief and value as they structure basic human interactions' (Kirschner, 1994: 241). Kirschner thus proposes that psychic development is in part dependent upon the mainte-nance of this third membrane (associated in his writing with Lacan's notion of the symbolic order), which provides a broader kind of containment in which optimal caretaking, object relating and interpersonal interaction can take place. The prevalence of trauma exposure in South Africa, and particularly of exposure to multiple traumatic events and to events of an apparently gratuitously violent nature, means that it may be difficult for people to feel that this third layer is sufficiently robust or indeed exists at all. At such times South Africans may feel that they are living in a somewhat crazy or chaotic world in which it is difficult to assess what is rational in their own thinking. One manifestation of this absence of a sense of a sound third layer of protection or order appears to be a kind of general low-level lawlessness or tolerance of transgression (such as excessive drinking or speeding while driving) that further contributes to a sense of living in a somewhat precarious society. Kirschner (1994) suggests that the role of the analyst lies in upholding the basic human right of 'access to a symbolic order' that entails not only protection and restoration of 'good objects' at the individual and social levels (both the good maternal object and the good maternal environment), but also resistance to attacks on those aspects of society that promote social cohesion. In this respect it is important that trauma interventionists in South Africa work to actively promote both individual and collective healing, as to some extent each is predicated upon the other. While it was perhaps somewhat easier for mental health workers to assume a complementary political commitment in their work in the anti-apartheid period, it is evident that many contemporary trauma practitioners still demonstrate a strong commitment to the politics of upholding human rights. Thus, for example, post-apartheid trauma interventionists have assisted victim groups to establish self-help groups and to generate self-help projects; have conducted psychosocial interventions with ex-combatants; have documented the torture reported by refugees from particular African countries; and have lobbied the government and business to take victim rights more seriously, among a range of other interventions. I believe that this kind of work is undertaken to contribute to the psychological integrity and sanity of service providers as much as it is to benefit victims. In order to continue to provide containment at a therapeutic level, it is important to have some sense of contributing to a socially cohesive environment.

Having examined some of the contextual features of South African society that have contributed to historical and collective trauma, and also those that account for the high prevalence of direct and indirect exposure to traumatic stressors, the discussion now moves to examine more directly clinical elements of trauma practice in the country. With the background painted, it is now possible to begin to focus on the foreground, in this instance on more individual aspects of trauma impact and treatment as understood psychodynamically.

CLINICAL AND INDIVIDUALLY ORIENTED CONSIDERATIONS IN TRAUMA WORK IN SOUTH AFRICA

This section of the chapter includes discussion of both trauma impact and presentation, and psychotherapy for trauma-related conditions, including some discussion of countertransference and therapist engagement in trauma work. Reading the more recent international literature on traumatic stress as represented in the widely cited *Journal of Traumatic Stress* and the material generated by the International Society of Traumatic Stress Studies and its European and Australasian counterparts, it is evident that psychodynamic approaches to traumatic stress have become somewhat marginalised. In part because of the shift to evidence-based practice and the emphasis on clinical guidelines in offering treatment for mental health conditions, including traumatic stress-related conditions, there has been a shift away from psychodynamically informed approaches in favour of cognitive behavioural therapy (CBT) and protocol- and technique-based approaches. In a recent overview article comparing clinical practice guidelines for the treatment of PTSD and related conditions across North America, Europe and Australia, it is evident that there is consensus that trauma-focused CBT (TFCBT) and EMDR are the psychological treatments of choice (Forbes et al., 2010). While psychodynamic psychotherapy is mentioned in two sets of guidelines, it is given a lower category rating as a desirable treatment for traumatic stress. In addition to difficulties in verifying psychodynamic interventions within the 'best practice' research guidelines of randomised control trials, it is also commonly believed that psychodynamic approaches are necessarily long term and therefore unsuitable for the short- or medium-term therapy interventions generally associated with traumatic stress conditions. The relegation of psychodynamic approaches to the periphery is somewhat surprising given that the majority of the early literature conceptualising traumatic stress impact was written by psychodynamic theorists such as Janet, Freud, Kahn, Lifton and Horowitz. This appears to reflect the orientation towards cost-effective and scientifically proven interventions, as influenced by medical models of practice. Within South Africa, although there are many practitioners who use TFCBT and EMDR in the trauma field, it is evident that psychodynamic ways of thinking and working still enjoy considerable support. The nature of traumatic stress presentations in South Africa, and the fact that many interventions are offered by non-professional counsellors, has meant that therapists have drawn upon a variety of models and approaches, some of them infused with psychodynamic constructs. While trauma-focused psychodynamic psychotherapy may not be practised with the same rigour or purity of approach as described by Tavistock Trauma Clinic practitioners (Garland, 1998a), it is nevertheless evident that psychodynamic theory occupies a central place in the work of many clinicians and community practitioners (Kaminer & Eagle, 2010). Some of the reasons for this are elaborated in the ensuing discussion.

PSYCHODYNAMIC CONTRIBUTIONS TO FORMULATING THE PSYCHOLOGICAL IMPACT OF TRAUMATIC STRESSORS

It is evident that 'trauma' has been understood relatively broadly within psychodynamic writing. Historically, the term has been used both to refer to developmental shocks and deficits (as in witnessing the primal scene, or experiencing a profound lack of mirroring), as well as to frame what would more commonly be understood by trauma practitioners as constituting a traumatic life stressor, for example exposure to stimuli of a sudden, life-threatening and/or injurious kind. For the purposes of this chapter, psychodynamic theory pertaining only to the latter kind of understanding is discussed. There are at least three theoretical traditions within psychoanalysis that have contributed significantly to the understanding of the impact of trauma of this kind, these being classical, ego-psychological and object relations perspectives, although it should be acknowledged that self and relational theorists have also made more recent useful inputs. As has been noted, Freud (1920/1948) made a seminal contribution to the theorisation of traumatic stress (although he did not explicitly use this terminology), arguing that exposure to catastrophic life events tended to produce some regression in psychic functioning, evidenced in the employment of more primitive defences, cognitive deficits (such as difficulties in symbolisation and articulation), and a propensity to dissociate. In addition, he argued that trauma was often implicated in repetition compulsion of various kinds, such as recurrent nightmares and trauma-related enactments. These ideas continue to remain useful to trauma practitioners and help to explain the sometimes rather dependant presentation of traumatised patients in psychotherapy. It has been widely observed that somatisation is a very common response to trauma among the South African population as a whole, and it is possible to understand this kind of presentation as representing signification of distress in a way that serves to protect the individual from the conscious knowing of the event which threatens to overwhelm psychic structures, in the kind of way suggested by Freud. In addition, recent neuroscience research confirms that one element of trauma impact is some compromise to verbal expression and symbolisation (Van der Kolk, 2006). When clinicians understand that somatisation may represent a strong defence suggesting the enormity of the underlying distress associated with consciously entertaining traumatic images, this can offer guidance as to how quickly they can work to uncover and process trauma-related memories, as well as to how supportive they may need to be in this kind of work. For example, a woman presented at a township outpatient clinic complaining of chest pains for which no medical cause could be determined. In exploring the onset of her symptoms and her recent life history, she revealed that her husband had been shot in front of her a month previously. In the course of a relatively brief therapy it was possible to draw links between her psychic and physical heart pain and to tie her somatic experience back to the horror and tension she felt at the time of his murder. Working through the psychological impact of the trauma led to an abatement of the chest pains.

Extending on Freud's formulation of an ego that becomes compromised and cannot retain the protective shield against external stimuli, ego-psychologists such as Horowitz (1992) argue that the intrusive force of traumatic experience is such as to destabilise meaning systems and to interfere with the normal integration of experience and laying down of memory traces. Combining insights from cognitive information processing theory and ego-psychology, Horowitz suggests that the manner in which trauma manifests in psychic functioning is in the vacillation between intrusion and avoidance of aversive contents. While the task of the ego is to assimilate and accommodate the new information, this requires engagement with unbearable contents that remained undigested, in the form of sensory associations and fragmented bits of memory that evoke massive anxiety. In consequence, there is a tendency to both behavioural and cognitive avoidance of trauma-related material. In his book *Stress Response Syndromes*, Horowitz (1992) thus anticipated and provided some theoretical rationale for the kind of symptom picture that is understood psychiatrically to be associated with traumatic stress (most notably the cluster B and C sets of symptoms – intrusive and avoidance/numbing respectively) (APA, 2000). I have also found it helpful to hold this model in mind in undertaking trauma work in South Africa, appreciating that the survivor is in some respects trapped in a cycle of avoidance and intrusion that precludes them from doing precisely that which is required in order for traumatic memories to be integrated into narrative or long-term memory. In contexts of multiple or poly-traumatisation and/or where external containment is lacking (as is frequently the case in South Africa), this kind of psychological vacillation may well be exaggerated or prolonged and again may require careful assessment on the part of the therapist. Part of the therapist's task then is to gauge what 'optimal dosing' (Horowitz, 1992: 125) in respect of engaging with trauma-associated contents might entail for a particular patient, dealing with a particular traumatic event, and in a particular context at a particular time.

From an object relations (as well as a more classical) perspective, it is understood that traumatic events will hold or take on specific meanings based on the way in which current events map back onto earlier developmental difficulties (for example, castration anxieties) and, perhaps even more importantly for such theorists, based on the manner in which parental or caretaker introjects or objects have taken up residence in the psyche. Garland argues that 'there is a way in which a current trauma can link up powerfully with events from the past, through long established internal object relationships' (1998b: 108). This perspective is poignantly illustrated in her discussion of a rape case in which she describes how the introjection of a contemptuous, intellectual and mocking father-part and a 'vulnerable, despised, contaminated female aspect of herself' (Garland, 1998b: 115) appear to be implicated in the experience and processing of the sexual assault. While it may not always be possible to unearth these types of connections in the kinds of brief-term trauma interventions commonly offered in South Africa, it is useful to entertain the notion that traumatic events will hold highly personalised meanings for individuals as well as carry commonly understood associations. It is interesting that in the comprehensive TFCBT model proposed by Ehlers and Clark (2000), considerable weight is placed upon the attributions that individuals have made in relation to both the circumstances of their traumatisation and the likely consequences this will hold for them in the future. This suggests that they also attach considerable significance to the meaning-making aspect of the trauma response, and that their exploration goes beyond assessing the kinds of trauma-related cognitions that would traditionally be the target of cognitive restructuring. Writing from a self-psychology perspective, and integrating aspects of schema theory, McCann and Pearlman (1990) also propose that an essential element of traumatisation is the rupturing of core schemas, specifically those pertaining to safety, trust, independence, power, self-esteem, intimacy and frame of reference. Although object relations theorists would probably maintain that more individualised depth work is necessary to the uncovering of the manner in which object-relational constellations articulate with traumatic experiences in the present, it is perhaps useful to view these kinds of approaches to grasping the meaning-related aspects of trauma impact as occurring along a continuum, and to remain alert to the possibility of achieving such insight-oriented connections even in more short-term trauma therapy.

A second strand in object relations theorisation of trauma concerns the association of traumatic experiences with the absence of, or abandonment by, 'good object' (usually maternal object) introjects. The fact that one has been allowed to suffer so terribly suggests the failure and/or impotence of good objects to protect one and this may lead to the sense that such objects have been destroyed or cannot be trusted.

> Trauma disrupts the link between self and empathic other, a link first established by the expectation of mutual responsiveness in the mother-child bond and 'objectified' in the maternal introject. Indeed we…proposed that the essential experience of trauma was the unraveling of the relationship between self and nurturing other, the very fabric of psychic life. (Laub & Auerhahn, 1993: 287)

In a rather poignant case example, a young woman who had been assaulted and raped in a house robbery described how when her brother arrived, having accompanied her through her medical examination, he took her home and placed her in a hot bath, washing her body and her hair as if she were a child. Her recollection of this very maternal form of care was such as to restore a good and containing object introject, and appeared to have aided remarkably in her recovery.

Paralleling Laub and Auerhahn's (1993) understanding, but drawing more explicitly on Bion's understanding of the importance of the containing function of the mother, Garland (1998a) concurs that a further dimension of traumatisation is the experience that the maternal object has failed one. She argues that this inevitably leads to problems in the area of symbolisation, resonating with the ideas of Freud and Horowitz about the negative impact of trauma on cognitive capacities, although understanding that the compromise to thinking stems not so much from regression and ego dysfunction as from the felt absence of a containing other.

> Both the external and internal containers are lost: the world itself has become unpredictable and dangerous, and the dangers are such that one's good internal objects are powerless to prevent the worst from happening. The capacity to symbolize, to use aspects of the actual world to represent internal

objects and object relationships for purposes of thinking and understanding, depends upon the proper functioning of an internal container. In a trauma that container is lost; in treatment an attempt is made to restore its function. (Garland, 1998b: 108–109)

This construction of the essence of traumatisation is also helpful to formulating traumatic stress responses in South Africa. In the first place, it is important to acknowledge the possibility, discussed elsewhere in this text, that for many traumatised individuals there may not have been the possibility for adequate attachment and early experiences of maternal/caretaker containment, given deprivation and a variety of stresses on maternal capacity and relating. In such cases, resources to deal with victimisation may be lacking from the outset and one may see a kind of resignation or passivity in the face of traumatisation (or intense anxiety and potential for disintegration). However, even for those who have benefited from good early containment, the experiences consequent upon attack may produce this sense of abandonment by one's good object/s. Many South African trauma victims describe bystander apathy and post-trauma isolation and rejection as a significant aspect of their trauma experience. Not only have they been the target of attack by the direct perpetrators, but those who might have intervened to prevent or assist them have often proved afraid or apathetic, or in some instances overtly exploitative or hostile. I am not sure if this kind of secondary violation is more prevalent in South Africa than in other contexts, but it is certainly not infrequent and may reflect something about a blunting to violence, and a lack of the kind of social cohesion that might allow for collective resistance to violence. There are also instances in which others do intervene in helpful and protective ways (as in the example described above) and in these cases it is less likely that good object introjects become completely unavailable to the psyche. However, in addition to bystander responses, the responses of those entrusted with law enforcement in the country are also implicated in the degree to which victims feel supported or let down by social containers. Again, it is not infrequent for victims to describe secondary victimisation at the hands of police personnel, or to detail incompetence, carelessness or a lack of concern from the criminal justice system. For example, a woman who had been involved in a motor vehicle accident and had been trapped for over an hour described her initial relief at being rescued from the vehicle, but her deep hurt at what she perceived as the deliberately sadistic treatment by a nurse in the emergency room who had put more pressure on her leg as she cried out that it was painful. This failure of an anticipated 'good object' had stayed with her more vividly in many respects than the actual accident. It is helpful in such instances to recognise that experiences like these may represent not only real but also symbolic failure in the mind of the victim, and to appreciate that the restoration of good object introjects may require considerable effort.

A further area that deserves brief mention in thinking psychodynamically about traumatised populations is that of what has been termed Complex PTSD (Herman, 1992). Although the category has not entered formally into diagnostic classification systems, the notion of Complex PTSD enjoys considerable conceptual and clinical support in trauma studies. Essentially, what is argued is that adaptation to a pathological and dangerous environment over an extended period of time requires the employment of particular defences and coping strategies that may become almost characterological over time. Thus one sees increased dissociation, somatisation, substance abuse, depression and pathological relationship enactment in victims of prolonged, multiple and inescapable abuse. It is apparent that an enormous body of psychoanalytic literature could be usefully drawn upon to appreciate the kinds of psychic structure and relational patterns that such survivors might manifest. Shottenbauer et al. (2008) have argued that psychodynamic approaches to treatment have a particularly meaningful role to play in the treatment of Complex PTSD, in part because other approaches have proved less successful in treating this kind of population. Given the number of people reporting poly- or multiple-event exposure in the country, it is also becoming increasingly common for more of those presenting for treatment at clinics and treatment centres to manifest complex trauma-like symptom patterns, suggesting that psychodynamic approaches might have increasing value in this context.

A final aspect of trauma impact that warrants discussion in terms of psychodynamic contributions to trauma intervention in South Africa is the common development of exaggerated intergroup prejudice, racism and xenophobia in many victims. Although these kinds of attitudinal shifts are common in survivors, this dimension of traumatic stress response has received minimal attention in the international trauma literature. Trauma counsellors and therapists in South Africa have reported that overt and intense prejudice against groups of people associated with the perpetration of violence is the norm rather than the exception (Fletcher, 2008, and Sibisi, 2008, both cited in Kaminer & Eagle, 2010). Such attitudes tend to carry behavioural consequences such as suspicion, avoidance and fearfulness, or the overt expression of aggression towards group members. In Benn's (2007) study into this phenomenon, he proposes that a Kleinian lens is useful in trying to make psychological sense of what are often egodystonic responses for individuals. Based on interviews with victims of violent attack he suggests that the regression associated with traumatisation brings about an increased propensity to operate from paranoid-schizoid states or positioning, leading to increased employment of projection, splitting and projective identification. Within psychoanalysis, racism (and prejudice in general) has been understood by some writers to stem from the need to project disowned or devalued parts of the self into others, as well as the need to protect good object introjects from 'bad objects' by employing processes of splitting and denigration directed at those who are seen as in some way different to oneself (Benn, 2007). It is then not difficult to appreciate how deliberate human-inflicted trauma may bring about a kind of marriage between these two pathological ways of functioning in the victim, leading to the development or exacerbation of particular kinds of social prejudice. Of course, it is important to acknowledge that these kinds of attitudes also often have their origin within historical patterns of relating within a social environment, and that, in this instance, intrapsychically generated conflicts may find expression in pre-existing South African social discourses (such as those holding foreigners responsible for crime or attributing particularly aggressive tendencies to Zulu men).

Recognising that some aspects of impact deserve greater elaboration than is possible within the scope of this chapter, it is important to move on to discuss some of the ways in which psychodynamic thinking has merit in informing trauma interventions and psychotherapy in South Africa.

TRAUMATIC STRESS INTERVENTION AND PSYCHODYNAMIC CONTRIBUTIONS

As discussed earlier, psychodynamic approaches to working with traumatic stress seem to have lost favour internationally, in part because of a lack of empirical evidence and perceptions that such approaches are necessarily long term. However, Shottenbauer et al. (2008) make a case for the value of psychodynamic treatment of PTSD, suggesting that such approaches may be better suited to working with more complex forms of trauma and perhaps with the not insignificant proportion of people who drop out of the protocol-based treatments assessed in randomised control trials. They argue that psychodynamic approaches may produce more lasting psychological shifts beyond symptom reduction, such as improved reflexive functioning and capacity to tolerate future anxiety. They also discuss two short-term models for working with PTSD. The first, elaborated by Horowitz (1997) and Krupnik (2002), entails a 12-session treatment model that includes three stages: establishing a working alliance and narration of the story; working through; and focusing on trauma-related loss and therapy termination (see Shottenbauer et al., 2008), as well as support and psycho-education.

The second rather similar model proposed by Lindy (1993) also involves three stages. The first stage focuses on developing a working alliance strong enough to allow the patient to shed his or her defences against confronting the feelings and memories associated with the traumatic event. The second stage is characterised by interventions aimed at understanding and working through the defences, feelings and memories associated with a specific traumatic event. This leads to the third stage, during which the patient restructures the memory of the event through a mourning-like process in which the trauma is endowed with a specific place and meaning in the life history of the individual, making for continuity and age-appropriate adaptive functioning (cited in Shottenbauer et al., 2008).

The authors present some evidence in support of the effectiveness of brief-term psychodynamic approaches but suggest the need to develop clearly defined manualised approaches to treatment that can be more easily researched. In addition, they make a strong case for the usefulness of specific aspects of psychodynamic practice in complex trauma work, including the need to work with attachment difficulties and to improve reflective functioning and mentalisation. Also writing about technical considerations in psychotherapy with traumatised patients, Nayar (2008) asserts the importance, firstly, of creating a safe holding environment (understood in Winnicottian terms) in order to create a context for the tolerance of trauma-related affects and memories. Secondly, he asserts the need for the therapist to be flexible in being used by the patient as 'transference object, developmental object and self object' (2008: 51). In Shottenbauer et al. (2008) and Nayar's (2008) papers there is an assumption that psychodynamically oriented trauma work necessarily involves the uncovering and narration of traumatic memories (what in CBT approaches might be understood as involving an element of 'exposure' to such material), and it is apparent that considerable initial work is undertaken to ensure that there is a context in which this can take place. However, it is worth cautioning that there is some room to debate whether in fact it is always therapeutic to work to uncover or recover repressed traumatic material. Writing primarily about those affected by the Holocaust, Rosenblum (2009) makes the argument that in some patients the magnitude of the horror associated with remembering, coupled with patient fragility, may mean that the encouragement of full telling could produce the risk of psychosis or breakdown. She goes so far as to suggest that in some instances repression, denial and splitting may need to be left unchallenged. McCann and Pearlman (1990) also suggest in their treatment model that in some instances the initial goal of therapy may be to strengthen compromised self-capacities, before any kind of trauma processing is initiated, and note that this may take a considerable period of time. It is interesting that from a different perspective Straker and the Sanctuaries Counselling Team (1987), in writing about the treatment of South African political activists in the context of ongoing risk and compromised safety in the real world, also suggest that the narration of traumatic experience needs to be undertaken with circumspection, focusing more strongly on reflective, less personalised aspects of the trauma experience rather than primarily on somatic and affective contents. While it is generally accepted that trauma cannot be fully processed without retrieval of memory contents into the present, it is important to assess the capacity of the individual to engage in such a process, both from the perspective of internal resources and from the perspective of external safety and freedom from potential harm.

A further debate in psychodynamically oriented trauma work concerns the role of interpretation, both of unconscious conflicts and of transference material. In some psychoanalytic writing about trauma there has been an inference that individuals may in some way invite traumatic events so as to establish a mechanism for representing pathological intrapsychic constellations, lending to the possibility of over-interpretation and a kind of victim blaming. In a previous paper, 'When objects attack in reality' (Eagle & Watts, 2002), Dr Jacki Watts and I aimed to contest this framing of trauma exposure within some psychoanalytic writings, asserting that while it might be important to explore what meanings individuals attach to such events, it is not necessarily helpful to insist that trauma responses can *only* and exclusively be understood in light of personal history and pre-existing intrapsychic conflicts and vulnerability. In keeping with Laub and Auerhahn, I would continue to maintain that modes of interpretation designed to unravel 'the manner in which a concern with external reality can serve as a defence against unconscious conflict' (1993: 300) are generally not appropriate in trauma work and may in fact produce iatrogenic effects, as they have suggested. 'Such a hermeneutic approach is effective when applied to non-victims, but disastrous with victims who can neither use their trauma defensively nor playfully, and experience such analysis of their reality as a conceptualization of all reality as fantasy and, hence, entrapment in the symptomatic level of knowing' (Laub & Auerhahn, 1993: 300). Without dismissing the importance of the personal interpretive lens that the survivor brings to bear on their experience, it is important to take account of the features of external reality, such as the characteristics of the actual event and social constructions of particular kinds of victimisation, that play an equally significant role in the trauma response. A delicate balance needs to be struck between the emphasis on the internal and the external and their interrelationship in trauma work. Similarly, although it is important to pay attention to transference dynamics in working with trauma survivors, it is often useful or even necessary to allow for the development of positive or even idealised transference responses since these tend to allow for the reintrojection or bolstering of good object introjects. This is part of what is entailed in establishing the strong working alliance referred to in the brief-term psychodynamic approaches above. It is also not generally advised to make transference interpretations in this kind of work as this is often likely to take the therapy in a different direction and may well be experienced as confusing rather than helpful by traumatised patients. However, this having been said, it is useful to bear in mind, as suggested by Herman (1992) and others (Wilson & Lindy, 1999), that in trauma work the therapist may not always automatically occupy the place of benign, validating, concerned or nurturing object in the mind of the patient, but may in fact be perceived in many guises, including that of violator or perpetrator, that of bystander, and that of powerful, undamaged object of envy. Such insights into the therapeutic process may be of use to the therapist without necessarily having to be shared within the therapy room, unless they represent insurmountable obstacles to therapy progress.

Among clinicians and counsellors working with traumatic stress in post-apartheid South Africa, there is little consensus about optimal therapeutic approaches and much of the research that has been conducted into local interventions has been case-study based (Edwards, 2005). It is evident that for most of those clinicians who have been trained within a general psychodynamic framework, their work with traumatised populations is broadly informed by this theoretical perspective. It is less evident that the kinds of short-term psychodynamic approaches described by Shottenbauer et al. (2008) are employed in a systematic way by South African practitioners, although they may well understand their interventions to include the establishment of a good working alliance, the processing of traumatic memories and the elaboration of the meanings attached to this, and some exploration of the perceived future consequences of having experienced the event/s. A model that is fairly widely employed by South African trauma therapists is the Wits Trauma Model, understood to represent an integrative approach to working with traumatic stress, drawing upon both psychodynamic and cognitive behavioural principles (Eagle, 2000). The components of the model are: telling the story, normalising symptoms, working with self-blame or survivor guilt (restoring self-respect), enhancing mastery (including the accessing of social support), and facilitating meaning (Eagle, 2000). For the purposes of this chapter, those aspects of the model that are of most interest from a psychodynamic point of view will be elaborated.

In the first instance, as noted, almost all trauma work involves the retrieval, rehearsal and processing of the traumatic experience, usually through the victim/ survivor's face-to-face narration of the experience, although writing, acting, drawing and other forms of artistic expression have also been used to access and symbolise traumatic material. In the case of the Wits Trauma Model, the element of telling and retelling is viewed as importantly undertaken in a relational context. Thus, unlike some TFCBT models in which exposure to the traumatic stimuli is viewed as significant in and of itself, in psychodynamically informed approaches it is the witnessing of the experience and the psychological accompaniment of the victim through the experience that is every bit as, if not more, significant. I cannot emphasise enough the degree to which this understanding of one's role and function as a trauma therapist is core to the process of healing. Undertaking this kind of witnessing and deep empathic engagement with traumatic experiences can be enormously emotionally taxing. I still hold in my mind the extended narrative of a patient who described the loss of his wife in a car hijacking from the point of receiving the telephone call to tell him that she had been shot, to sitting with her while paramedics tried unsuccessfully to revive her, to having to identify her body in the mortuary. Each part of the narrative was described in great personal detail, including, for example, his impulse to clean away the smudged mascara from under his dead wife's eyes.[3] There is something profoundly moving about this aspect of trauma work and I have sometimes experienced deep therapeutic engagement during retelling to be akin to a kind of maternal reverie. While this holding function of the mother is generally understood to be important in various ways in the course of normal child development (including in the development of a sense of a cohesive self), it may also be important to the process of beginning to gather oneself together as the (survivor) narrator of an enormously damaging or psychically taxing event in which one is a central actor. The narration in the presence of another who provides both a holding and a containing function allows the patient to regain a sense of 'ongoing being', including that of an identity continuous with their pre-trauma self, as well as to begin to process unbearable fantasies, thoughts and affects. In respect of the latter, it may well be that the therapist has to be open to projective identifications that initially allow the victim to void themselves of the worst aspects of the experience by projecting them into the therapist or by stimulating fantasies in the therapist that represent a kind of identification with their traumatised being. Given the nature of trauma, this may well mean tolerating powerful feelings of helplessness, impotence, despair, fear, anxiety, terror, anger, aggression, guilt, humiliation, shame, disgust and horror. Although these form part of the emotional repertoire of all human beings, such affects are not easy to bear and manage, as written about ubiquitously in the psychoanalytic literature. The therapist needs to find an optimal balance in retaining good-enough ego boundaries so as neither to over-identify nor to emotionally distance from the patient (Wilson & Lindy, 1999), while at the same time remaining sufficiently open or permeable to the patient's conscious and unconscious communications so as to be felt to be willing to 'bear' the experience together with the patient. Rosenblum, referring to Laub's work, suggests that the analyst may play three kinds of interrelated roles in this respect, those of 'the authenticating witness, the sanctuary provider, and the experience-sharing companion' (2009: 1335), and quotes Laub as writing that the therapeutic listener 'shares the journey into the eye of the hurricane' (2009: 1335). Although therapists and counsellors employing the Wits Trauma Model may not always be trained to draw upon such deeper psychodynamic levels of understanding about what listening to the telling of the trauma might be about, it is important that they nevertheless understand their role to be a receptive and active one in the sense of psychologically accompanying the traumatised individual through their remembered experience. Going back to psychodynamic understandings of trauma impact, it is apparent that this aspect of intervention is designed to rebuild the sense of available and accessible good object introjects that are willing to help bear the experience retrospectively, even if they could not prevent it happening in the first instance. Since trauma involves considerable re-experiencing, representing the reliving of past experience in the present, being available to the patient at these times as a sharing, reparative or protective good object is not insignificant. In the role of 'authenticating witness' it is also apparent that the therapist assists with reality testing and potentially with the restoration of the third, symbolic register of meaning. From a more classical psychodynamic perspective it can also be argued that the detailed narration of the events, together with accompanying sensations, affects and fantasies, allows for some catharsis or expression of inhibited affects and anxieties, and also helps to restore cognitive coherence through the sequential and careful recounting of what took place and associations to various elements of the event. Although I have chosen to focus on interventions with adult survivors, it is also worth noting that psychodynamically informed play therapy for traumatised children entails many of the same processes, including psychological accompaniment, assistance in symbolising the experience, opportunities for emotional catharsis and attention to fantasies associated with the trauma and its impact.

The second feature of the Wits Trauma Model that is heavily influenced by psychodynamic understandings is that of 'meaning making' (linked also in some instances to addressing self-blame and threats to self-respect). A real strength of psychodynamic approaches is their attention to the ideographic meanings that people attach to experience, the way in which this reflects their inner worlds and how these map onto the external environment (although, as discussed above, interpretation of these relationships needs to be undertaken with some circumspection). The psychodynamic formulation of trauma-related responses assumes the importance of exploring the particular meaning that each individual attaches to the traumatic event. Although this kind of exploration is generally associated with longer-term work, it is possible to achieve aspects of this even in short-term trauma interventions. By listening carefully to the manner in which patients talk about the traumatic event and its impact, including the kinds of words and language employed, evidence of strong affect, repetition of material, and apparent avoidance of key issues, among other aspects, it may be possible to tap into core meaning-related issues. In Ehlers and Clark's (2000) comprehensive TFCBT model, they talk about working with trauma 'hotspots', usually those aspects of the traumatic event discussed with most intensity in the session. It is possible that these hotspots represent those aspects of the event that carry most weight or currency for the individual in terms of the meaning the trauma has come to assume for them. Also, in the assessment phase of EMDR treatment, a key element is the identification of the core 'negative cognitions' associated with the event. Although these latter two approaches may approach the notion of meaning making at a more conscious level than that pursued in more psychodynamically oriented treatment, it is evident that an important part of trauma intervention is to uncover and identify the specific ways in which patients have made sense of their victimisation. In some cases, meanings may be more event driven (as in taking on board the idea that 'these people really intend to hurt or even kill me'), and in others more personally driven (as in 'my father has always doubted my competence and now I have confirmed this by losing his money in succumbing to this armed robbery'). In addition, making sense of human-inflicted trauma often involves an attempt to understand the perpetrators' motives and the selection of oneself as victim. Psychodynamic theory allows us to appreciate that these kinds of interpretations may involve processes of projection and of identification and disidentification. For example, victims may struggle to resist the abjection inflicted upon them by attackers and may internalise feelings of self-disgust (as is common in rape survivors) or, alternatively, identify with the powerful aggressor position by indulging in violent revenge fantasies (as is more common in masculine-identified victims). It is also important to explore how cultural attributions for misfortune (Eagle, 2005) might shape personal meaning making. For example, more traditional African people may view falling victim to traumatic events as an indication that they have alienated their ancestors or have become the target of bewitchment (Eagle, 2005). Again, psychodynamic ways of thinking allow one to explore how there may be an articulation between personal history, prior personality functioning, the characteristics of the traumatic event, and the social and cultural frameworks within which these events may be commonly understood. Psychodynamic approaches allow interventionists to be sensitive to cultural difference, and to appreciate the many features of both the internal and external world that come to shape the patient's interpretation of the event. Wherever possible, even in short-term trauma work, it is useful to identify and point out the kinds of interpretive links that the trauma appears to have evoked, and to spend some time exploring how this impacts upon the ability to integrate and live with the implications of traumatisation.

Accompanying the client through the traumatic retelling and exploring the meaning-related associations to the event can be taxing to trauma therapists. Providing the sense of a safe, supportive, containing and holding environment during the course of therapy may be particularly difficult when therapists themselves are subject to the same kinds of risks and frustrations as their clients. As will be evident from the introduction to the chapter, therapists in South Africa are very likely to have been either directly or indirectly affected by traumatic events in their personal lives and may struggle with issues of over-identification and vicarious traumatisation. Although this is an element of trauma work that deserves deeper exploration, suffice it to say that an awareness of countertransference and its multiple vectors as well as its place in psychotherapy, may go some way towards helping psychodynamically oriented therapists to be open to exploring the difficulties posed in undertaking such work without shame. Psychodynamically influenced supervision may be invaluable in assisting to identify and usefully employ such countertransference-generated insights.

In conclusion, it is hoped that this discussion of how psychodynamic thinking may be important to understanding both collective and individual aspects of traumatic stress has allowed for a greater appreciation of the value of this kind of theorisation in working in the context of post-apartheid South Africa. As a final note, I emphasise that while the discussion of traumatic stress inevitably involves a focus on the disabling and damaging aspects of such experiences, there is also an increasing interest in the traumatic stress literature in the phenomenon of post-traumatic growth (Tedeschi & Calhoun, 2004). It has been suggested that it is only in transcending experiences of damage and loss that human beings can develop a true sense of resilience and hope. This way of thinking resonates with some notion of what is achieved in the resolution of the depressive position as understood by Klein. Coming to terms with trauma may indeed offer an arche-typical opportunity to recognise the interrelationship between good and bad objects and the necessity for repair and restoration in response to psychic damage (even if in this case one experiences oneself as the one transgressed against rather than the transgressor). However, post-traumatic growth is not an automatic outcome of trauma events and should not be assumed to be a necessary goal of therapy or a sign of patient health. Trauma workers perhaps need to hold tena-ciously to the good objects in their own internal worlds, and to cherish those aspects of the social that offer them a sense of cohesion and connection, if they are to sustain themselves in conducting such work in the multifaceted context of post-apartheid South Africa, and may find it helpful to be open to vicarious growth opportunities as well as the demands of such practice.

NOTES

1   See www.apartheidarchivesproject.co.za.
2   See http://www.issafrica.org/crimehub/uploads/3_crime_situation.pdf.
3   Some details have been altered to protect confidentiality.

REFERENCES

Adams, RE & Serpe, RT (2000) Social integration, fear of crime, and life satisfaction. *Socio-logical Perspectives*, 43(4): 605–629.

APA (American Psychiatric Association) (2000) *Diagnostic and Statistical Manual of Mental Disorders (DSM-IV-TR)*. Washington, DC: APA.

Barbarin, OA, Richter, L & De Wet, T (2001) Exposure to violence, coping resources and adjustment of South African children. *American Journal of Orthopsychiatry*, 7: 16–25.

Benn, M (2007) Perceived alterations in racial perceptions of victims of violent crime. Unpublished master's dissertation, University of the Witwatersrand, Johannesburg.

Danieli, Y (1985) The treatment and prevention of long-term effects and intergenerational transmission of victimization: A lesson from Holocaust survivors and their children. In CR Figley (ed.) *Trauma and Its Wake*, pp. 295–313. New York: Brunner/Mazel.

Eagle, G (2000) The shattering of the stimulus barrier: The case for an integrative approach to short-term treatment of psychological trauma. *Journal of Psychotherapy Integration*, 10(3): 301–324.

Eagle, G (2005) Therapy at the cultural interface: Implications of African cosmology for traumatic stress interventions. *Journal of Contemporary Psychotherapy*, 35(2): 199–210.

Eagle, G & Watts, J (2002) When objects attack in reality: Psychoanalytic contributions to formulations of the impact and treatment of traumatic stress incidences: Part 1. *Psychoanalytic Psychotherapy in South Africa*, 10(1): 1–24.

Edwards, D (2005) Treating PTSD in South African contexts: A theoretical framework and a model for developing evidence-based practice. *Journal of Psychology in Africa*, 15(2): 117–124.

Ehlers, A & Clark, DM (2000) A cognitive model of posttraumatic stress disorder. *Behavior Research and Therapy*, 38(4): 319–345.

Forbes, D, Creamer, M, Bisson, J, Cohen, J, Crow, B, Foa, E, Friedman, M, Keane, T, Kudler, H & Ursano, R (2010) A guide to guidelines for the treatment of PTSD and related conditions. *Journal of Traumatic Stress*, 23(5): 537–552.

Freud, S (1920/1948) *Beyond the Pleasure Principle*. London: Hogarth Press.

Garland, C (ed.) (1998a) *Understanding Trauma: A Psychoanalytical Approach*. London: Duckworth.

Garland, C (1998b) Issues in treatment: A case of rape. In C Garland (ed.) *Understanding Trauma: A Psychoanalytical Approach*, pp. 108–122. London: Duckworth.

Gobodo-Madikizela, P (2008) Trauma, forgiveness and the witnessing dance: Making public spaces intimate. *Journal of Analytical Psychology*, 53: 169–188.

Grootenhuis, K (2007) Therapeutic dilemmas in working with African refugees in South Africa. Unpublished master's dissertation, University of the Witwatersrand, Johannesburg.

Herman, J (1992) *Trauma and Recovery: From Domestic Abuse to Political Terror*. London: Pandora.

Horowitz, M (1992) *Stress Response Syndromes*. Northvale, NJ: Jason Aronson.

Jolly, R (2010) *Cultured Violence: Narrative, Social Suffering, and Engendering Human Rights in Contemporary South Africa*. Pietermaritzburg: University of KwaZulu-Natal Press.

Horowitz, M (1997) *Stress Response Syndromes (third edition)*. Northvale, NJ: Jason Aronson.

Kaminer, D & Eagle, G (2010) *Traumatic Stress in South Africa*. Johannesburg: Wits University Press.

Kirschner, L (1994) Trauma, the good object, and the symbolic: A theoretical integration. *The International Journal of Psychoanalysis*, 75: 235–242.

Kometsi, K (2008) Coloured subjectivities and black Africanness. Unpublished doctoral thesis, University of the Witwatersrand, Johannesburg.

Krupnik, JL (2002) Brief psychodynamic treatment for PTSD. *Journal of Clinical Psychology*, 58: 919–932.

Laub, D (1998) The empty circle: Children of survivors and the limits of reconstruction. *Journal of the American Psychoanalytic Association*, 46: 507–529.

Laub, D & Auerhahn, N (1993) Knowing and not knowing massive psychic trauma: Forms of traumatic memory. *The International Journal of Psychoanalysis*, 74: 287–302.

Lindy, JD (1993) Focal psychoanalytic psychotherapy of posttraumatic stress disorder. In J P Wilson & B Raphael (eds) *International Handbook of Traumatic Stress Syndromes*, pp. 803–809. New York: Plenum.

McCann, L & Pearlman, L (1990) *Trauma and the Adult Survivor*. New York: Brunner Mazel.

Nayar, M (2008) Technical considerations in the psychotherapy of traumatized individuals: A psychoanalytic perspective. *The American Journal of Psychoanalysis*, 68: 50–65.

Nightingale, V, Sher, T & Hansen, N (2010) The impact of receiving an HIV diagnosis and cognitive processing on psychological distress and posttraumatic growth. *Journal of Traumatic Stress*, 23(4): 452–460.

Pharoah, R (2008) *National Victims of Crime Survey: South Africa 2007*. Institute for Security Studies Paper 175. Pretoria: Institute for Security Studies.

Posel, D (2006) The TRC's unfinished business. In C Villa-Vicencio & F du Toit (eds) *Truth and Reconciliation in South Africa: 10 Years On*, pp. 86–95. Cape Town: David Philip.

Rosenblum, R (2009) Postponing trauma: The dangers of telling. *The International Journal of Psychoanalysis*, 90: 1319–1340.

Shottenbauer, M, Glass, CR, Arnkoff, DB & Grey, SH (2008) Contributions of psychodynamic approaches to treatment of PTSD and trauma: A review of the empirical treatment and psychopathology literature. *Psychiatry*, 71(1): 13–34.

Straker, G & the Sanctuaries Counselling Team (1987) The continuous traumatic stress syndrome: The single therapeutic interview. *Psychology in Society*, 8: 48–79.

Tedeschi, RG & Calhoun, LG (2004) Posttraumatic growth: Conceptual foundations and empirical evidence. *Psychological Inquiry*, 15(1): 1–18.

TRC (Truth and Reconciliation Commission) (1998) *Truth and Reconciliation Commission of South Africa Report*. Cape Town: CTP Book Printers.

Van der Kolk, B (2006) Clinical implications of neuroscience research in PTSD. *Annals of the New York Academy of Science*, 1071: 277–293.

Van der Walt, C, Franchi, V & Stevens, G (2003) The South African Truth and Reconciliation Commission: 'Race', historical compromise and transitional democracy. *International Journal of Intercultural Relations*, 27(2): 251–267.

Williams, SL, Williams, D, Stein, D, Seedat, S, Jackson, P & Moomal, H (2007) Multiple traumatic events and psychological distress: The South Africa Stress and Health Study. *Journal of Traumatic Stress*, 20(5): 845–855.

Wilson JP & Lindy, JD (1999) Empathic strain and countertransference. In MJ Horowitz (ed.) *Essential Papers on Posttraumatic Stress Disorder*, pp. 518–543. New York: New York University Press.

SECTION III

SOCIAL ISSUES

CHAPTER 6

UNCONSCIOUS MEANING AND MAGIC:
Comparing psychoanalysis and African indigenous healing

Gavin Ivey

Nearly two decades after the transition to democracy in South Africa, the mental health field has revealed itself to be a fascinating attractor for a range of cultural, political, legal and philosophical debates, inevitably shaped by the country's turbulent past and questions about its future. Two recent events establish the context for this chapter. In 2009 the South African Psychoanalytic Association was accredited as an official International Psychoanalytical Association study group, with the ultimate aim of training psychoanalysts in accordance with international standards. Five years earlier the South African parliament passed the Traditional Health Practitioners Act (No. 35 of 2004), aimed at recognising and integrating traditional healers into the country's official healthcare system. The historical juxtaposition of these two events invites a consideration of the relationship between psychoanalysis and indigenous African healing.

The existing meagre comparative local literature focuses more generally on biomedicine and indigenous healing, the politics of mental health, or on the role of indigenous beliefs in the context of integrative trauma therapy (Eagle, 2004; Straker, 1994). Few authors (I know only of Buhrmann, 1986, and Maiello, 1999) have published comparative work on psychoanalysis and traditional healing in the South African context. The aim of this chapter is to extend and sharpen the comparative discussion of these two healing systems. In the course of doing so I will not simply examine traditional healing from the perspective of psychoanalysis, but also highlight the peculiarities of psychoanalysis and consider its 'place' in the South African context.

My interest in comparing psychoanalysis and indigenous healing has three professional tributaries. Firstly, my role in training South African clinical psychologists in psychoanalytic psychotherapy has exposed me to the tensions between traditional African belief systems and those informing the psychoanalytic worldview. Many African trainee psychologists, particularly those raised in rural communities, have consulted indigenous healers and been raised in cultures imbued with these healing practices and their attendant philosophies. Comparisons between psychoanalytic and indigenous healing thus arise regularly in seminar discussions about the nature of the therapeutic enterprise. These discussions have required that I, a white psychoanalytically oriented therapist, acquaint myself with the culturally embedded healing traditions familiar to my students. Secondly, a recent requirement for professional registration as a clinical psychologist in South Africa is a year of post-qualification community service. Many recently qualified psychologists find themselves in remote rural clinics, where they frequently encounter patients concurrently treated by indigenous healers. These psychologists are forced to negotiate potentially fraught professional dilemmas arising from the collision of differing belief system healing modalities. An example of this is presented later in the chapter. In such circumstances a considered awareness of the commonalities and differences between these modalities is a prerequisite for ethically informed professional action. Thirdly, as noted in the legislation referred to above, formerly suppressed and marginalised traditional healing has been accorded new respect and legal recognition. This behoves Western psychotherapists to reflectively engage indigenous healing practices, both out of respect for these 'new' professional colleagues (who, ironically, pre-date psychotherapy practitioners by centuries) and because some formal cooperation between psychotherapists and indigenous healers may well arise in future. The form such cooperation may assume is currently being debated and I will offer my perspective on this toward the end of the chapter.

A BRIEF OVERVIEW OF AFRICAN INDIGENOUS HEALING

There has been a recent increase in the amount of literature on African cosmology and indigenous healing in South Africa, driven largely by two post-apartheid imperatives. The first involves efforts to restore the dignity of African philosophies and cultural practices following their marginalisation by hegemonic Western biomedical ideology and decades of racist stigmatisation (Holdstock, 2000; Kruger et al., 2007; Mkhize, 2004). The second concerns attempts to establish collaborative relationships between Western biomedical and allied practitioners (including psychologists) and traditional healers. This is aimed at addressing the pressing mental health needs of a country where a large percentage of the population consults both Western practitioners and indigenous healers (Campbell-Hall et al., 2010; Mkize, 2009).

The first initiative typically endorses the culturally embedded differences between African indigenous healing practices and Western therapeutic modalities, but does so proudly, countering the latter colonising ideologies by asserting the legitimacy of African cultural realities. The second is aimed at reconciling racial divisions evident in the biomedical–indigenous healing schism, not merely to redress historical ideological injustice, but also to build bridges between contrasting healing frameworks in order to improve health service delivery. However, the question of where to locate psychoanalytic theory and practice in all of this is seldom addressed in the literature referred to. Before discussing this matter, it is necessary to describe indigenous African healing and to locate it in the context of traditional African culture.

Indigenous healing refers to traditional therapeutic practices that tend to share four characteristics (Tseng, 2001). These practices are (1) embedded in local cultural traditions, (2) magico-religious in terms of mobilising supernatural forces, (3) tend to function independently of official healthcare systems, and (4) are validated in terms of subjectively experienced benefits rather than scientific procedures.

While a variety of indigenous healers exists in South Africa (e.g. herbalists and spiritual healers), it is the *isangoma*'s (*isiZulu* term for 'diviner' or 'witchdoctor') work that most invites comparisons with psychoanalytic therapy. The term 'diviner' refers to the central activity of divining the cause of the person's misfortune or suffering. The nature of these causes is embedded in the traditional 'African worldview', a 'psychological reality referring to shared constructs, shared patterns of belief, feeling and knowledge...which members of the group carry in their minds as a guide for conduct and definition of reality' (Makwe, 1985: 4). This worldview is expressly supernatural as magical and spiritual figures and forces are believed to exert both benevolent and malign influence. Of foremost importance are the ancestors – omnipresent spirits of significant deceased relatives who continue to play a life-preservative role in the activities of the living (Mbiti, 1990; Ngubane, 1977). Ritual contact with and adherence to the wishes of the ancestors is considered imperative for continued well-being. Withdrawal of ancestral protection leaves the individual spiritually alienated and vulnerable to misfortune, whether opportunistic or intended by the ancestors to teach the 'victim' a lesson.

The *sangoma*'s ancestors are particularly significant as it is they who summon the individual to the diviner's vocation and confer upon him or her healing powers. Becoming a *sangoma* is not a matter of individual choice, but rather an ancestral decree made evident in the individual's experience of *thwasa* sickness. This 'syndrome', while varied in its manifestations, is typically characterised by alarming physical and psychological symptoms, often including psychotic states. Only a *sangoma* can diagnose *thwasa* sickness and the symptoms will persist until the afflicted person accepts the calling. The *sangoma*'s training is protracted and arduous, requiring a long period of apprenticeship to a senior *sangoma* who instructs the neophyte in medicinal preparation, purification rituals, animal sacrifice, dream interpretation, ceremonial dancing, diagnosis and divination. All these interventions require the *sangoma* to be a conduit for the ancestral spirits – both the *sangoma*'s and the patient's – as it is the ancestors who ultimately restore the patient to health (Buhrmann, 1986).

Misfortune is never accidental but is usually the consequence of 'pollution' or witchcraft. Pollution refers to a contaminating mystical force that may afflict a person who comes into contact with persons or objects considered taboo, such as menstruating women, meat from a diseased animal, or a foetus that has not been properly buried (Hammond-Tooke, 1989). Ritual purification is required to remove the polluted state.

While good magic involves the use of supernatural power to positive ends, witchcraft – typically motivated by envy, jealousy and malice – involves the intentional deployment of malignant spirits or magical substances to harm others. The latter substances are collectively referred to as *muti*, an ambiguous term denoting supernaturally imbued objects or potions capable of magically healing or harming, depending on their application and the intentions of their user (Ngubane, 1977). *Sangomas* typically use good *muti* to counteract bad *muti* and heal afflictions, whereas witches only use bad *muti* to destructive ends. They concoct this from symbolically poisonous substances such as ground-up ants that have eaten meat deposited in graveyards, thereby capturing vengeful spirits of the dead (Niehaus, 2000) or 'bodily exuviae, such as nail parings and hair clippings, or even the earth from footprints' (Hammond-Tooke, 1989: 78). *Muti* exerts its influence through contact with the victim or being unknowingly imbibed, thereby 'poisoning' them.

Being bewitched may be indicated by a variety of dramatic somatic or psychological symptoms, or simply evident in what westerners attribute to 'bad luck' – becoming unemployed, miscarrying, failing in a business venture, and so on. While acknowledging a role for natural causes (particularly in the case of common minor ailments), significant adverse life events are typically attributed to someone's actions and the diviner's 'diagnostic' task is to ascertain *who* is responsible.

Another aspect of the African worldview that is important concerns the culturally prevalent form that selfhood assumes. The African conception of self is a collectivist, as opposed to individualist, conception – 'a being-with-and-for-others' (Mkhize, 2004: 26). In other words, the self is socially constituted and maintained in terms of a network of interdependent familial and community relationships and identifications. The meaning of one's life is defined by means of communal recognition and engagement, captured in sayings such as 'I am because we are, and since we are, therefore I am' (Mbiti, 1969, quoted in Mkhize, 2004: 24). The implication of this collective self is that individual well-being is subordinate to and contingent upon harmonious relationships with familial and community members, that relational disharmony inevitably produces individual dysfunction, and that the repair of disharmonious familial and community relationships is a central aim of healing interventions.

These three integral aspects of the African worldview – collectivist selfhood, the existence of supernatural entities and forces, and the causal attribution of misfortune to malevolent others – all inform the *sangoma*'s diagnostic and therapeutic practices.

COMPARING PSYCHOANALYSIS AND INDIGENOUS HEALING

Psychoanalysis and indigenous healing do share some characteristics, features that distinguish them from biomedical interventions. Firstly, in diagnostic terms, both are concerned with the underlying *meaning* of symptoms, which invariably relates to the life context of the sufferer. Secondly, both are forms of symbolic healing. Rather than resorting to biomedical cures, symbolic healing employs words, rituals or symbolic actions as therapeutic interventions. Thirdly, both analysts and *sangomas* are 'wounded healers' in that their respective apprenticeships require their own personal acquaintance with psychic suffering and their treatment by a senior healer in their respective traditions. Fourthly, both approaches consider the patients' dreams to be meaningful communications and an important resource in the treatment process.

The search for commonalities between apparently divergent therapeutic approaches appeals to the 'common factor' literature that has proven popular for at least six decades in Western psychotherapy. It began with Rosenzweig's (1936) observation that although psychotherapy in general is effective in the alleviation of psychological distress, no one theory-driven psychotherapy approach is more effective than another across a variety of symptom presentations. This must mean that despite overt theoretical and technical differences, it is the underlying factors common to all psychotherapy treatment contexts that are largely responsible for facilitating psychological change.

Relevant to our purposes is the fact that the common factor literature has also been employed to argue for a cross-cultural theory of psychological healing. Thus, despite radically different cultural assumptions and intervention modalities, traditional healing and psychotherapy are argued to be equally effective in their respective cultural settings because the healing agents responsible for alleviating distress are essentially the same. In the 1960s, Frank and Frank (1991) advanced a model that is still influential today. Arguing that all psychological disturbance is either the cause or the consequence of demoralisation (a state of hopelessness, helplessness and perceived failure to cope with life), they claimed that symbolic healing practices include four interrelated aspects that combine to combat demoralisation: (1) a professional relationship between a socially sanctioned healer and a sufferer, in which the healer inspires belief that positive change can be effected in the sufferer's life. This creates a hopeful expectancy in the sufferer that the relationship will bring about change; (2) treatment takes place in a designated healing setting demarcated from the rest of the environment; (3) every therapy needs to provide a culturally meaningful explanation for the suffering, thereby making symptoms meaningful; and (4) the sufferer must participate in a task, procedure or ritual that is emotionally arousing, requires some effort or sacrifice and is consistent with the explanation for the symptoms. Successfully accomplishing these tasks enhances the sufferer's sense of mastery, interpersonal competence or other capability.

This framework democratises diverse healing practices by revealing a common cross-cultural structure that establishes the necessary and sufficient conditions for psychological healing to occur. Fuller Torrey champions this position by asserting, '[T]he apparent differences between types of psychotherapy within a culture or between cultures are more illusion than substance and are due to differences in techniques used to enhance the basic components' (1986: 231).

While other cross-cultural common factor theories of symbolic healing have been advanced (e.g. Dow, 1986; Fuller Torrey, 1986; Kleinman, 1988), these tend to be mere clarifications or elaborations of the model Frank and Frank published 50 years ago. While this healing structure undoubtedly applies to both indigenous healing and psychoanalysis, it is worth noting how the model flattens and obscures the signature features and functions of different therapies. This point will be addressed later, but we first need to consider the distinctions between psychoanalysis and indigenous healing.

To begin with, psychoanalysis and all forms of psychotherapy are distinguished from indigenous healing by their emphasis on verbal transactions focused on the patient's states of mind: '[T]hey use explicit talk about the person's thoughts, feelings, emotions and relationships to effect change. They thus demand the ability and willingness to participate in a conversation about private experiences or interpersonal events, objectifying the processes of one's own mind' (Kirmayer, 2007: 233).

Psychoanalysis, both as a theory of selfhood and as a treatment method, was occasioned by a historical convergence of social factors that, while influenced by Enlightenment philosophy, produced a new form of subjectivity in 19th century Europe. Industrial capitalism separated work and family life; brought strangers together in urban environments; fostered democratic political arrange-ments; destabilised traditional roles, relationships and institutional loyalties; and established autonomous personal identity as both a valued creation and ongoing discovery. The result was a dislocated and problematic *private self* defined by individuality, interiority, conflicting possibilities and heightened awareness of burgeoning personal complexity. This historically unprecedented division between public and private life created both the personal unconscious and a new therapy for treating the consequent psychic afflictions (Zaretsky, 2004).

Following Freud's (1923) famous conceptualisation, in these circumstances contradictions between human desires and the normative demands of culture are internalised as personified forbidding and punishing parental presences, thereby constituting the superego. The conflicting demands of instinctual life and the superego result in unpleasurable anxiety states, requiring the operation of defence mechanisms to reduce the unpleasure and banish the conflict from awareness. Where this repression is severe, insufficient instinctual gratification is permitted. Consequently, where desire was there is now a symptom and a system of defences that minimises anxiety while producing self-alienation and distortion of one's perception of others. Psychoanalysis proceeds by sequestering the individual from the social gaze in the privacy of the therapeutic setting, suspending all normative judgement and facilitating a quality of self-observation that allows unconscious derivatives a disguised manifestation as seemingly incidental and decontextualised thoughts, images and memories. Drawing patients' awareness to defensive interruptions of this process occasioned by irrational impressions of the analyst intensifies their self-awareness, prompting new self-understanding that the symptom was self-inflicted, thereby rendering it superfluous once the underlying conflict has been worked through. Self-alienation is slowly replaced by self-insight and a new freedom to respond adaptively to the inherent conflicts that are the price of individuality. Anyone reading this overly concise and simplified description of traditional psychoanalytic therapy will be struck by the repeated references to self: self-alienation, self-observation, self-awareness, self-insight, self-inflicted. This focus on the self, a socio-historical product of a valorised Western individuality, is aimed at making the patient even more of an individual in order to maximise their personal freedom to engage with relationships and societal demands more on their own terms.

How strikingly different this egocentric self is from the *sociocentric* or collectivist African self, and how different the therapeutic objectives and treatment strategies. From an indigenous healing perspective it is ruptured communality that is the problem, whether due to relational friction between the patient and others, prompting the latter to bewitch the patient, or due to the individual's failure to honour traditional customs and observe the wishes of ancestral spirits. This sociocentric self locates the healing emphasis on repairing communal rupture and reconnecting the alienated patient, rather than facilitating his or her individuation. Consequently, the psychoanalytic focus on fostering self-awareness in order to liberate the person from conflicted enslavement to internalised social authority is not only misdirected but guaranteed to further alienate the individual from the collective self that is the measure of health and humanness.

Levin notes that all 'cultural formations have a relationship to the unconscious, but only in the unusual circumstances of modern living are unconscious forces gradually transformed into the personal responsibilities of individual citizens, as special features of their private lives' (2001: 189). This distinguishes psychoanalytic therapy from forms of healing in cultures characterised by collective identifications and ritual containers of instinctual life. Levin's observation is apt and, with this in mind, I must disagree with the rhetorical claim that psychotherapy 'is the bastard progeny of a long tradition of neo-religious and magical practices that have risen up in every…human culture' (Calestro, in Fuller Torrey, 1986: 12). This is not to deny the presence of ritual aspects in psychoanalytic treatment, necessary to facilitate therapeutic regression, but merely to emphasise that such ritual elements are not focused on abreaction and social integration. Indeed, while psychoanalysis is tolerated by Western societies, its persistent critical interrogation of patients' internalised moral assumptions and group identifications means that it necessarily exists in uneasy tension with societal norms, unlike traditional healing practices (Levin, 2001).

Instead of simply comparing these abstract portrayals of different healing modalities, it may be useful to examine a clinical case that highlights an apparent collision of culturally distinctive healing approaches.

BOILING BLOOD: A comparative case study

A male patient, S, was referred to a female psychologist completing her community service year in a rural clinic (for more detail, see Ivey & Myers, 2008). S, a married black man in his twenties, worked as a gardener. He was referred by his employer, who noted his poor work performance and wondered if he was depressed. S had a gentle bearing, spoke English fluently and responded enthusiastically to the invitation to talk about his difficulties. S had a tertiary diploma and considered his menial work situation to be an unacceptable compromise born out of having to support his family. He described his difficulties, namely feeling 'down' and anxious, as stemming from the financial and emotional strain of supporting his immediate family and his mother. S was the youngest of five children and, as he stood to inherit the family home, was responsible for its upkeep. Although claiming to have a close relationship with his mother, S clearly resented the demands she regularly made on him. He could not express the extent of his resentment, however, and was seemingly resigned to a situation dictated by tradition.

S spoke about feeling dissatisfied with his wife, who had embarked on a university course at the time, adding to S's financial burden. S described her as unreasonable and demanding, leaving him feeling resentful and uncertain about how to satisfy her. This perceived general inability was also physically manifest in the form of erectile dysfunction. His wife's response to this was to complain that he was 'not man enough' and he feared ridicule should his friends find out. He already felt foolish having to ask his wife for sex while his friends simply demanded it from their wives.

S's father lived with his second wife and was estranged from the family. S felt that his father had abandoned the family for this woman, putting a further burden on S's shoulders and leaving him with the responsibility of managing the family. Although S would seek advice from him, he increasingly believed that his father was disinterested in him and the family's difficulties.

S's bewitchment beliefs were pervasive and strongly influenced his under-standing of the world and his interactions with others. He cited various familial and personal examples of witchcraft. Firstly, S's one brother suddenly displayed excitable and destructive behaviour, attacking the family home and breaking all the windows. Medical treatment had no impact and a *sangoma* was consulted. Various treatments (steaming, purging, etc.) were administered and the brother reportedly recovered.

At the same time, a second brother was convinced his wife was having an affair and so shot and injured his wife's alleged lover. In order to understand the family turmoil, a number of *sangomas* were consulted and it was divined that a female relative was bewitching the family. As their mother was related to a *sangoma*, two of the brothers believed the mother to be the witchcraft perpetrator, leading to disagreement and division between the siblings.

Further consultations with *sangomas* resulted in the source of the family hostility being identified as a pot of boiling blood buried beneath the gate of the family home. Various attempts were made to remove the pot of boiling blood, but the patient was informed that only a *sangoma* would be able to perform the required ritual, and at a significant cost.

The third family incident of bewitchment related to the death of one brother, whose body was found lying next to the road in a twisted position without any trace of blood. Soon after this the mother complained of hearing strange noises at night and they discovered that food left uneaten the previous night had disappeared by morning. After relating how their brother had died, a *sangoma* informed them that he had been transformed into a zombie by a witch in order to do her bidding. They were instructed to leave food out for him every night. This was done and after a short while the family was no longer troubled by the nocturnal visits.

S also felt himself to be bewitched on a personal level, claiming that this was instigated by people who were envious of him. He felt that witchcraft was responsible for his not being selected for a job, and for his perception that his employer no longer favoured him.

S similarly used bewitchment as an explanation for his erectile dysfunction, claiming that *muti* once used on him still negatively affected his erections. He attributed his condition to the sorcery of a former lover who betrayed him by having a sexual relationship with another man. When he commenced a subsequent relationship, he had difficulty achieving 'powerful' erections. He confronted the previous girlfriend, who admitted having used magical potions to bind him to her. After having sex with her he was able to have a 'powerful' erection, but his potency problems resumed thereafter.

The patient was also convinced that envy-induced bewitchment hindered his career advancement. When a work application was unsuccessful, a *sangoma* informed him that *muti* had been put on his certificates, rendering them invisible to the selectors. Although unsure about the actual perpetrator of this act, S believed that various people wished him harm.

S also had difficult relationships with his employer and a co-worker, who he suspected of secretly maligning him. He claimed his co-worker collected the earth from their employer's footprint and took this to a *sangoma*, who performed certain rites on the soil, resulting in the employer favouring the co-worker and turning against the patient. He saw evidence of this in the employer's behaviour and recent treatment of him.

A COMPARATIVE FORMULATION OF THE CASE

The following hypothesised indigenous healing construction, inferred from the patient's accounts of his interactions with various *sangomas*, is largely consistent with the published literature. Familial enmity caused by witchcraft has sundered relational ties, caused illness and misfortune, destroyed family life and damaged ancestral relations. Divination has revealed a pot of boiling blood beneath the homestead, which must be removed before the sick family can be healed. Other disturbed relationships, involving jealousy (the work colleague), possessiveness (the former girlfriend) and competition (the successful job applicant), have motivated the individuals concerned to use witchcraft to cause S misfortune. The ostensibly deceased brother is not really dead but rather a revitalised corpse (zombie) enslaved by a witch.

The above formulation is striking in a number of respects. It is short, simple (very few concepts employed, linear cause–effect relationships identified), supernatural in its appeal to magical entities and forces (*muti*, witchcraft, zombies, spirits), interpersonally focused in its emphasis on disturbed relationships, and makes no reference to the subjectivity of the sufferer (his wishes, conflicts, feelings, etc.), who is presented as the innocent victim of others' evil machinations.

From a psychoanalytic perspective, S's difficulties are readily comprehended in terms of unresolved Oedipal conflicts exacerbated by current familial difficulties. Despite being the youngest child, he is thrust into the role of surrogate husband when his father leaves the family. This understandably evokes Oedipal anxieties, hostility toward his abandoning father, and mixed erotic and aggressive feelings toward his dependent mother. S's gentle bearing belies the intensity of his animosity toward close family members, which is turned inward on himself in order to obviate the guilt associated with both his Oedipal 'victory' over his father and his hatred of the latter for leaving him with an unbearable burden. His wife is experienced as a materially and sexually demanding maternal object who he feels incapable of satisfying. His combined Oedipal anxiety and hatred toward her is expressed bodily in his erectile dysfunction, a useful compromise which precludes him from having aggressively charged sex with her (and thereby damaging her) while simultaneously punishing her by depriving her of sexual and relationship satisfaction. It may be further surmised that S unconsciously associated two previous miscarriages with his destructive 'sexual attacks' on his wife's body, which would further impair his ability to have satisfactory intercourse with her. These aggressive wishes not only elicited fears that he might hurt and damage her, but also contradicted his cherished conscious self-image of being a kind and gentle man.

S cannot escape the Oedipal structure of his world, finding himself located in different corners of various triangular relationships. The loss and rejection experienced when his lover leaves him for another man cannot be tolerated and so he has to sexually repossess her in order to repair his injured self-esteem. This potency, saturated with Oedipal fantasy, is anxiety provoking and so cannot be sustained. S's interactions with his employer and work colleague (another Oedipal triangle) also illustrate his hostility and jealousy and how his bewitchment beliefs protect him from owning these uncomfortable feelings. Instead, he projects them into his employer and co-worker. The latter is thought to have sinister intentions towards him and wishes to destroy the relationship between S and his employer (a paternal transference figure), using evil magic. By believing himself bewitched, S can locate his own destructive feelings in others, but only at the expense of becoming a 'victim' of his colleague's sorcery. In fact, it is S who wishes to destroy the relationship between his colleague and his employer and to become the favoured 'child'. Given S's disappointing relationship with his own father, this transference dynamic is hardly surprising.

The evocative image of the pot of boiling blood accurately symbolises the patient's aggression. Inside of him is a cauldron of boiling angry feelings that threatens to annihilate his good internal objects and his interpersonal connection with significant others. These hostile feelings cannot be accepted and are instead projected into other family members and various alleged perpetrators of witchcraft.

THERAPEUTIC IMPLICATIONS OF DIVERGENT CASE FORMULATIONS

Psychoanalysis is essentially concerned with the pursuit of the emotional truth about our own experience of ourselves in relation to others (Ivey, 2009, 2011). This is a realist, rather than a relativist, conception of truth in that the object of inquiry (psychic reality) is held to be both autonomous of, and resistant to, the understanding of a specific interpreting subject (Rustin, 2001). Truth, in this sense, is discovered rather than created (Ogden, 2003). To the extent that the above psychoanalytic formulation of S captures the emotional reality of what is happening, both internally and interpersonally, it is true, although its validation would ultimately depend on the patient's response in the therapeutic context. Is the alternative cultural explanation, one that appeals to *muti*, witchcraft and zombies, then untrue? My answer would be that this depends on the extent to which the context-specific interpretation of events functions to either apprehend or evade psychic reality. Using this criterion, I would say that the claim that S was not awarded the job he applied for because a competitor made his certificates invisible, is definitely untrue. However, the *sangoma*'s 'diagnosis' that S's difficulties relate to a pot of boiling blood buried beneath the family home is true in so far as it metaphorically presents the psychic reality of boiling and buried feelings associated with conflicted familial relationships. But the literalisation of metaphor (Ivey, 2010), in which the identity of analogous phenomena (a psyche containing 'boiling' feelings and a pot containing boiling blood) eclipses the difference between them and results in concrete action (removing the pot), signals a departure from psychic truth.

It should be evident that I am not speaking about truth in the scientific sense of accurate statements about relationships between observable or measureable entities. In this regard we cannot engage in epistemological one-upmanship by claiming that the psychoanalytic account is superior to the magical one by virtue of any scientific status. Numerous critics have frequently dismissed psychoanalysis on precisely the grounds that its fundamental explanatory constructs – the dynamic unconscious, Oedipus complex, internal objects, etc. – have the same epistemological status as supernatural entities because they cannot be empirically observed, measured or used to derive accurate predictions of future behaviour. Today, given the hegemony of cognitive behavioural therapy and evidence-based practice, one could easily substitute the word 'psychoanalysts' for 'native healers' in the chauvinist sentiment expressed by one Dr Margett, a psychiatrist with experience of working in Africa:

> [N]ative healers can do little good in a mental health program…They can have no rational place in the modern technological world and as the educational level of African natives improves and as time affords them the cultural wisdom…[they] will drift away from the primitive attractions of magic and seek help in science. (quoted in Fuller Torrey, 1986: 228)

Ironically, from the perspective of the scientific establishment, both psychoanalysis and indigenous healing are repudiated and marginalised discourses. Most psychoanalysts, however, would object to the category analogy between psychoanalytic and indigenous healing concepts. From the outset the psychoanalytic model was both secular and naturalistic, explicitly rejecting the idea that there may be supernatural entities or forces exerting an influence on humankind. Instead, Freud assumed that all supernatural entities and figures are psychological realities: 'I believe that a large part of the mythological view of the world, which extends a long way into the most modern religions, is nothing but psychology projected into the external world' (1901: 258). He further argued that religious myths and rituals are the collective expression of the same unconscious dynamics found in the dreams and neurotic symptoms of individuals. In other words, religious myths and rituals serve a defensive function. Struck by the impression that ordinary people's religious observances had an obsessive and compulsive quality, Freud turned his mind to the relationship between religion and obsessional neurosis. Both the obsessive's rituals and those common to religious practices, he contended, indirectly express anxiety-provoking unconscious wishes: 'In view of these correspondences…one might venture to regard obsessional neurosis as a pathological counterpart to religious formation, neurosis as an individual religion, religion as a universal obsessional neurosis' (Freud, 1907: 126–127). Just as obsessional rituals defend against psychological anxieties, religious beliefs and rituals serve to protect people from helplessness and vulnerability in the face of natural events, fate and the evils of society. All magical beliefs, whether religious or otherwise, are entertained in order to 'subject the process of nature to the will of man, protect the individual against enemies and dangers, and give him the power to injure his enemies' (Freud, 1998: 67).

Implicit in this perspective is the notion that a measure of psychic health is the extent to which someone comes to understand the defensive function of magical beliefs and surrenders these in favour of more rational interpretations of events. We could refer to two significant aspects of our case study relevant to this criterion. Firstly, S's belief that his certificates had been made invisible and that this had resulted in him not getting a job. From a psychoanalytic perspective this signals an inability to face reality and accept his limitations in a competitive world. While it may be consoling to believe that a competitor got what we wanted because they resorted to sorcery, is it not healthier and more realistic to acknowledge that we hate them for the relatively superior aptitude and experience that made them a better job prospect?

A second example relates to the importance of mourning in psychoanalytic treatment and the various ways this is defended against. From this perspective, aggressive feelings are always unconsciously associated with loss as we fear that our destructive impulses have harmed or killed off our good internal objects and valued relationships with significant others. Losses of various kinds become symbolically associated in this way, and it is clear that S has indeed experienced a number of losses. Loss and its acknowledgement is necessary for the developmental shift from the paranoid-schizoid to the depressive position (Klein, 1940), bringing with it the ownership of experience, withdrawal of projections and the ability to distinguish between reality and fantasy. Bewitchment may be viewed as a consummate defence against feeling loss and having to do the work of mourning. A good example from our case is the witchcraft-related belief in zombies. As a zombie, the brother resides in the world between the living and the dead, that is, in limbo. There is also the belief that zombies can be brought back from the dead through the use of magic potions. In keeping the brother partially alive in their own minds, or at least the hope that the brother may return from the dead, the family does not have to properly confront the loss of the brother and mourn him.

The figure of a zombie also has a sinister aspect as it is connected to evil and witches. This aspect of the zombie figure reveals the fear and guilt that the survivors experience, especially with regard to their ambivalent feelings toward the deceased. By blaming the deceased's zombie fate on witches, the patient's hostile feelings toward his brother, and his associated guilt, need not be confronted. All the bad feelings are projected into the witches and he is spared dealing with the fantasy that his own aggression is somehow implicated in his brother's suspicious death.

Proponents of the common factors approach would contend that although the interpretive frameworks and specific interventions may differ, the healing effects are the same. In Frank and Frank's (1991) terms, the demoralised patient becomes 'remoralised' after receiving an explanation for their suffering, becoming open (suggestible) to an authoritative healer's influence and experiencing some form of catharsis after participating in a socially sanctioned healing ritual that increases expectant faith that something will change for the positive. Whatever the posited differences between psychoanalysis and indigenous healing, they are functionally equivalent in that they are equally effective in terms of their 'remoralising' effects (Kleinman, 1988).

The psychoanalyst may object to this argument, saying that while they may both be effective, precisely how they exert their healing influence and precisely what constitutes positive change differ fundamentally. Regarding the first issue, Freud rejected his own original cathartic model of psychological change (the discharge of blocked libido), supplanting it with an emphasis on the analysis of unconscious wishes in the patient's transference to the analyst and resistance to the treatment relationship. Even Kleinman (1988: 122) concedes that there are 'few non-Western analogues' to psychoanalytic treatment. I would argue that there are none.

In this regard, while the common factors model claims that suggestion – implicit or explicit – is a universal aspect of the healing relationship, psychoanalysts would argue that it is the avoidance of suggestion that distinguishes psychoanalysis from other treatments. Caper defines suggestion as promoting 'the belief in an idea based not on its logic, or on the evidence for it, but on who has expressed it' (1999: 10) and states that any suggestive influence exerted by the analyst is consciously unintentional and betrays some countertransference resistance to the real analytic work. Other healing frameworks, in contrast, capitalise on the healer's authority to heighten patients' suggestibility and influence them to think and act in certain ways.

The previous point brings us to another problem with the common factors approach, namely the question of divergent treatment goals. Psychoanalysts would reject the claim that the aim of psychoanalytic therapy is to 'remoralise' patients and alleviate their symptoms, although these may be common by-products of treatment. In fact, claims Caper (1999: 24), the analyst does not even attempt to 'cure the patient of anything (except perhaps unconscious self-deception)', but merely to assist him or her integrate split-off parts of their personality. The belief that one can or should heal the patient betrays collusion with the patient's fantasy that the therapist possesses magical curative powers that will obviate the need for the patient to struggle with and solve their own internal difficulties. Thus, while indigenous healing fosters and exploits the patient's idealising transference (the illusion that the healer has magical curative powers), psychoanalysis *disillusions* the patient by analysing the patient's omnipotent projections and their unconscious origin, thereby promoting a more realistic appraisal of both self and others.

A good example of this relates to the *sangoma*'s explanation that S's difficulties were caused by a pot of boiling blood located beneath the gate to the family home, and that the family's problems would persist unless the *sangoma* removed it. This is a powerful metaphor of S's boiling anger and his therapist attempted to interpret it as such. However, while S listened to the interpretation he still wished to have a *sangoma* remove the pot from beneath the gate. This indicates a failure to properly own, experience and integrate the projected hostility. From an indigenous healing perspective, witchcraft, zombies and pots of boiling blood are realities to be acted on rather than symbols to be thought about. In contrast, psychoanalysts would say that the illusion that the pot of blood actually exists and that only a *sangoma* can remove it prevents the patient from integrating their split-off aggression and assuming responsibility for these feelings and the resolution of the internal conflict resulting from them.

It is important to emphasise that I am not questioning the effectiveness of the *sangoma*'s approach in terms of indigenous healing objectives. Over time S reported that the family had been discussing ways of removing the pot of blood and that it had been agreed that all the siblings would contribute toward the payment of the *sangoma*. This cooperative task, involving a sharing of familial responsibility, clearly had some therapeutic benefit. In fact, though probably unintentional, this resembles a systemic family intervention, bringing warring family members together in a collaborative task that unites them, at least temporarily. The point I wish to make is simply that psychoanalysis and indigenous healing, as pure forms, differ fundamentally regarding both their therapeutic intentions and the methods for accomplishing these.

PROBLEMS POSED BY REIFYING CULTURES AND THERAPEUTIC MODALITIES

Emphasising the contrasting aspects of psychoanalysis and indigenous healing carries a number of risks. The first is that these two modalities, portrayed as polarised ideal types, misrepresent their more varied manifestation in the day-to-day work of practitioners. For example, many or most psychoanalytic therapists, while they may aspire to the analytic ideals espoused above, may not work consistently in the transference and may occasionally make interventions considered to be educative, supportive or even suggestive. Indeed, analysts representing different theoretical traditions may not even subscribe to the same analytic ideals, as the heated ideological battles characterising the discipline's history attest to. The same may hold true for indigenous healers in terms of treatment deviations from the magico-religious ideal type.

The second risk is that cultures are presented as static, reified and uniform, thereby supporting stereotyped portrayals of individuals in those cultures. Yen and Wilbraham, critiquing the ideological construction of the 'African personality' in the cross-cultural literature, note that the dualistic classification of cultures as individualist or collective 'posits cultures as discrete and homogenous, and is then employed in interpreting the comparative thoughts, emotions and behaviours of different groups of people' (2003: 567). African people are thus assumed to be dependent, non-rational, lacking individuality and incapable of self-reflection. Those advocates of African belief systems and indigenous healing in turn often portray all westerners as selfish individualists, bereft of spiritual values and a sense of community. Psychoanalysis and indigenous healing are then consigned to either side of a splitting divide, with one side idealised and the other denigrated.

Kakar, an Indian psychoanalyst famous for his comparative investigations of selfhood in Indian and Western cultures, makes a relevant observation:

> I am...not advancing any simplified dichotomy between a Western cultural image of an individual, autonomous self and a relational, transpersonal self of Indian society. These prototypical patterns do not exist in their pure form in any society. Psychotherapy with middle-class western patients tells us that the

autonomy of the self is as precarious as is the notion of the Indian self that is merged in the surroundings of its family and community. *Both are fictions; their influence on behaviour derives not from their actual occurrence but from their enshrinement as cultural ideals.* (2008: 36, emphasis added)

Research by Ensink and Robertson (1999) into African psychiatric patients' illness conceptualisation and satisfaction with their treatment by Western psychiatric services and indigenous healers in a South African metropolitan area yielded some interesting findings. Firstly, most of these patients made parallel use of both biomedical and indigenous practitioners; secondly, most respondents considered their problems to be psychosocial in origin and only 14% identified 'indigenous causes' as solely responsible; thirdly, the respondents who had consulted *sangomas* had largely negative views of these indigenous practitioners, considering them exploitative and unable to deliver on their promises to effectively treat the sufferers' difficulties. There was also little evidence of *sangomas* actually conforming to their popular positive depiction as holistic in their approach to patient treatment. The authors conclude that:

> [T]he majority of African patients and their families interpret mental-health problems in terms of a combination of indigenous, psychosocial and other causes. Even when indigenous names are used, indigenous causes are often not prioritized…patients and their families construct multiple, complex and seemingly contradictory understandings of mental illness in which indigenous and other lay understandings are combined to construct meanings that cut across the relatively discrete indigenous categories depicted in the literature. (Ensink & Robertson, 1999: 38)

This research undermines the notion of a reified 'African personality' who invariably subscribes to magical causation, shuns Western mental health treatment and is an uncritical consumer of indigenous healing. It also undermines the positive stereotyped portrayal of indigenous healers as wise custodians of cultural tradition, employing holistic healing practices while in communion with ancestral spirits.

The lesson here is to avoid the proclivity for identifying the individual with his or her cultural background or, rather, our assumptions about this background. Furthermore, not only is the assumption of a 'pure' culture and its psychological prototypes inherently problematic, but previously firm cultural 'borders' are becoming increasingly porous. Kirmayer, referring to the social impact of globalisation, observes:

> Older theories of the fit of healing practices with ethnopsychological, socio-moral or religious systems of meaning are insufficient to address the common predicament of the person moving between cultural worlds. We need new models to understand the potential effectiveness of culturally based healing in a world in which cultures are in constant flux, transformation and hybridization. (2004: 45).

In the case study, S exemplifies such a person. His education, vocational aspirations, conflicted masculinity and striving for relative independence from his family are consistent with those of young Western adults. At the same time, his beliefs in magical causation, supernatural entities and the relevance of indigenous healing locate him in a more traditional African worldview. These accentuated cultural conflicts, alongside the universal internal conflict between love and hate, instinctual expression and prohibition, etc., require a model of healing sensitive to the tensions of his cultural hybridisation.

Here is another example of competing internalised cultural assumptions emerging in the therapeutic context (Read, 2005). A young black female patient was contemplating the relationship between two recent events – her marriage and her father's death from natural causes. The family had consulted a *sangoma*, who said that someone in the community had been 'jealous' of her marriage and so had bewitched her father, thereby causing his death. She wondered if this made her responsible for his death, but added, 'It is difficult for me to believe these superstitions because they are not scientific. I have this western view – but another part [of me] believes in superstition because my mother believes and always has…' (Read, 2005: 120). The patient then mentioned her reluctance to employ a domestic worker in her home, saying that the worker could 'do things to me in my marriage, using witchcraft' (2005: 120).

A further risk is that emphasising the differences between psychoanalysis and indigenous healing may lead to the conclusion that not only are these two modalities fundamentally incompatible, but that African people cannot benefit from psychoanalytic therapy because of their cultural heritage. Yen and Wilbraham observe that the danger here is of 'reproducing the old racialized division of care', which also 'legitimates a lack of serious attention to adapting western psychotherapy…as interventions for African patients' (2003: 558).

THE PSYCHOANALYTIC CHALLENGE OF ENGAGING WITH INDIGENOUS AFRICAN BELIEFS AND HEALING PRACTICES

In his intriguing account of psychoanalysis in Japan, Parker observes that, 'Distinctive patterns of child-rearing, local conceptions of self in relation to others and culturally bound possibilities for change raise questions about the place of psychoanalysis there...' (2008: 1). Of course, this applies equally to psycho-analysis in South Africa. Psychoanalysis entered Africa as a colonial import and the expectation that Africans should welcome its traditionally Westerncentric philosophy and treatment methods is both arrogant and unrealistic. However, the claim made by some critics that psychoanalysis has no place in Africa because of its Western provenance and cultural underpinnings is equally problematic, endorsing the essentialist notion of culture criticised above. A more useful question is what sort of place psychoanalysis can negotiate for itself through a genuine dialogue with African cultural realities, including indigenous healing frameworks. This means that certain adaptations in how psychoanalytic thera-pists think and practice may prove necessary to accommodate the more collec-tivist self-formations, extended family allegiances and magico-religious beliefs that form a part of most South Africans' cultural heritage.

There are three levels of adjustment needed when any psychotherapy is employed in a cultural setting different from the one in which it originated, namely philosophical, theoretical and technical (Tseng, 1999). The philosoph-ical level is probably the most important for the focus of this chapter. Roland observes that psychoanalysis is guilty of ignoring 'the influence of the cultural world without realizing how much psychoanalysis, itself, is related to it' (1996: 85). The psychoanalytic emphasis on introspection, self-assertion, rationality and individual freedom and responsibility, because these are pervasive Western ideological assumptions, permeates psychoanalysis as universal normative expec-tations. From this perspective, African supernatural beliefs, proximity to the spirit world and tendency to externalise responsibility may appear inherently abnormal. However, it is important for Western therapists to acknowledge these as cultural realities rather than symptoms.

At the same time, however, therapists need to be aware of how patients may use cultural beliefs to support their defensive avoidance of internal conflict. In this regard, African patients who attribute their symptoms to bewitchment are analogous to Western patients who blame all their psychological difficul-ties on neurochemical imbalances, heredity or childhood trauma. It is not *what* we believe that is important, but *how* we use our culturally contingent beliefs to avoid owning and taking responsibility for anxiety-provoking or painful thoughts or feelings. This is very different from pathologising others' cultural beliefs because they appear 'primitive' or 'irrational'. Earlier I discussed Freud's argument that supernatural belief systems serve a defensive function, hindering the process of accessing difficult feelings and attaining a 'truer' understanding of one's psychological life. While this is often true and certainly seems to be so in S's case, it is not necessarily always so, and the danger exists that *all* supernatural beliefs are pathologised as manifestations of defensive psychological processes.

In some respects the demands on the therapist confronting culturally supported defences are similar to those arising when patients present with rigid defences that are not part of cultural belief systems. Timely interpretation of their protective function and the underlying feelings should reduce the need to cling to defensive beliefs and allow a closer focus on the person's emotional reality. In this way, the beliefs themselves are not directly challenged and the therapeutic alliance is thus not compromised by interventions that appear to be insensitive to, or critical of, some valued aspect of the patient's cultural reality. An illustration of this is the therapist's approach to S's erectile problems. By claiming that his former girlfriend had used witchcraft to make him impotent, S externalised the source of his distress, rather than seeing a connection between his erectile dysfunction and the feelings of loss and rejection that resulted from her choosing another lover. This made him doubt his masculinity and left him hurt and humiliated. By linking the experience of betrayal and the associated feelings to the somatic symptom, the therapist redirects the patient's awareness from the perceived witchcraft-related activities outside of him to the emotional processes 'inside' him.

However, in the eyes of Western psychotherapists, the status of witchcraft beliefs as the epitome of pathological irrationality means that when such material arises in the therapy dyad it becomes a precipitant for the therapist's *cultural countertransference*. This refers to 'the reactive arousals, biases, and anxieties that emerge [in the therapist]…in the presence of an ethnic stranger' (Perez Foster, 1998: 267). What makes these countertransference proclivities cultural is that they concern the therapist's feelings and fantasies regarding the patient's cultural positioning and ethnic identity, as well as the therapist's relationship to their own cultural identity. The cultural countertransference may assume many forms depending on the therapist and the dynamics of the specific therapeutic dyad. For example, the white male therapist treating the recently married black female patient who wondered if witchcraft killed her father may respond to this in various ways. He may distance himself emotionally from his patient, appeal to the 'scientific' aspect of her mind, interpret her supernatural suspicions as defensive avoidance of her own fantasies of having killed her father, remind her that he died of natural causes, become overly interested in learning details of her worldview, or suddenly find himself anxiously wondering whether sorcery is real and can actually bring about a person's death. All of these different reactions may suggest idiosyncratic countertransference responses to the emotional arousal elicited by the experience of cultural dissonance.

Another manifestation of cultural countertransference, particularly on the part of white therapists, is to adopt an uncritical and romanticised view of traditional healing. Swartz (1999) notes the intellectual expression of this attitude in the largely descriptive and uncritically positive view of indigenous healing in the literature, typically without any appeal to supporting evidence. Furthermore, the more problematic aspects of indigenous healing, such as the destructive impact of witchcraft accusations, are often ignored by sympathetic advocates.

Given the racial history of South Africa, white therapists' moral investment in avoiding any suggestion of racism on their part makes the issue of cultural countertransference in relation to traditional healing particularly fraught. This cultural superego, as we may label it, can obstruct therapists' mental freedom and impose self-censorship whenever dissonant thoughts about traditional healing arise in therapeutic settings with African patients.

A further challenge to psychotherapists is how to relate to the indigenous healers who promote beliefs concerning evil magic, particularly when the patient consults these healers while concurrently seeing a psychotherapist. For example, what is our attitude to the *sangoma* who tells S that his not getting the job was due to a competitor using sorcery to render S's certificates invisible? In situations like this it is not merely a case of analyst and healer having different understandings, but that these understandings are fundamentally antagonistic. Here is a collision of incompatible cultural assumptions: either the patient must confront the emotional injury of losing out to a superior Oedipal rival *or* he accepts that he was the better applicant and sorcery unfairly deprived him of a job that was rightfully his.

We could view this situation as analogous to the frequently arising professional differences between psychoanalysts and organic psychiatrists, who attribute all psychological difficulties to some somatic disturbance. However, whereas rivalry between biomedicine and psychotherapy is often partially resolved through a respect for a natural division of labour – psychiatrists treating the presumed somatic dysfunction and therapists treating the accompanying 'problems in living' – a similar resolution may not be possible when the indigenous healer claims to treat the 'whole' of the patient.

While appreciating the reparative impulse at work in the often heard plea for collaboration between psychotherapists and indigenous healers, I question how realistic this possibility is. The psychoanalyst Maiello (1999) provides a thoughtful account of her interaction in South Africa with Makaba, a *sangoma*, which illustrates both the therapeutic efficacy of indigenous healing and the challenges to collaboration. Having been introduced to the *sangoma*, Maiello, through interpreters, inquired into Makaba's treatment of a psychotic male patient (named Maboete) who lived with her in her hut until he was cured. Initially the *sangoma* spent some weeks just observing her patient, after which she prepared *muti* to cleanse him internally and rubbed another *muti* into his legs to prevent him running away. The actual treatment commenced with the nocturnal introduction of *muti* into her patient's nose and ears while he slept. This allowed healing substances to carry the ancestral voices into his head in order to 'stop the patient from hearing "his own stuff" and bring him back to hearing and listening to his fellow human beings' (Maiello 1999: 221). Once able to recognise and communicate with Makaba, a verbal phase of treatment began. The *sangoma* gave simple instructions to her patient (such as fetching specific objects), working with his inability or refusal to comply 'until he was "right" again, i.e. until objects and names, words and actions matched as they had done before the illness' (1999: 222). Six months later the young man was no longer psychotic, had been reintegrated into his community and was undergoing vocational training.

When the *sangoma* asked Maiello how she would treat such a patient, Maiello explained that:

> the only *muthi* I used were my words. From what the patient did or said, I tried to understand what his illness was about. Then, I transformed into words what I thought was hidden in his behaviour or speech that made him ill. And if I found the right words for him, they would enter into his ears and go into his head. Gradually he would hear me, and the words would have the effect of a *muthi*. (1999: 222)

Makaba, after responding that their respective treatments were similar, offered to exchange a *muti* recipe for one of Maiello's *muti* words. Maiello concludes the story:

This was one of the moments when I painfully perceived the depth of the gap between our cultures. None of my English words would have been any use to her. I expressed my gratitude and my appreciation for the effectiveness of Maboete's treatment, but we parted without exchanging any of our therapeutic tools. (1999: 222)

This poignant disjuncture in a discussion between healer and analyst marks the intrinsic difficulties with any proposed collaboration and attempt to translate the *sangoma*'s treatment into psychoanalytic terminology. Verbal interchange between patient and therapist, with its signature emphasis in psychoanalysis on self-deception, self-discovery and the articulation of the transference relationship, is absent in the *sangoma*'s treatment. Here the significance of words does not lie in the illumination of personal meaning, but in the induction of hypnotic states through incantation, to instruct patients to perform certain rituals, to transmit ancestral demands, and so on.

In psychoanalysis the work of mourning applies not merely to the loss of loved ones but also to acknowledging guilt, limitation, separateness, difference and the realisation that wished for forms of connectedness with others is not possible in reality. This is why the phrase 'painfully perceived' in Maiello's account of her parting from Makaba is so important. Apartheid was a potent socio-political expression of splitting and projective identification, polarising people along racial lines while justifying the denigration and oppression of black Africans who seemed to embody the antithesis of white Western 'civilised' beliefs and values. Given South Africa's history, the desire to put the past behind us and minimise the cultural differences that were once destructively exaggerated is understandably strong. However, with regard to the relationship between traditional healing and psychoanalysis, it is important to acknowledge difference and think about its meanings, looking for points of contact while accepting that mutually respectful coexistence, rather than collaboration, might be a more realistic and good-enough outcome.

CONCLUSION

In South Africa, perhaps more than anywhere else, comparing African and Western healing systems is unavoidably a political activity as apartheid ideology deployed the comparative emphasis on the 'irrational' aspects of African healing to further its racist agenda (Swartz, 1998). Given this history, some may question the right of a white South African, who does not even speak an African language, to write about traditional African healing and emphasise the distinctions between this healing system and psychoanalysis. Moreover, while I have cited psychoanalysts, psychologists, researchers and anthropologists, conspicuously absent in the chapter are the 'voices' of indigenous healers themselves. I cannot engage here the ideologically charged issues of legitimacy, othering, and absent voices, though these concerns were never far from mind in the writing.

Readers will have noted that parts of this chapter focus on similarities between the two healing modalities, while other parts emphasise apparently irreconcilable differences. I would suggest that this is not due to contradictory assertions in my argument but, rather, attests to the inherent complexities and paradoxes that arise when comparing symbolic or non-biomedical healing systems. Any attempt to evade these complexities results in the adoption of problematic discursive positions: either polarising the two approaches by denying common ground (the intellectual equivalent of splitting), or denying substantive differences in order to pursue a conflict-free integrationist vision. Both of these positions, I believe, close down dialogue and productive inquiry. A respectful but critical curiosity about the theoretical and practical commonalities and differences between healing modalities suggests itself as a healthy alternative perspective. Who knows what may emerge from psychoanalysts and *sangomas* talking and listening to each other about their healing practices?

Part of the ongoing challenge of racial reconciliation in South Africa is the collective failure of white people to demonstrate openness to engaging with the cultural values and practices of black South Africans. Psychoanalysis' history of excluding systematic consideration of non-Western cultures in its theoretical models and therapeutic practice has not helped in this regard. My hope is that as formalised psychoanalytic training takes root in South Africa, psychoanalytic practitioners will be sufficiently interested and socially aware to create inclusive opportunities for discussions on the role of culture, ethnicity and professional identity in their work and in their relationships with other healing systems. This chapter serves as an invitation to those interested in the relationship between respectively new and ancient healing modalities in South Africa to add their voices.

REFERENCES

Buhrmann, MV (1986) *Living in Two Worlds.* Wilmette, Illinois: Chiron Publications.

Campbell-Hall, V, Petersen, I, Bhana, A, Mjadu, S, Hosegood, V & Flisher, A (2010) Collaboration between traditional practitioners and primary health care staff in South Africa: Developing a workable partnership for community mental health services. *Transcultural Psychiatry*, 47(4): 610–628.

Caper, R (1999) *A Mind of One's Own.* London: Routledge.

Dow, J (1986) Universal aspects of symbolic healing: A theoretical synthesis. *American Anthropologist*, 88(1): 56–69.

Eagle, G (2004) Therapy at the cultural interface: Implications of African cosmology for traumatic stress intervention. *Psychology in Society*, 30: 1–22.

Ensink, K & Robertson, B (1999) Patient and family experiences of psychiatric services and African indigenous healers. *Transcultural Psychiatry*, 36(1): 23–43.

Frank, JD & Frank, JB (1991) *Persuasion and Healing.* London: Johns Hopkins University Press.

Freud, S (1901) The psychopathology of everyday life. In J Strachey (ed. and trans., with A Freud) *Standard Edition of the Complete Psychological Works of Sigmund Freud, Volume 6*, pp. 239–279. London: Hogarth.

Freud, S (1907) Obsessive actions and religious practices. In J Strachey (ed. and trans., with A Freud) *Standard Edition of the Complete Psychological Works of Sigmund Freud, Volume 9*, pp. 117–127. London: Hogarth.

Freud, S. (1923). The ego and the id. In J Strachey (ed. and trans., with A Freud) *Standard Edition of the Complete Psychological Works of Sigmund Freud, Volume 19*, pp. 12–66. London: Hogarth.

Freud, S (1998) *Totem and Taboo.* New York: Dover Third Editions.

Fuller Torrey, E (1986) *Witchdoctors and Psychiatrists.* Northvale: Jason Aronson.

Hammond-Tooke, D (1989) *Rituals and Medicines.* Johannesburg: AD Donker.

Holdstock, TL (2000) *Re-examining Psychology: Critical Perspectives and African Insights.* London: Routledge.

Ivey, G (2009) Wilfred Bion: Thinking, feeling and the search for truth. In J Watts, K Cockcroft & N Duncan (eds) *Developmental Psychology (second edition)*, pp. 112–137. Cape Town: UCT Press.

Ivey, G (2010) Plying the steel: A reconsideration of surgical metaphors in psychoanalysis. *Journal of the American Psychoanalytic Association*, 58: 59–82.

Ivey, G (2011) Bion's therapeutic applications. *Psychoanalytic Psychotherapy*, 25(1): 92–104.

Ivey, G & Myers, T (2008) The psychology of bewitchment (Part 2): A psychoanalytic model for conceptualising and working with bewitchment experiences. *South African Journal of Psychology*, 38(1): 75–94.

Kakar, S (2008) Culture and psychoanalysis: A personal journey. In J Mimica (ed.) *Explorations in Psychoanalytic Ethnography*, pp. 25–44. New York: Berghahn Books.

Kirmayer, LJ (2004) The cultural diversity of healing: Meaning, metaphor and mechanism. *British Medical Bulletin*, 69: 33–48.

Kirmayer, LJ (2007) Psychotherapy and the cultural concept of the person. *Transcultural Psychiatry*, 44(2): 232–257.

Klein, M (1940) Mourning and its relation to manic depressive states. In M Klein *Love, Guilt and Reparation: And Other Works 1921–1945*, pp. 344–369. London: Hogarth Press.

Kleinman, A (1988) *Rethinking Psychiatry*. New York: The Free Press.

Kruger, J, Lifschitz, S & Baloyi, L (2007) Healing practices in communities. In N Duncan, B Bowman, A Naidoo, J Pillay & V Roos (eds) *Community Psychology: Analysis, Context and Action*, pp. 323–344. Cape Town: UCT Press.

Levin, C (2001) The siege of psychotherapeutic space: Psychoanalysis in the age of transparency. *Canadian Journal of Psychoanalysis*, 9: 187–215.

Maiello, S (1999) Encounter with an African healer: Thinking about the possibilities and limits of cross-cultural psychotherapy. *Journal of Child Psychotherapy*, 25(2): 217–238.

Makwe, ER (1985) Western and indigenous psychiatric help-seeking in an urban African population. Master's dissertation, University of the Witwatersrand, Johannesburg.

Mbiti, JS (1990) *African Religions and Philosophy (second edition)*. London: Heinemann.

Mkhize, N (2004) Psychology: An African perspective. In N Duncan, K Ratele, D Hook, N Mkhize, P Kiguwa & A Collins (eds) *Self, Community and Psychology*, pp. 4.1–4.29. Cape Town: UCT Press.

Mkize, DL (2009) Bringing together indigenous and western medicine in South Africa: A university initiative. In M Incayawar, R Wintrob & L Bouchard (eds) *Psychiatrists and Traditional Healers*, pp. 207–214. London: John Wiley and Sons.

Ngubane, H (1977) *Body and Mind in Zulu Medicine*. London: Academic Press.

Niehaus, I (2000) *Witchcraft, Power and Politics: Exploring the Occult in the South African Lowveld*. Cape Town: David Philip.

Ogden, TH (2003) What's true and whose idea was it? *International Journal of Psychoanalysis*, 84: 593–606.

Parker, I (2008) *Japan in Analysis: Cultures of the Unconscious*. New York: Palgrave Macmillan.

Perez Foster, R (1998) The clinician's cultural countertransference: The psychodynamics of culturally competent practice. *Clinical Social Work Journal*, 26(3): 253–270.

Read, GFH (2005) Psychoanalytic psychotherapy and the analytic attitude: A cross-cultural case study approach. PhD (Psychotherapy), University of Pretoria.

Roland, A (1996) *Cultural Pluralism and Psychoanalysis*. New York: Routledge.

Rosenzweig, S (1936) Some implicit common factors in diverse methods of psychotherapy. *American Journal of Orthopsychiatry*, 6: 412–415.

Rustin, M (2001) *Reason and Unreason: Psychoanalysis, Science and Politics*. London: Continuum.

Straker, G (1994) Integrating African and Western healing practices in South Africa. *American Journal of Psychotherapy*, 48(3): 455–467.

Swartz, L (1998) *Culture and Mental Health: A Southern African View*. Cape Town: Oxford University Press.

Swartz, L (1999) Multiculturalism and mental health in a changing South Africa. In P Pedersen (ed.) *Multiculturalism as a Fourth Force*, pp. 93–110. Philadelphia: Brunner/Mazel.

Tseng, W-S (1999) Culture and psychotherapy: Review and practical guidelines. *Transcultural Psychiatry*, 36(2): 131–179.

Tseng, W-S (2001) *Handbook of Cultural Psychiatry*. San Diego: Academic Press.

Yen, J & Wilbraham, L (2003) Discourses of culture and illness in South African mental health care and indigenous healing, Part 2: African mentality. *Transcultural Psychiatry*, 40(4): 562–584.

Zaretsky, E (2004) *Secrets of the Soul: A Social and Cultural History of Psychoanalysis*. New York: Alfred Knopf.

CHAPTER 7

INTIMATE PARTNER VIOLENCE IN POST-APARTHEID SOUTH AFRICA:
Psychoanalytic insights and dilemmas[1]

Tina Sideris

INTRODUCTION

South African statistics reveal alarmingly high levels of violence in intimate partner relations. Figures from the Gender Links Gender Based Violence Indicators Project, conducted in Gauteng province between April and July 2010, found that 51% of women have experienced some kind of violence in their intimate relationships. The same project found that 75% of partnered men admitted to perpetrating violence (Gender Links, 2011: 2). A report examining masculinities and public policies in South Africa quotes figures showing that in 2000, violence and homicide were the second most common causes of unnatural death of men and women (Redpath et al., 2008). The same report notes that half the women killed were killed by intimate partners (Redpath et al., 2008). Intimate partner violence or domestic violence is neither a new nor a uniquely

South African phenomenon. However, the transition to political democracy in South Africa laid bare the connection between the public and the private and, in so doing, provoked new questions about how we understand intimate partner violence and its prevention.

This chapter explores a theoretical framework for understanding the psychosocial conditions that create the possibilities for intimate partner violence and how such theoretical insights might inform interventions in the public sphere that are aimed at preventing domestic violence. The chapter argues that by calling attention to the interface between socio-political conditions and the psychic dynamics of gender, psychoanalytic feminist and intersubjective theories provide a more complex understanding of domestic violence in post-apartheid South Africa. An intersubjective account of gender violence has significant implications for programmes of intervention that have proliferated post-apartheid to address issues of gender rights and gender violence. In particular, this chapter argues that where the focus is on 'education' and training, psychodynamic conceptions of the subject unsettle the conviction that by addressing rational cognitive processes, attitudes and behaviours will change. Psychodynamic theory challenges us to consider that questioning established gender hierarchies evokes anxiety and that defences against anxiety complicate the reception of public messaging.

Research on men's responses to the focus on gender rights in the aftermath of the transition to democracy raises questions for which an exclusive focus on social and political factors is not sufficient – in particular, how and why men who are frustrated by the failure of the promises of political transformation convert the women with whom they are intimately involved into threats. This raises the question of what is at stake in the 'private' sphere of intimate relationships that fuels the continuity of domestic violence.

The latter question is approached through the work of psychoanalytic feminist Jessica Benjamin who, from an intersubjective perspective, places 'recognition' of the other as a separate but *equivalent* entity at the centre of violence.

> The question – Can a subject relate to the other without assimilating the other to the self through identification? – corresponds to the political question, Can a community admit the Other without her/him having to already be or become the same? What psychoanalysis considers the problem of overcoming omnipotence is thus always linked to the ethical problem of respect and the political problem of nonviolence. (Benjamin, 1998: 94)

Transition to democracy in South Africa generated tensions between domains and forms of recognition.[2] This chapter is organised into four sections, taking as a starting point that recognition of women as equal legal persons in the public domain exposed a crisis of recognition in the private sphere. The first section provides a brief background on research with men that explored the association between masculinity and violence. The research is located against the background of the social and political changes that have taken place in South Africa. Reference to the gender rights project and sexual violence reveals how, in the process of political transformation, men's sexual and relational practices have been exposed to public scrutiny. While the chapter draws on research with individual men, it does not examine the unique combination of psychic, familial, interpersonal and social factors that results in violence between particular men and women. Instead, the research findings provided the impetus for exploring what psychodynamic theory brings to our understanding of violence perpetrated by men against women in intimate partnership, as a social phenomenon. This suggests that, paradoxically, psychoanalytic theory, which is conventionally considered a theory of the individual, provides critical insights into a socio-political phenomenon, shifting our thinking away from viewing violence as simply an effect of individual pathology. In other words, the school of psychoanalytic theory on which this chapter draws suggests connections between the psychic contents of gender relations, and the social dimensions of violence between individuals.

The second section discusses Benjamin's (1995, 1998) theory of recognition. Addressing the Hegelian master–slave dialectic, Benjamin (1998) draws on the work of child psychoanalyst Donald Winnicott (2002) to give an account of the tension between dependence and independence that characterises recognition. While she seeks mutual recognition as an ideal, using the psychoanalytic concept of omnipotence, Benjamin (1998) emphasises the point that recognition is subject to constant breakdown. Her integration of feminist questions of power, subordination and domination with object relations and intersubjective theory makes her work particularly relevant for examining domestic violence in the context of South Africa's political transition.

The third section looks at what social conditions might do to the breakdown and repair of recognition. Looking more closely at masculinity, this section draws on theoretical work, examining how broad social changes in the order of gender relations may render the masculine defence of projecting vulnerability onto women unworkable. Considered against recent changes that have unsettled gender relations in South Africa, this view provides important insights into the sense of insecurity that some men express, and the crisis of recognition in the private sphere of intimate relations.

The power of psychodynamic theory to clarify intimate partner violence presents dilemmas at the level of practice. In the fourth section a focus on training and awareness-raising interventions highlights the dilemmas of applying psychodynamic theory. This section suggests that it is in practice that the friction between the psychic and the social becomes most evident. How do those involved in the daily struggle to prevent violence facilitate processes which enable ownership of dependence? This is especially difficult when social conditions reinforce antagonism and foster anxieties, which conspire against holding the tension between dependence and independence that allows for recognition. The section concludes that psychodynamic theory cautions against high expectations of interventions that address rational cognitive processes, and highlights the difficulty of effecting social change. This perspective could be interpreted as pessimistic. Nevertheless, a sobering account of the human struggle for recognition can be invaluable for practitioners. Winnicott (2002) alerts us that the struggle with omnipotence is ongoing. As Benjamin (1995) emphasises, there is no ideal context that can eliminate the anxiety evoked by the encounter with the other, which inevitably challenges omnipotent control. For those working to prevent gender violence, psychodynamic theory provides clues for how to bear anxiety and imagine repair.

BACKGROUND

South Africa's transition from apartheid to political democracy has been marked by a sudden and intense disruption of norms and identities. Challenges to previously held values made their way into the personal and private domains of people's lives, making practices in intimate relationships sites of contestation. In the aftermath of the transition to democracy sexual violence became an unprecedented focus of public concern and debate, with relational and sexual practices, in particular those of men, increasingly interrogated.[3]

Against the background of the constitutional endorsement of gender equality and accompanying legislation, research was conducted over a two-year period to explore the association of masculinity and domestic violence.[4] The research was conducted through a women's crisis centre[5] in the Nkomazi district, a remote rural region on South Africa's borders with Mozambique and Swaziland. Founded in 1994, the centre was established to assist survivors of rape and domestic violence access legal rights and medical care. In-depth life history interviews and four focus group discussions were held with a group of seven men living in the Nkomazi district. In addition, semi-structured interviews were conducted with 25 men who hold leadership positions, including traditional leaders, politicians and influential businessmen, to provide contextual detail on dominant notions of manhood and the dynamics of power that structure gender relations. This chapter draws on both sets of interviews.

The seven men who participated in the study constitute a purposive sample, in the sense that they were invited to take part in this research because they were known to openly reject violence against women and children. They came to join the study in different ways. Two of them initially made contact with Masisukumeni Women's Centre around assistance to abused women. One of the other men referred a young girl, who he suspected was a victim of incest, to the centre for help. A short time after sending her for help, the child's uncle tracked him down and physically assaulted him for interfering in their family affairs. Two of the group had frequently visited the centre to have photocopies made. They engaged staff in discussion about the services offered and the kinds of questions they asked reflected a concern about the way women are treated. One of these men, in a separate discussion with members of the centre's staff, expressed his frustration about the attitudes of men around him.

The group of seven men comprises a convenient sample, small enough to allow for detailed case studies. However, the size of this sample in no way implies they are the only men in the Nkomazi district who aspire to relational care and equity in their intimate relationships. The number of men in the district who are changing their views on gender violence and their practices in intimate relationships has not been empirically evaluated.[6]

Intimate partner violence is an aspect of men and women's relationships in a wide variety of societies, cutting across class, race, culture and ethnicity. Nevertheless, the forms it takes and the extent and content of the violence are greatly elaborated by social context. Not all men are violent, neither is domestic violence enacted with the same frequency and intensity in all social settings. This chapter speaks about gender relations in a particular social context and does not presume 'men' or 'masculinity' in South Africa as fixed, essential and unchanging categories. The chapter takes as a theoretical starting point the significance of social context and assumes the notion established by Connell (1995) that 'masculinity' is not homogeneous. Though there may be a hegemonic model of masculinity in social settings, there is always a multiplicity of masculine positions and practices. Equally, although this chapter examines intimate partner violence in a rural area of South Africa as it occurs among poor and working-class people, it should not be read to suggest domestic violence is not a problem in urban areas, and among affluent and privileged classes.

The social realities of the Nkomazi region inform masculine practices in important ways. Patriarchal ideology holds sway and a history of underdevelopment manifests in high levels of poverty and unemployment. Occupying a superior position in the household is central to patriarchal ideals in this social context and is captured in the notion that being the head of the household defines manhood. Being the head of the household requires the capacity to provide and control the resources needed by the household, a requirement that is destabilised by economic factors. The following testimony illustrates the association of manhood with being the head of a household and how, in complex ways, poverty and unemployment combine to threaten male domination.

> To be considered a man you must have a woman. If you are not married, you can't go to the places where men are discussing problems. Without a wife and a child, you are still a boy...Lack of work is a problem for men who want to marry, build a house and have children...To be a real man you must be respected by your wife. If the man does not work and the wife does, things that undermine a man are to do cooking, wash clothes and clean. Then there is no difference between.

> I also see that she is worried about my not being able to maintain the family. She looks at me. Even if I speak with her, there is no respect. I do not feel like a proper man.

Where social constructions portray masculinity as dependent on dominance and power, threats to these can be cause for violence. Hagemann-White and Mincus put this more strongly when they argue that, 'The inclination to use violence against known women can thus be operationally defined as having a concept of "being a man" that requires dominance and specific kinds of recognition and respect, such that it is open to being threatened or potentially lost' (1999: 2).

Notwithstanding the threats that economic conditions and the new constitutional order pose in the Nkomazi area, traditional ideas about gender hierarchies permit violent forms of reasserting control, albeit as a last resort.

The community does not just accept that violence. What is acceptable is that a woman must submit. Nowadays there are laws. Before there were *indunas* and they put him at the *ibandla* (traditional court). If he is wrong they penalise him. You cannot beat your wife for anything. After you have undergone certain stages of disciplining and they don't work, then you can beat her.

The research revealed that despite the authorisation of a dominating and at times violent expression of masculinity, there are men grappling to embrace change and establish new practices in their intimate relationships (Sideris, 2005). A discourse of human rights and Christian principles provides the moral framework in which these men locate their changing practices. They seek equity and reciprocity in their intimate relationships with women and with their children, and are motivated by what they describe as the possibility of a harmonious and peaceful family life. Indeed, there is ample evidence to show that in diverse South African social contexts men are grappling with change (Reid & Walker, 2005). Masculinity is contested and dynamic. The challenges to the gender order that have accompanied political transition in South Africa have resulted in the emergence of new and diverse understandings of masculinities and masculine practices (Morrell, 2001).

Of particular relevance for this chapter, the research shows that those groups of men who seek to reassert control, and those who are trying to forge new models of manhood, are both confronted, in different ways, with the fragile foundations on which masculinity rests (Frosh, 1994). Men who embrace rights are confronted with the contradiction between equity in the household and the dominant idea that being the head of the household is a principal mark of manhood. Embracing equity without alternative role models and social support, they are left feeling uncertain about what it means to be a man. For those men who aspire to the hegemonic ideal, the limits to the legitimacy of male authority posed by the constitutional endorsement of gender equality (Posel, 1991, 2005) combine with economic factors to expose the emptiness of the promise of men's unlimited access to power (Segal, 1990).

Gone are the days of a man being in power. We are inheriting Western style. As African we are lost. As men we are feeling it. As African we don't know where we are.

We are moving to equity very fast. Even in the work sphere there is equity. Men feel threatened by this. We don't know what the role of men is anymore.

This is a challenge. If you look at a man's status culturally, it was above, also in the church and in religion. One has to prove oneself. Some men resort to force to protect their status.

You have to change and you don't know how. The government is confusing things. They say let's go back to our culture and then they say let's go forth, (mean)while they are legalising polygamy they say women have equal rights.

Hence, while the new constitutional order in South Africa endorses gender equality, neither the structural foundations of inequality nor the ideology that makes access to power an ideal has been dismantled (Segal, 1990). Therefore, for many men the gender rights project evokes potential loss. Social conditions, particularly economic marginalisation, can result in what appear to be feelings of envy among some men, of what they experience as women's privileged access to the benefits of political transformation. Equally obvious in the research findings is the sense of threat that men feel, an anxiety that the women they are involved with will start to persecute them. The assumption that a woman who has access to rights will *obviously* turn against him is clearly illustrated in the following excerpt from an interview with a man who took part in the study.

Mmm, you see these equal rights, I think sometimes for men they are a burden. Especially when you find that a woman is working at home and the man is not working. Or maybe they are both working but the woman is earning more than the man and obviously she turns to undermine her husband you see.

In defence against a socially generated condition of material dependence, this man converts the woman he is involved with into the threat. Does this statement bear witness to the panic that separateness evokes, because the other who can no longer be controlled is still needed (Benjamin, 1998) and is a constant reminder of the fear of being abandoned (Mercader et al., 2003)?

WHAT IS AT STAKE IN THE 'PRIVATE DOMAIN'?

Winnicott (1958) argues that it is the relationship of total dependence on the mother figure that explains men's fear of women. The fact that, as infants, we all experience absolute dependence leaves a residual fear of dependency which, because the primary caretaker is usually a woman, translates into fear of women. This fear can be managed by identification, by internalising the feminine – a task that is easier for women because they can become mothers. Ideologies render this identification difficult for men, thus intensifying their fear of women in general. This, Winnicott (1958) suggests, provides an explanation for cruelty towards women and the tendency to demand total control of women.

Over half of the men interviewed for the study were raised by their mother, who was either the principal or only breadwinner. The same number regard their mother as the most influential figure in their lives. Hence, these men who feel so threatened by the prospect of independent women identify women, their mothers, as the people who autonomously provided for their subsistence needs, education, care and wider development.

For example, one man said about gender rights, 'This thing of rights of a women, I do not like them.' Yet he recalled with enthusiasm the capacity his mother demonstrated to care for him and his siblings under very difficult conditions.

> We were six in my family. Then my mother had to bring us up from the moment my mother and father got separated. We went to stay with my mother at our grannies. Because of some reasons, problems, due to, I can say my father was not quite responsible for maintaining us, we grew up in very hard times. So my mother decided to take us with her. I am like my mother, I mean how she cared for us, how she thinks for other people you know. I am that kind of person.

Similarly, a young man commented on gender equality:

> I take gender rights as a threat to the family. It is a threat to me for instance, when it is said that the wife has a right to do whatever she thinks is good. I think that shouldn't be the way. ...

Yet, in an apparent contradiction, he describes how close he is to his mother:

> I have grown up with my mother. She was closest to me. She used to teach me how to do things…It was much easier for me to conduct a relationship with my mother than my father. My father was a bit apart from me…We usually didn't have time to talk or to be together and he was so strict.

Benjamin (1998) seeks a reversal of theories of gender differentiation and thereby challenges cultural assumptions about motherhood contained in psychoanalytic theory. She develops a perspective through which mothers can be represented as subjects and not simply objects, and mothers and fathers may each become figures of separation and identification for children of both sexes. In other words, she categorically rejects the notion that male children cannot identify with the mother and, with equal emphasis, the complement, that fathers should not constitute figures of identification for girls.

She makes the important theoretical point that in the pre-Oedipal phase the father is able to support increasing separation from the mother, as well as an active sense of desire in children of both sexes. Simultaneously, both children may continue to identify with the mother as a 'source of goodness' (Benjamin, 1998: 61). Even when children begin to recognise, through anatomy, that there is a system of sexual difference, they can still imagine containing the opposite thereby permitting 'fluid and contradictory' forms of identification (1998: 62).

Benjamin (1986) locates relations of domination in the rupture of the tension, the splitting of self-assertion and recognition. Where there is adherence to only one side of self-assertion or recognition, relationships of control and submission are generated. For Benjamin (1998), recognition requires tolerating the externality and difference of the other. As a resolution to the Hegelian master–slave dialectic whereby the assertion of independence clashes with the need for recognition, resulting in domination, she seeks mutual recognition. This means recognising the externality of the other on whom we depend for our own recognition. Drawing on Winnicott's (1958, 2002) theory of destruction and survival, she introduces negation as the opposing term of recognition.

It is through negation that Winnicott (1958, 2002) leads us to the externality of the other. The other who survives destructive impulses is discovered as having an independent existence outside the world of fantasy. Crucially, this discovery of separateness also allows for the experience of self as real. In Hegelian terms, the subject recognises itself in the object (Mills, 2000). The outcome of destruction determines recognition or, in Benjamin's (1998) terms, recognition is dependent on how negation is processed.

The idea of the externality of the other is clarified by Winnicott's (2002) distinction between intrapsychic and intersubjective constructions. In contrast to internal representations of the self's relations to its objects, he seeks an other who is '…part of a shared reality, not a bundle of projections' (2002: 88). To this extent he celebrates the discovery of the other. The significance of Winnicott's theory of development is that it establishes a conceptual basis for an ethics of relating in which there is mutual recognition between equal subjects (Benjamin, 1998; Honneth, 1995).

As a result of socially constructed gender categories, the splitting of self-assertion and recognition becomes equivalent to male domination and female subordination. Patriarchal ideologies, whereby gender difference is hierarchically constructed, prescribe male autonomy or, more accurately, associate individuality and absolute autonomy with masculinity. Women, defined as the other of men, are associated with dependence and subordination. Yet as is emphasised by Benjamin (1995, 1998) and Winnicott (2002), the fact of dependence reasserts itself. In other words, the will to absolute autonomy does not do away with the need for recognition. The assertion of complete autonomy involves domination and control of the other from whom recognition is demanded or forced (Benjamin, 1990). In essence, then, domination is based on the denial of dependency.

BREAKDOWN AND REPAIR OF RECOGNITION IN SOCIAL CONTEXT

Recently there has been a growth in psychoanalytic perspectives which seek to theorise how the social and psychic intersect. Layton, reflecting on subjectivity, makes a strong case for a contextualised perspective:

> Thus do psychological structures such as dependency, agency, vulnerability, reason, etc. become gendered, raced, classed and sexed. The way they become so differs, of course, in different cultures and subcultures and in different historical moments. To understand the way cultural hierarchies influence the development of subjectivity in any given culture, researchers must carefully attend to local and historical specificity. (2007: 148)

Winnicott was exceptional among traditional theorists in moving away from a purely intrapsychic focus and emphasising the 'environment'. However, his writing tends to equate the 'environment' with the mother/caregiver. While from the perspective of the infant the mother is the 'environment', a wider angle of vision takes in how social factors construct 'motherhood' and shape mothering. Walls observes: 'Even traditional object relations theorists such as Winnicott and Kohut view the parent–child dyad as a decontextualised universe of its own without reference to the historical and political forces that shape it' (2004: 621).

Appealing for a psychoanalytic treatment modality that acknowledges the social – culture, language, systems of belief, institutional participation and customs – as inherent to 'human nature', Walls (2004) refers to the relational or intersubjective turn in contemporary psychoanalytic thought as encouraging. This is because it gives social context a place in explaining psychopathology, and because it may make therapy more applicable across race, culture and class.

Viewed from this angle, how might the tension between dependence and independence be torqued by specific historical conditions and particular social circumstances in South Africa? The site of the research fieldwork to which this chapter refers is characterised by poverty, and in many instances scarcity of resources in the household precipitates violence.

The testimony of one of the men interviewed reveals how the frustrations generated by scarcity meet with gendered assumptions about respect and submission, resulting in him beating his partner.

> I asked her to give me food. She said, where do you think I must get food? You can see there is no food. There was a little that I bought. She took it and gave it to the children. She didn't answer me in a good way – she shouted at me. It's the way she spoke and behaved. Then I beat her.

The question arises how violence of this kind, which in reality renders the mother's survival precarious, might elaborate children's unconscious aggressive and destructive fantasies. In the unconscious world of fantasy, actual deprivation – scarcity of food, lack of clothing and mothers who are absent due to competing demands on their attention – may easily be interpreted as persecutory. Of course, even mothers severely constrained by environmental conditions can provide the 'devotion' that defines success in infant care. They can and do have times of caring interaction with their children which 'mend' the deprivations imposed by external realities (Winnicott, 1958: 238).

But where external deprivations include the violation of women, the mother's capacity to be consistently available, reliable and giving is more forcefully undermined. By the logic of the unconscious, her vulnerability can be interpreted as a failure to survive and ongoing abuse decreases her capacity to repair the effects of deprivations. As a result, the infant is prevented from experiencing the caregiver as a subject, an entity in her own right, whose independence and nurturance are equally trustworthy. Thus, the child who is left feeling ineffectual and in a continued search for recognition from the other, may carry on trying to destroy, establishing the foundation for future relations in which recognition is coercively extracted without reciprocity (Benjamin, 1998; Hageman-White & Mincus, 1999).

The rural area in which the fieldwork was conducted was previously a 'homeland' created through apartheid policy, as a resettlement area for people removed from their land for wildlife conservation and commercial farming. The 'homeland' system was such that men were forced to seek employment and as a result migrated out. During their periods of absence women remained as 'heads' of households, where they constituted powerful figures in the lives of children. As is illustrated by the testimony quoted above, notwithstanding their limited access to resources and the arduous conditions under which they lived, women managed to sustain their families, and by managing the household economy they exercised significant degrees of power (Posel, 1991).

Despite women's powerful presence in the household, ideology constructed women as subordinate to men. And social and institutional practices, in particular the apartheid state, legitimised male domination over women and children. Thus, in spite of the absence of actual fathers, the father's eminence was kept alive in the image of the head of a family, even though many actual patriarchs did not, or could not, fulfil the responsibilities to provide and protect attendant on this role. The consequences of virulent forms of racial domination and class exploitation for men's sense of themselves in public life gave domestic life a special significance as the site of successful manhood. Polarised notions of masculinity and femininity dominated the cultural content of gender categories. These underscore anatomical difference and invoke bodily symbols of strength and weakness.

For example, the account a young man gives of the passage to manhood is couched in such metaphors: 'A boy has to suffer. He has to go through difficulties. If he grows up soft he won't be able to think.' In contrast, the feminine is associated with submission, yielding in the service of the patriarch. The same young man describes the ideal relationship of a wife to her husband: 'When she brings him food or something she must go down on her knees and say, "Here's your food father."'

Arguably, under such conditions the psychological passage to manhood demands a defensive repudiation of dependency and a vigorous rupture of connection to the feminine. The image of the patriarch who holds the promise of autonomy and casts the feminine as subordinate encourages an internal disconnection between dependence and independence – the feminine becoming the container for projections of painful feelings of vulnerability, the paternal representing autonomy (Benjamin, 1998). In this way the fragile tension between dependence and independence is undermined. Hence we could argue that the family forms produced under apartheid, and the gender norms mediated by these families, intensify the tendency in men to discharge vulnerability into women.

This raises two questions. Firstly, how viable is this defence in the face of the social and political changes that defy the representation of women as weak, vulnerable and dependent? And where then does the threat posed by the political obligation to recognise women's externality lie? In other words, wherein lies the threat of the recognition of women as equal legal persons?

Changes in social and political conditions that have resulted in women taking on and performing what are assumed to be masculine roles are not uniquely South African. In East Africa, social anthropologist Silberschmidt documents the increasing economic independence of women and the consequent 'disempowerment and marginalisation of men in practice' (2004: 240), despite the continuation of patriarchal ideology. Her research findings show increasing numbers of men seeking psychiatric help, and a growing economy in the field of interventions to assist men with depression and loss of sexual power (Silberschmidt, 2004).

The European Research Network on Men, a group of researchers using a gender perspective, point to the effects of massive social and economic transformation on attitudes towards men and their practices. Issues of concern include crime, fatherhood, men's physical and mental health, lifestyles and risk, violence towards women, and anxieties around family (Pringle et al., 2001). Similarly, Jefferson (2002) references studies that describe the destabilisation of masculinity and reveal the problematic implications for individual men.

Reflecting on the British context, psychoanalyst Minsky (2004: 3) argues that growing unemployment among men, increasing numbers of women in the job market, and the welfare state's appropriation of the roles that fathers play lead to a 'cultural peeling away' of the need for men to protect and provide for women. Consequently, 'for the first time' there is a risk of men's vulnerability being exposed (Minsky, 2004: 3). Could it be that we are witnessing a similar risk in South Africa?

Among the least expected outcomes of the human rights discourse and political transformation in South Africa has been the challenge posed to the legitimacy of men's privileged status over women. The state's recognition of women as equal legal persons combines with the presence of growing numbers of successful women in the public domain to reveal men's vulnerability. As Minsky argues, these factors operate to undermine the effectiveness of masculine defences: 'Highly significantly, this development in women has meant that many men can no longer unconsciously project culturally unacceptable feelings of loss and lack onto women because it so obviously flies in the face of all the evidence to the contrary' (2004: 2).

To recognise women as independent subjects, equally entitled to rights, belies projecting them as the weak other. Mutual recognition confronts men with their dependence on women, who are repositioned as independent and beyond omnipotent control. Without support for negotiating this encounter with the other, significant anxieties are provoked. As a defence, men may construct women as threats to be blamed for men's insecurity. And as has been suggested above, where culture permits, violent control of women, albeit as a last resort, may be used to disavow dependency.

SOCIAL CHANGE: Psychoanalytic insights and dilemmas

How might the knowledge generated by the intersubjective account of domestic violence be translated into action? A variety of forms of action can be imagined, not least work in the clinic with individuals and couples. Beyond clinical work, the history of community-based interventions in South Africa informed by psychoanalytic theory provides creative models to inform interventions in the gender-based violence sector (see for example Swartz et al., 2002). More specifically, however, what insights does psychoanalytic theory bring to public-sphere interventions that seek prevention of domestic violence? This section examines the dilemmas posed for gender education and 'training'.

The thorny debates among psychoanalysts on whether and how to engage in political action would form the subject of a separate chapter. Nevertheless, it is important to bear in mind that the intersubjective theory of domination and submission challenges psychodynamic practitioners to view gender as relational, and to account for the hierarchies of power that organise gender relations. Initiatives aimed at preventing violence form part of the gender equality project and, to this extent, constitute political action. Schlapobersky (1993), noting that rehabilitative work with torture survivors is part of a commitment to human rights, asks, 'What remains of the therapist's neutrality?'

Historically, activists, particularly in the gender violence sector, have viewed psychologists and psychoanalysts with caution at best, suspicion at worst, because privileging the intrapsychic frequently leads to excusing or absolving perpetrators. Furthermore, conventional psychoanalytic practice has failed to take account of social context, that is, to the experience of race, class and culture, what Altman terms the 'blind spots' of psychoanalysis (Medscape, 2005). Hence, from the activist's perspective, psychoanalysis risks reducing political problems to issues of individual psychopathology.

By giving centre stage to the nexus of relationships out of which violence emerges, the promise of the intersubjective account lies in its challenge to discourses that construct the individual as a discrete and bounded entity. The psychoanalytic challenge to the over-socialised conception of rational 'man' is equally important because it warns about the difficulties involved in effecting social change. At the most obvious level, psychoanalytic theory alerts us to the limitations of interventions which rely on rational intellectual processes.

South African public-sphere organisations, both government and civil society, analogous with counterparts in other countries, have turned to 'education' as a core strategy in the struggle to prevent domestic violence. This is well illustrated in the South African 365 Day National Action Plan to End Violence against Women and Children (2007), a document endorsed by the deputy president.[7] This plan outlines an initiative of cooperation between national and local government, community and non-government organisations, traditional leaders, donors, the arts and sports communities, and the private sector. Priority actions noted in the document include media and marketing, training for government personnel, and lifestyle- and mindset-changing workshops.

Publicly disseminating information about human and legal rights, and how to pursue these, is critical in transitional societies. Combined with exposing the negative effects of violence, raising awareness about gender rights has opened up space for reflection and criticism of conventional gendered practices. This kind of messaging has the potential to disrupt thinking. Nevertheless, it generally remains at the level of persuasion, such that participants exposed to this form of education may engage with concepts without having to take on critical self-reflection.

Feminist critiques argue against the assumption that knowledge can be transferred in a linear way, such that transmitting information will translate into changed behaviours (Mukhopadhyay & Wong, 2007). From a feminist perspective, much gender education has become depoliticised because it avoids the uncomfortable issues of power and conflict, and fails to destabilise personal, interpersonal and institutional patterns of domination and submission (Dasgupta, 2007).

From a psychoanalytic perspective if, as has been suggested, resisting relations of domination and submission requires men to take back the vulnerable parts of themselves, then education of the kind that simply presents new information is unlikely to result in changed minds. Similarly, educational content that focuses on gender equality is unlikely to dismantle the patriarchal thinking found among women, for whom relinquishing submission represents a risk to significant attachments and recognition.

A review of gender education and training programmes reveals that the best do not simply rely on the notion of providing information in the hope that participants will implement new ideas about relationships. Indeed, there is a strong tradition of challenging conventional methods of education in favour of experiential forms. One example in the feminist movement has been consciousness raising, that process whereby reflection on life stories and personal experiences unsettles assumptions and brings to conscious awareness known but unthought about experiences of oppression. In this tradition, the limitations of conventional modes of training identified by feminists are congruent with the insights of psychodynamic practice in privileging process over content.

However, the difficulties involved in effecting changes in attitudes and behaviour extend beyond the form that education takes. Indeed, modes of education that rely on excavating lived experience illustrate the problem well. Interventions of the kind that unsettle assumptions and hold up a mirror to reflect vulnerability inevitably provoke anxiety and defences against it. Hoggett, in reference to Bion's work on the capacity for thinking, captures the potential for trauma astutely: 'Experience always outstrips our capacity to contain it' (1992: 61).

At a workshop[8] in which men and women from civil society organisations gathered to reflect on how to work with men to effect changes in their practices, the concept of gender was debated. Considered critiques were made of conceptualisations of gender which universalise the concept of 'woman' and the oppression of women. Critics pointed to the differences that exist between women and the variety of forms of their oppression, noting that some forms can only be understood as they coincide with race, class and ethnicity. At the same time, a discourse of resistance emerged within the group, one which cast gender in opposition to African culture. The rejection of gender was accompanied by appeals to the moral codes of 'tradition' and the regulations of 'culture'.

As the discussion progressed it became evident that some participants were experiencing acute anxiety, which derailed the group's conversation. Reflecting on this anxiety, the facilitator invited deliberation on what gender equality means.

For those who saw gender as natural, a fixed, biological difference between polar opposites – men and women – equality was interpreted literally to mean 'to make the same' or 'to do away with difference' (Connell, 1995). From this position equality constitutes a profound threat to individual identity, a potential annihilation and a threat to social stability, provoking unbearable vulnerability.

Bhasin's reflection on experiences of working with men on gender captures the vulnerability: 'They seem to be trapped in insecurity, based on a fear of the family structure collapsing, and their safe position disappearing from under their feet' (2001: 33). The retreat to the fixed codes of 'culture' is a defensive manoeuvre – a defence against anxiety, which is simultaneously a defence of privilege. By disputing the notion of gender categories as essential and fixed, the potential value that an intersubjective perspective brings to this situation is obvious.

Less obvious might be the crucial insights that psychoanalytic theory and practice bring to critical reflection. Krips (2008), in reference to the written text, argues that for an essay to be politically radical it must challenge readers to reflect on their investment in how they interpret and evaluate the text.

> In other words, the essay must produce in its readers the momentous meta-shift that Freud initiated in the concept of interpretation, when he turned from merely sending Dora interpretative messages (which she promptly rejected) to asking her the key meta-question that signals his break from psychology to psychoanalysis: What is your investment in opposing me on the field of interpretation? (Krips, 2008: 6)

Phillips, in his exploration of psychoanalysis as education, notes that education and teaching inevitably confront resistance: 'Something in people is unyielding; there are truths to which they will not surrender' (2004: 794). Drawing on Freud, he argues that psychoanalysis reveals the internal imperative to resist because learning, knowing, consciousness – the reality principle – require sacrifice. Thus he casts psychoanalysis as education 'to make education possible' (Phillips, 2004: 794).

Change involves relinquishing old investments and risking uncertainty – giving up omnipotence, acknowledging dependency and bearing frustration. Paradoxically, it is the capacity to tolerate vulnerability and bear frustration that facilitates learning. But, crucially, this requires containment of anxiety – an other or an environment that can hold and *digest* the unbearable, and thereby facilitate the capacity for thought – the kind of containment that Hoggett refers to as 'the labour of love' (1992: 54).

Most immediately the question arises of how public sector organisations, in particular civil society organisations – most of which struggle to survive in hostile social and economic environments – can provide containment. They are largely dependent on funding from donors who demand short-term interventions and 'measurable' outcomes, a methodology that runs counter to the longer-term, process-oriented techniques required by psychoanalysis. The task of containment is made even more difficult in social contexts where omnipotence is presented as an ideal, dependency is shamed and immediate gratification is expected.

Returning to the theme of how the psyche and the social, the private and the public, traverse each other, it is important to bear in mind the feminist dictum 'the personal is political'. While this section has emphasised the imperative of resistance in the logic of the unconscious, the force of the social is equally evident. In the research to which this chapter refers, material conditions and cultural proscriptions stand out. The links between socio-economic deprivation and violence have been described. In Hoggett's (1992) terms, economic marginalisation and poverty emerge as experiences that exceed the emotional capacity to contain them. They can fuel intense anxiety and thereby restrict the ability to symbolically represent or think about the other as non-threatening, as separate, and as equally entitled to recognition.

Culture and tradition exercise similarly powerful effects. Some men who participated in the study sought alternative practices in their intimate family relationships. While they noted the benefits, they also reported on the pressure that tradition and culture exerted. On the basis of engaging in behaviours which are associated with the feminine, some of these men were described by kin as having been bewitched by their wives.

> They say you have been given something poisonous to eat. They say you are a fool – not okay in the head. It is not easy.

> We have few friends. They say we are pompous. They think of us as people who think we are better than others.

As Minsky notes, referring to men who change their practices, 'they risk a decline in status in their own and others' eyes' (2005: 2). Equally, it must be added that social exclusion carries material effects. Thus, the idealisation of culture provides a defensive structure and wields pressure to abandon change, to conform.

The force of culture becomes even clearer when viewed from the perspective of the Marxist cultural theorist Williams (1977: 110), who argues that the influence of dominant beliefs, meanings and values derives from the ways in which they organise and pattern people's material lives and bodily selves, as 'lived' systems of meanings and values. He emphasises that changes in practice involve complex struggle, '...not casting off an ideology, or learning phrases about it, but confronting a hegemony in the fibres of the self and in the hard practical substance of effective and continuing relationships' (1977: 212).

The challenge for psychodynamic practitioners engaging in the public sphere is how to work creatively in the tension between the social and the psychic. At a minimum this requires an awareness of the socio-political context, at best earnest cooperation with other disciplines. Twemlow and Wilkinson argue, 'When addressing social problems, the analyst is no longer at the hub, but one among many collaborators' (2004: 2). Could it be that such forms of collaboration occupy *potential space* where, in Winnicott's (2002) terms, no questions are asked about what is inner or outer – a space that is cohabited by multiple ways of knowing and understanding? The capacity to cooperate in this way requires psychoanalysts and training institutions to address the 'blind spots' of psychoanalysis (Medscape, 2005).

In summary, psychoanalytic theory provides critical insights into the intractability of social problems, and the limitations of interventions in the public sphere that appeal to individuals who are constructed as bounded and whose attitudes and behaviours are determined simply by rational interests. Paradoxically, it is precisely these insights that give psychoanalysis subversive potential as a vehicle for critical reflection. With the theoretical means of identifying resistance and unconscious motivations, psychoanalytic practitioners may be urged to think with others about conditions that facilitate investment in alternative practices and contain anxiety. Although mindful that unsettling emotional investments is threatening and evokes defences against anxiety, by naming the experience of anxiety psychoanalytic practice provides the potential for containment and the facilitation of learning.

Finally, intersubjective theory of domination and submission provides a complex account of intimate partner violence, and presents us with notions of subjectivity which have practical and political implications. Benjamin's (1998) theory insists on the mother as subject. Assigning agency and authorship to women not only comprises a challenge to conventional wisdom, but simultaneously requires that women also take ownership of their tendency to negate.

Focusing on the literary, Haaken (2008) argues that psychoanalytic–feminist cultural theory expands the terrain of narratives of domestic violence, allowing a shift from the *script* of the unidimensional victim and villain, thus allowing women agency.

Similarly, the intersubjective view provides a more complicated under-standing of male violence, one that allows us to keep in mind the inequities of power that constitute a necessary condition for violence. At the same time it alerts us to the anxieties and defensive splitting that socially defined gender categories produce, and thereby problematises men's relation to power. From a feminist point of view, Segal (1990) argues that men's relation to power is illu-sive, an 'empty category' in the experience of many men.

CONCLUSION

The violence of racism and sexism in South Africa's history provides a constant reminder of the breakdown of reciprocal recognition. With specific reference to domestic violence, this chapter has argued for an approach to the problem that takes account of the psychic and relational dimensions of gender. For those concerned with the prevention of gender-related violence, the direction in which theoretical approaches point us has implications. Claims for recognition framed by discourses that assume discrete individuals tend to focus largely on crises in identity. An intersubjective perspective invites us to extend our view to the complex contradictions that inhere in the relation of self to other.

With the concepts of destruction and negation, both Winnicott (1958) and Benjamin (1998) warn against the ever-present danger of assimilating the other. Hence Benjamin (1998) emphasises the importance of owning the tendency to negation so that we acknowledge our impact on the other and the other on the self. This leads us to enquire what conditions might allow men to more effectively symbolise the negation that is contained in the recognition of women's rights. Under what circumstances might they register the impact without retaliating? How can they survive and negotiate difference?

Equally, this perspective, by allowing women agency, invites thinking about how the previously silenced holds the silencer accountable without negating his subjectivity. In Benjamin's (1998) terms, women must take ownership of their own capacity to negate if they are to intervene and assert themselves as agents and not as victims. Accepting that negation is always involved in the encounter with difference, we do not aim for ideal forms of reconciliation. The question becomes, how do we keep 'me' and 'not me' separate yet interrelated without yielding to the defence of converting difference to same or threat (Benjamin, 1995, 1998; Winnicott, 1958)? The challenge lies in fostering conditions that make loss of omnipotence more bearable.

Considering social conditions returns us to thinking about how structural inequalities elaborate the negotiation of difference. Evidence in this chapter attests to the impact of economic marginalisation on the capacity for recognition. The men on whom this chapter focuses are simultaneously silenced and silencers, exploited and oppressors: the 'other' of racial projections and the agents of subordinating constructions of women; subjected to the exploitation of their labour power and consumers of the unpaid labour and sexuality of women. While no perfect environment removes the complexity of dealing with otherness (Benjamin, 1995), it remains important to look at where and how recognition between self and other is linked to the injustices of *maldistribution* (Fraser, 2000).

A theme running through the reflections of gender activists and trainers on their experiences of conducting workshops is the anxiety and resistance that appeals for change evoke. Locating gender equality/inequality and gender-related violence in relational systems preserves the political content of violence, and shifts the focus from individual pathology or antagonisms between individual men and women, to a focus on the systems by which relations of domination and submission are perpetuated. Nevertheless, this should not become a mechanism for denial of individual anxiety.

Psychoanalytic theory provides a compelling account of anxiety and the defences through which the external world is encountered. From this perspective the difficulty of achieving social change is emphasised. Correspondingly, the psychoanalytic record of psychic resistance warns against views that rely exclusively on changes in social and political conditions to effect transformation of human relations. It is these cautions that render psychoanalytic theory valuable for working in the public sphere. For psychoanalytic practitioners who elect to reflect together with others working in the public domain, the challenge lies in accounting for change – what enables resistance to social norms, disidentification and critical reflection?

NOTES

1   This chapter uses the concepts of intimate partner violence and domestic violence to refer to the violence that occurs between men and women involved in intimate sexual relationships. In South Africa, the Domestic Violence Act (No. 116 of 1998) includes reference to wider sets of relationships, including children and people living in the same household but who are not related.

2   Political philosopher Axel Honneth (1995) draws on Hegel to outline an intersubjective approach to recognition between self and other. Noting three domains of recognition, he posits forms of recognition particular to each domain: recognition of the unique needs and desires of the other in primary or intimate relationships; recognition of universal equal rights in the legal sphere; and recognition of the contribution that the unique abilities of the other make to a concrete community.

3   Posel argues that unlike the secrecy surrounding sexual violence under apartheid, by 2001 public discussion of sexual violence in media talk shows, the press, magazine articles and other forms of social commentary was 'incessant and prominent' (2005: 13). She notes that consequent to the spate of baby rapes publicised in the media, sexual violence represented a fundamental political and moral challenge to the new nation, with men becoming the focus of shame and scandal. Arguably, the vitriolic exchange in the media between political opponents in 2009 around Jacob Zuma's rape trial typifies the public scrutiny of men's sexual practices as a mark of moral leadership.

4   The findings of the research form the basis of published work in journals and edited collections on masculinity and violence, masculinity and change and development in South Africa, including Clarke et al. (2006) and Sideris (2004a, b, c).

5   Masisukumeni Women's Crisis Centre, Mpumalanga province.

6   This discussion of the research sample and methodology can be found in Sideris (2004a).

7   See http://www.justice.gov.za/VC/docs/campaings/2007_365actionplan.pdf.

8   Workshop on the challenges of 'working with men' to end gender-based violence, 21 November 2005, Constitution Hill, Johannesburg.

REFERENCES

Benjamin, J (1986) A desire of one's own: Psychoanalytic feminism and intersubjective space. In T de Lauretis (ed.) *Feminist Studies/Critical Studies*, pp. 78–101. Indiana: Indiana University Press.

Benjamin, J (1990) *Bonds of Love: Psychoanalysis, Feminism and the Problem of Domination*. Ithaca: Cornell University Press.

Benjamin, J (1995) Recognition and destruction: An outline of intersubjectivity. In J Benjamin *Like Subjects, Love Objects: Essays on Recognition and Sexual Difference*, pp. 27–48. New Haven: Yale University Press.

Benjamin, J (1998) *Shadow of the Other: Intersubjectivity and Gender in Psychoanalysis*. London: Routledge.

Bhasin, K (2001) Gender workshops with men: Experiences and reflections from South Asia. In C Sweetman (ed.) *Men's Involvement in Gender and Development Policy and Practice: Beyond Rhetoric*, pp. 20–34. Oxfam Working Paper Series. Oxford: Oxfam.

Clarke, S, Hahn, H, Hoggett, P & Sideris T (2006) Psychoanalysis and community. *Psychoanalysis, Culture & Society*, March, 11: 199–216.

Connell, RW (1995) *Masculinities*. Cambridge: Polity.

Dasgupta, J (2007) Gender training: Politics or development? A perspective from India. In M Mukhopadhyay & F Wong (eds) *Revisiting Gender Training. The Making and Remaking of Gender Knowledge: A Global Sourcebook*, pp. 27–38. Oxford: Oxfam.

Fraser, N (2000) Rethinking recognition. *New Left Review* 3, May–June: 107–120.

Frosh, S (1994) *Sexual Difference: Masculinity and Psychoanalysis*. London: Routledge.

Gender Links (2011) *Roadmap to Equality*, Issue 14, February. Preliminary results of the Gauteng Gender Violence Indicators Project by Gender Links and the Medical Research Council. Accessed from http://www.genderlinks.org.za/article/roadmap-to-equality-issue-14-february-2011-2011-02-04 on 28 October 2012.

Haaken, J (2008) Too close for comfort: Psychoanalytic cultural theory and domestic violence politics. *Psychoanalysis, Culture & Society*, 13: 75–93.

Hagemann-White, C & Mincus, C (1999) Explaining the inclination to use violence against women. Paper presented at Council of Europe seminar 'Men and Violence against Women', Strasbourg, France. Accessed from http://www.europrofem.org/o2.info/22contri/2.o4.en/4en.viol/77en-vio.htm on 3 July 2004.

Hoggett, P (1992) *Partisans in an Uncertain World: The Psychoanalysis of Engagement*. London: Free Association Books.

Honneth, A (1995) Patterns of intersubjective recognition: Love, rights, and solidarity. In A Honneth *The Struggle for Recognition. The Moral Grammar of Social Conflicts*, Chapter 5. Cambridge: Polity Press.

Jefferson, T (2002) Subordinating hegemonic masculinity. *Theoretical Criminology*, 6(1): 63–88.

Krips, H (2008) Editorial introduction: Politics and psychoanalysis. *Psychoanalysis, Culture & Society*, 13: 1–7.

Layton, L (2007) What medicine means to me: What psychoanalysis, culture and society mean to me. *Mens Sana Monographs*, 5(1): 146–157.

Medscape (2005) Race and class considerations for care after hurricanes Katrina and Rita: An expert interview with Neil Altman, MD. *Medscape Psychiatry & Mental Health*, 10(2). Accessed from http://www.medscape.com/psychiatryhome on 29 November 2005.

Mercader, P, Houel, A & Sobota, H (2003) *Perspectives on Intimate Partner Murders*. Accessed from http://www.aletta.nu/epublications/2003/Gender_and_power/5thfeminist/paper_656.pdf on 28 October 2012.

Mills, J (2000) Hegel on projective identification: Implications for Klein, Bion, and beyond. *The Psychoanalytic Review*, 87(6): 841–874.

Minsky, R (2004) *Beyond Nurture: Finding the Words for Male Identity*. Accessed from http://human-nature.com/free-associations/minskynurture.html on 28 October 2012.

Minsky, R (2005) *'Too Much of a Good Thing': Control or Containment in Coping with Change*. Accessed from http://human-nature.com/free-associations/minskychange.html on 28 October 2012.

Morrell, R (2001) *Changing Men in Southern Africa*. London: Zed Books.

Mukhopadhyay, M & Wong, F (eds) (2007) *Revisiting Gender Training. The Making and Remaking of Gender Knowledge: A Global Sourcebook*. Oxford: Oxfam.

Phillips, A (2004) Psychoanalysis as education. *The Psychoanalytic Review*, December, 91(6): 779–799.

Posel, D (1991) Women's powers, men's authority: Rethinking patriarchy. Paper presented at Conference on Women and Gender in Southern Africa, 30 January–2 February, Johannesburg.

Posel, D (2005) 'Baby rape': Unmaking secrets of sexual violence in post-apartheid South Africa. In G Reid & L Walker (eds) *Men Behaving Differently: South African Men since 1994*, pp. 21–64. Cape Town: Double Storey Books.

Pringle, K, Hearn, J, Oleksy, E, Mueller, U, Pitch, T, Kolga, V, Ferguson, H, Ventimiglia, C, Novikova, I, Chernova, J, Gullvåg Holter, O, Lattu, E, Olsvik, E & Millet, J (2001) The European Research Network on Men in Europe: The social problem of men. *Journal of European Social Policy*, 11(2): 171–173.

Redpath, J, Morrell, R, Jewkes, R & Peacock, D (2008) Masculinities and public policy in South Africa: Changing masculinities and working towards gender equality. A report prepared by Sonke Gender Justice Network, Johannesburg, October. Accessed from http://www.engagingmen.net/files/resources/2010/Bridget/Masculinties_and_Public_Policy_in_South_Africa_FINAL_250509_0.pdf on 4 November 2012.

Reid, G & Walker, L (eds) (2005) *Men Behaving Differently: South African Men since 1994*. Cape Town: Double Storey Books.

Schlapobersky, J (1993) The reclamation of space and time: A political application of psychotherapy. Paper presented to a seminar 'The Political Psyche' at the Institute of Contemporary Arts, London, November. Accessed from http://www.torturecare.org.uk/UserFiles/File/publications/Schla_1.rtf.

Segal, L (1990) *Slow Motion: Changing Masculinities, Changing Men*. London: Virago.

Sideris, T (2004a) You have to change and you don't know how! Contesting what it means to be a man in a rural area of South Africa. *African Studies*, January, 63(1): 29–49.

Sideris, T (2004b) Boas Mabiza and the long walk to freedom: The diary of an abused and neglected boy as a 'potential space' – implications for therapeutic practice. *Psycho-analytic Psychotherapy in South Africa*, 12(2): 72–86.

Sideris, T (2004c) Men, identity and power. A case study of the re-invention of 'tradition': Implications for involving men in training and education about gender. *Agenda*, 18(60): 88–93.

Sideris, T (2005) 'You have to change and you don't know how': Contesting what it means to be a man in a rural area of South Africa. In G Reid & L Walker (eds) *Men Behaving Differently: South African Men since 1994*, pp. 111–138. Cape Town: Double Storey Books.

Silberschmidt, M (2004) Masculinity, sexuality and socioeconomic change in rural and urban East Africa. In S Arnfred (ed.) *Re-thinking Sexualities in Africa*. Uppsala, Sweden: Nordiska Afrikainstitutet.

Swartz, L, Gibson, G & Gelman, T (2002) *Reflexive Practice: Psychodynamic Ideas in the Community*. Cape Town: HSRC Press.

Twemlow, S & Wilkinson, S (2004) Topeka's Health Community Initiative: A psychoanalytic model for change. In B Sklarew, S Twemlow & S Wilkinson (eds) *Analysts in the Trenches: Streets, Schools, War Zones*, pp. 103–136. Hillsdale, NJ: Analytic Press.

Walls, GB (2004) Toward a critical global psychoanalysis. *Psychoanalytic Dialogues*, 14(5): 605–634.

Williams, R (1977) *Marxism and Literature*. Oxford: Oxford University Press.

Winnicott, DW (1958) *Collected Papers: Through Paediatrics to Psycho-Analysis*. New York: Basic Books.

Winnicott, DW (2002) *Playing and Reality*. New York: Brunner-Routledge.

CHAPTER 8

SERIAL MURDER AND PSYCHOANALYSIS IN SOUTH AFRICA: Teasing out contextual issues amid intrapsychic phenomena in two case studies

Giada Del Fabbro

CRIME AND SOUTH AFRICA

Crime, especially violent and sexual crimes such as rape and murder, pose particular problems for the South African context. According to the South African
Police Service (SAPS) Crime Statistics published for 2010,[1] there were approximately 2 million reported crimes that year. Of the overall tally of crimes that
took place in South Africa from April 2009 to March 2010, 16 834 occurrences
were of murder and 68 322 of sexual crimes. Both of these crimes fall under the
contact crime category of criminal acts, which accounts for 31.9% of total crimes
reported in South Africa; murder accounts for 2.5% of all contact crimes and
sexual crimes for 10% of all contact crimes.[2]

Additionally, the United Nations Office on Drugs and Crime's survey of international homicide rates for 2009 found that South Africa has a homicide rate of

36.5 per 100 000 population, ranking ninth internationally (UNODC, 2009). Murder as a sub-category of criminal behaviour consequently features prominently among important issues to be addressed in the South African context, and frequently as an issue of considerable concern in the daily lives of South Africans.

Working therapeutically with criminal populations poses challenges both in terms of developing effective strategies for pre-emptively addressing psychological and social factors that increase vulnerability to criminal behaviour, as well as providing rehabilitative interventions for individuals already incarcerated or apprehended. Psychoanalytic theory and approaches have provided a plethora of texts and formulations of personality structure together with the defence mechanisms and ego functioning of the criminal and, notably, the antisocial personality (Bluestone & Travin, 1984), but they are still relatively deficient in providing suggestions as to how one may work therapeutically with such individuals, if this is at all possible. The majority of existing and early psychoanalytic literature in this area emphasised intrapsychic factors, especially libidinal and aggressive drives and the role of the superego, and neglected the role played by contextual factors and the external world. Fitzpatrick (1976) describes a change in psychoanalytic studies of criminal motivation as shifting to encompass contextual diversity in the manifestation of antisocial character, as well as emphasising the etiological significance of character development, adaptational functions of the ego and the role played by environment. He highlights the extensive changes made from prior approaches stemming from Freud's essay 'Criminals from a Sense of Guilt' in 1916, which minimised social and economic factors and prioritised unconscious psychosexual conflict.

A cursory review of some of the published work on psychoanalysis and murder includes Abrahamsen (1973), who alluded to the role of environment, albeit minimally, when he described the torment of individuals who commit murder as involving a persistent internal conflict between the external world and the internal world of sexual and libidinal drives. Tanay (1972) developed a classificatory typology of murder, which has been applied and included in *Federal Bureau of Investigation* typology profiling techniques for serial murderers. He distinguished between egosyntonic, egodystonic and psychotic murders. Egosyntonic and egodystonic murderers can be differentiated on the basis of how acceptable the act of murder is for the individual at a conscious level, whereas the egodystonic is differentiated from the psychotic on the basis of the extent to which the individual has to dissociate in order to commit an act that is intolerable to his/her ego and harsh, over-controlling superego.

Several authors have emphasised lapses in ego control and explosion into consciousness of aggression (Menninger, 1963; Satten et al., 1960). Others have introduced the idea of murder as a means to discharge unmanageable rage to avoid psychotic decompensation and to cope with excessive intrapsychic or external stress (Guttmacher, 1960; Lanzkron, 1963; Podolsky, 1956; Reichard & Tillman, 1950). Kohut (1973) states that narcissistic rage often functions to satisfy an overwhelming need for revenge and to undo a narcissistic injury. This rage is not 'integrated with the mature purposes of the ego' but is rather 'mobilized in the service of an archaic grandiose self and is deployed within the framework of an archaic perception of reality', with the potential victim identified as a 'recalcitrant part of an expanded self over which he expects to exercise full control' (1973: 365). Theorists have also conceptualised of murder as symbolic suicide (Fenichel, 1945; Freud, 1917; Guttmacher, 1960), with primitive defence mechanisms of splitting and projection coming to the fore.

In summary, the psychoanalytic literature on murder emphasises the heightening of the normal tension between one's internal drives or needs and the expectations or norms of the external social world in the individual who commits murder; lapses in normal controls within the ego; intense rage and aggression; and, from Kernberg specifically, the introduction of narcissistic elements related to the grandiose self and needs for omnipotence and control.

SERIAL MURDER AS A SPECIFIC CRIME OF INTEREST

A category of criminal behaviour that attracted some scientific and much popular attention for the greater part of the 20th century is serial murder (Hickey, 2006a). Serial murder constitutes a very specific category of criminal behaviour. After emerging and increasing rapidly in prevalence in the United States of America during the 1960s and 1970s, figures for serial murder prevalence in the United States show that 50% of the known cases occurred between 1975 and 2004 (Hickey, 2006a).

Gorby (2000) found the same pattern for most non-European countries, in comparison to European countries that showed a slight decrease from 1975 to 1995, after peaking between 1950 and 1974. It would thus appear that serial murder as a type of criminal behaviour has been noticed and attended to largely during the last and current centuries. South Africa shows a similar pattern to the United States in terms of the proportion of murders accounted for by serial murder (less than 1%, with 55 recorded cases of serial murder between 1994 and 2004).

Serial murder can be defined as multiple murders committed over a period of time by one or more individuals (Del Fabbro, 2006). It should be differentiated from spree killing and mass murder. Spree killing involves the killing of many victims with brief time intervals between murders (at most hourly intervals) and mass murder involves the killing of several victims at one location and at one point in time (Lane & Gregg, 1992).

The central role of fantasy or intrapsychic phenomena in those who commit serial murder has been proposed by a number of individuals working in the field of investigative psychology and profiling (Claus & Lidberg, 1999; Myers et al., 1998). Psychoanalytic perspectives lend themselves easily to this discussion by virtue of their emphasis on internal processes, drives and sexual energy or libido (Smith, 1996), all of which can be used to explain different elements of fantasy. Prentky and colleagues define fantasy as 'an elaborated set of cognitions characterized by preoccupation anchored in emotion, and originating in daydreams' (1989: 889). Burgess et al. (1986) developed a fantasy-based motivational model for serial sexual murder. This model consists of five components: impaired development of early attachments; formative traumatic events; patterned responses that serve to generate fantasies; a private, internal world consumed by violent thoughts that leave the person isolated and self-preoccupied; and a feedback filter that sustains repetitive thinking patterns. Hazelwood and Warren (1995) elaborated upon the structure of sexual fantasy and also argued for five components: relational (a relationship between individuals), paraphilic (some form of deviant sexual behaviour), situational (taking place in a particular location), self-perceptual (furthering the individual's sense of self in some manner) and demographic (specific details about the other individuals involved, such as age and/or race and/or gender). Schlesinger (2001) highlights childhood maltreatment and eroticised maternal relationships as indicators of potential for sexually motivated crimes. Stein (2000) elaborates on this by stressing the role that dissociated trauma in early childhood plays in establishing the fantasy's content and compelling one to act on these fantasies.

Meloy (2000) argues that the manner in which a sexual fantasy is structured along the above lines is useful in establishing how sexual murders will be carried out by a particular individual, as well as the types of victims that such an individual will search for. This can be usefully applied to investigative operations in terms of guidance with regard to type of offender and victim. The fantasy may also be a useful guide to gaining insight into developmental experiences of the offender that may have contributed to both the shaping of the fantasy as well as the serial murder behaviour. Along similar lines, Hickey (2006b) coined the term 'relational paraphilic attachment' to describe the manner in which the attachment styles of individuals who commit serial murder influence their paraphilic preferences and proclivities in the evolution and eventual committing of their crimes.

In terms of diagnostic understandings of serial murder with regard to personality pathology, individuals who commit serial murder have been understood as pathological narcissists on account of demonstrating underlying feelings of inadequacy and humiliation which are defended against narcissistically with self-glorifying compensatory fantasies that restore a shattered self-esteem. Serial murderers under-report violence or abuse in early childhood and may exhibit typical abuse victim patterns of egosyntonic identification, identifying with the bad, and feeling that the abuse is justified.

Turco (2001) states that it is essential to understand the integration of aggression within the personality to access the motivation of individuals who commit serial murder. The actual reasons for committing serial murders are frequently unclear, and it is therefore important to examine the underlying psychopathology and personality of the murderer to comprehend the repetitive drive to kill (Liebert, 1985). Both Turco (2001) and Liebert (1985) have highlighted narcissistic and borderline conditions as clinical foundations for understanding the personality and behaviour of the individual who commits serial murder. These theorists hold that narcissistic pathology in the personalities of serial murderers is an intrinsic aspect of generating the motivation to murder. Specifically, these theorists, together with others working in the field of offender profiling and investigative psychology, have highlighted sadism, malignant narcissism, fantasies of power and narcissistic insults, along with the underlying sense of inferiority, the need for control over others and a history of animal cruelty in such individuals (Fromm, 1973; Gacono, 1992; Hickey, 1991; Liebert, 1985; Lowenstein, 1992; Marohn, 1987; McCarthy, 1978; Palermo & Knudten, 1994).

Kernberg (1984, 1992) describes malignant narcissism as an extreme variant of narcissistic personality disorder and as an intermediate form of character disorder between narcissistic and antisocial personality disorders. Malignant narcissism is characterised by narcissistic personality disorder, unrestrained aggression, antisocial behaviour and egosyntonic sadism, together with an impaired conscience, psychological need for power, grandiosity, and a paranoid approach to interpersonal relationships. As a result, feelings of aggression are integrated with a grandiose self-structure, and egosyntonic sadistic behaviour is directed against the self or others in a triumphant and destructive manner (Pollock, 1978). Developmentally, such an individual's parental and other objects were experienced as cruel, attacking, destructive and oppressive of any self-development, with the subsequent development of a defensive self characterised by the formation of a grandiose self-structure and an integrated hostility in the form of self-righteous aggression. The cruel behaviours and mutilation of others appear to be an endeavour to obtain a sense of superiority and triumph over life and fear. For those who commit serial murder, the rewards for killing are a confirmation of the needs for recognition and power. Hickey (1991) argues that experiences of rejection in childhood were experienced as intensely traumatising for male serial murderers, mainly on account of their pairing with experiences of humiliation and debasement.

Turco (2001) holds that serial murderers have absorbed the elements of badness through the aggression of the mother. The destructive elements of the early mother–child relationship are introjected and split and then projected with a recycling of this badness through projection and displacement towards female targets. The female victim then becomes the target of aggression displaced from the mother. There is a fusion of destructive impulses and disorganised sexual impulses that evolve out of the pre-Oedipal matrix. There is a lack of empathic bonding in such individuals, who may be superficially adapted to society but in an unintegrated manner. The sadism often demonstrated by these individuals is characterologically integrated and justified by chronic sadistic arrogance, and the reprojection of the primitive persecutory superego features onto others who are classified as inferior or dangerous enemies. Such individuals often experience a sense of emptiness and dissatisfaction due to the malignant transformation that impoverishes internal life as a result of devaluation and a failure of early object integration.

SERIAL MURDER IN SOUTH AFRICA

South Africa has a unique social, cultural and political heritage. As with other psychological phenomena, these factors play a role in shaping the manifestation, occurrence and proliferation of various types of criminal behaviour. As noted, serial murder has featured prominently on the criminal landscape of South Africa. Since approximately 1992, South Africa has borne witness to over 100 serial murderers who have targeted victims varying in race, gender and age.

Serial murder features frequently in the popular media[3] – in the form of newspaper articles, television programmes, non-fiction crime literature and fictional works – and has been the focus of a limited number of research initiatives in

South Africa (De Wet, 2005; Del Fabbro, 2006; Du Plessis, 1998; Hodgskiss, 2001, 2002, 2004; Hook, 2003; Labuschagne, 2001; Pistorius, 1996).

My experience in the field of forensic psychology, together with my psychodynamic/psychoanalytic theoretical orientation and interest in attachment, prompted me to explore and investigate the phenomenon of serial murder in South Africa from this perspective. I drew on data that formed part of my doctoral dissertation (Del Fabbro, 2006), which I obtained from five individuals currently incarcerated for committing serial murder. The sample used is outlined in Table 8.1.

As part of my research, I spent considerable time interviewing the individuals in the sample (five interviews each of two hours duration) as well as members of their respective families. Bearing the preceding discussion in mind with regard to various theoretical perspectives on the psychoanalysis of serial murder, so to speak, I will discuss my experiences with two individuals who formed part of the sample, making links to existing theory and generating new postulates.

CASE STUDY 1: John

John is a white, Afrikaans-speaking South African male of average height and slim build. On first meeting him, I was struck by his apparent dullness and blunted affect. His voice was monotonous and soft and he engaged in long, drawn-out mumbled monologues detailing his childhood and later criminal behaviour. I immediately found myself thinking of Hannah Arendt's 'banality of evil' (1994). John is unassuming, lacking in charm and quite inadequate on the whole. John murdered five women and raped seven.

John is an only child. He grew up in a white, Afrikaans working-class family where his father, a civil servant, was the primary breadwinner. John described himself as a loner who did not have any friends. He preferred the company of adults, mostly his parents' friends, and was always a quiet, softly spoken and introverted boy.

John had minimal interaction with his father, an emotionally distant and withdrawn man who was relatively absent from the family home. John's relationship with his mother was characterised by greater ambivalence. He experienced her as strict and punitive during his early childhood and more intrusive and clingy in his adolescence. Throughout both developmental periods, the relationship between John and his mother was quite enmeshed and he frequently served as a

	Mr V	Mr W (Jacob in this chapter)	Mr X (John in this chapter)	Mr Y	Mr Z
Gender	Male	Male	Male	Male	Male
Racial/ethnic background	Black	Black	White	White	White
Age (at time of research)	Late thirties	Early forties	Early forties	Early forties	Early forties
Sexual orientation	Heterosexual	Heterosexual	Heterosexual	Homosexual	Homosexual
Sentence	Life imprisonment	Life imprisonment	Death penalty (converted to life imprisonment)	Death penalty (converted to life imprisonment)	Life imprisonment
Victims	Black females – all ages	Black females in their twenties	Females – various ages and all races	White males, predominantly homosexual	Males – all races, predominantly homosexual
Nature of crimes	Worked alone Rape and murder	Worked alone Rape and murder	Worked alone Rape and murder	Worked with partner Murder	Worked with partner Murder
Family characteristics					
Structure	Multiple caregivers in extended family	Multiple caregivers within nuclear family	Traditionally nuclear	Single-parent household; later with step-father	Traditionally nuclear
Primary relationship type	Triadic around various caregivers	Dyadic with maternal aunt and elder sister	Triadic, with mother and father	Fused, dyadic with mother	Triadic, with mother, older brother and father
Sibling position	Second born	Second born	Only child	Two older half-siblings	Youngest child

TABLE 8.1 A SAMPLE OF SERIAL MURDERERS IN SOUTH AFRICA (Del Fabbro, 2006)

substitute for his absent father. John shared this role with his maternal grandfather, with whom his mother would spend considerable time outside of the family home as she cared for him when he was in between his various relationships with other women. As such, John's early relationship with his mother appears to fit Kernberg's (1984) description of the parental relationships that characterise the early and ongoing experiences of violent individuals in that these figures are experienced as oppressive, attacking and destructive, which fosters the entitlement, grandiosity and rage evident in the commission of the crimes in question.

John and his parents were quite isolated from extended family (other than the maternal grandfather), due to perceptions on the part of both his father and mother that these family members thought too highly of themselves and looked down on them. Throughout John's early life, his parents carried a considerable degree of narcissistic sensitivity to appearances and awareness of how they might be perceived by others. John suffered from encephalitis as a young boy and was left with considerable learning difficulties. This became a source of shame to his mother, who responded by putting more pressure on him to do his homework and to excel in a mainstream school setting. When John could not cope with the increased pressure, she would beat him severely as punishment. The repeated narcissistic injuries that John experienced as a result of this overly punitive, critical and harsh treatment by his parents, specifically his mother, may easily have fostered the overwhelming need for revenge postulated by Kohut (1973). This may have been paired with John's constitutionally increased sensitivity to these experiences.

If one considers John's relationship with his primary caregiver, his mother, in light of the discussion above, one can begin to see the origins of a combination of aggressive and libidinal components in a sadistic fusion, where closeness or 'intimacy' is paired with punitiveness and strictness, and pain or suffering is eroticised in the context of an enmeshed relationship. This is accompanied by fears of annihilation, engulfment and obliteration as part of an enmeshed relationship dyad with the characteristic primitive defences to avoid such a fate, as can be seen in John's isolation, withdrawal and emotional detachment from those around him. This interpersonal attitude may also reflect his attempts to identify with his father and thereby activate his role in an impending and necessary negotiation of the Oedipal dilemma. The containment and holding of John's infantile and germinal emotional development was also compromised by his mother's immense sensitivity and vulnerability to any disruptions of her own intrapsychic emotional milieu. John's mother presents as a fragile and weak woman in need of protection and holding in the face of life's stressors. One can hypothesise that this presentation may have been at odds with the harsh, strict and puni-tive mother John experienced, resulting in considerable confusion, ambivalence, mistrust and paranoia regarding superficial presentation, especially with respect to female figures, and underlying reality. For John, vulnerability in others is not to be trusted as it belies a persecutory and attacking other and as such needs to be obliterated. One can observe how John replays these self–object dyads in his rela-tionships with his victims, and displaces aggressive feelings toward his primary object (his mother) onto them. Interestingly, he repeated this dyad with me, as evidenced by my mistrust of his tears, and thereby his presentation of vulner-ability, in his expression of 'remorse'.

    Shame and humiliation also played central parts in John's early experiences. He experienced considerable feelings of inadequacy and humiliation when he could not perform satisfactorily at school (possibly evoking deeper notions of masculine inadequacy in his difficulty with sexual performance). He also recounted being caught masturbating by his mother when she entered the bath-room unannounced while he was in there. He was severely punished for this inci-dent and felt embarrassed and ashamed for having caused his mother so much distress. In recounting these incidents, John never alluded to the rage that inevi-tably accompanied these experiences of being shamed, and I began to get a sense of how prevalent his defensive denial of such feelings has been in negotiating and maintaining his relationship with his parental figures. It appears that John's aggression and rage were left unmodified, uncontained and unmetabolised by a Bionic alpha mother,[4] and instead responded to with shock, horror and decom-pensation by a maternal figure who presented as too weak and fragile to negotiate her infant's early aggressive experiences. John consequently had to find other avenues and objects upon which to displace the intense rage, largely denied, that accompanied cumulative early experiences of shame and humiliation, as discussed by Turco (2001).

    When he recounts his criminal acts, the manner in which he recounts the details is coloured by the same bland, blunted tone that characterised all his other conversation. He speaks of the thrill and excitement that the murders and rapes made him feel, but there is no faint stirring of the affective space between us or within me to indicate the presence of a titillation or arousal of any sort. In fact, I am more alarmed at my lack of shock, horror or repudiation and my identification of sorts with John's inner emptiness or deadness. If I experience any feeling in relation to his retelling of his crimes, it is irritation with him for his inadequacy or incapacity to stimulate some sort of 'living' or libidinal response in me. This perplexes me and I spend some time reflecting on it, eventually putting it down to John possibly recreating an early relationship with a disappointed and potentially punitive mother and an inadequate son in the transference, but recognise that I may also be identifying with his projected frustration and rage at a dead and unavailable, unresponsive parental figure.

I find at various points in my interviews with John that I am able to access my empathy for him, but it is one of many points of difference between us. He is not capable of empathy. My ability to empathise with John stirs considerable feelings of shame in me. It feels as though, in empathising with him, I am complicit in his criminal acts and tainted with his badness, his 'evil'. I become quite paranoid and guarded in how I speak of my work to others, not wanting to reveal my empathy for John for fear that others will perceive this as condoning his behaviour. Speaking of serial murder evokes pronounced responses in others and I am aware of the considerable splitting that takes place both intrapsychically and externally in order to manage the stirrings evoked by such individuals of archaic pre-Oedipal libidinal and aggressive impulses. The individual who commits murders, predominantly those of a sexual nature, repeatedly signifies a return to pre-Oedipal primitive states of being and an undoing of defences, collective and individual, that have evolved to keep these in check for the benefit of society and societal evolution. The response of others to my accounts of my work with serial murderers – in the form of splitting and denial of any identification with the individuals concerned – reflects paranoid-schizoid themes where the annihilation of good parts by bad is feared and needs to be defended against. In my opinion, this is testament to the collective perception of a serial murderer as 'prime evil' due to his repetitive violation and disrespect for social taboos and law regarding sexual and aggressive elements. In fact, the serial murderer himself frequently internalises this split by presenting a superficial façade to the external world that is socially acceptable and frequently desirable, but which is strikingly juxtaposed to the 'monster' beneath.

John speaks of this contradiction between the son his parents knew and the monster that was revealed. He says that:

> you could say that I led two lives, what people saw was a very sweet little boy and what came out was the monster and I take it as part of the ugly person and it doesn't bother me because it's in the past now…and it wasn't just my parents who were surprised, there were many other people who were shocked, who knew me…

In Tanay's (1972) typology, John would fall into the category of egodystonic murderer, which would explain the necessitated splits in his presentation to the external world as well as internally to allow him to continue to rape and murder as vehicles for more pressing deep-seated unconscious repressed aggression.

I am left wondering what it means to 'know' John and struck by how fragmented and split his internal object world is. He has a striking lack of remorse for his actions and when at one point he does break down in tears, I get the feeling that it is out of self-pity rather than any sense of guilt towards an integrated victim-object. One cannot know John – one can meet certain parts of him but I imagine the threat of annihilation and disintegration is too pronounced for him ever to integrate the internal splits.

Throughout my interviews with John, I am struck by his significance as an almost outdated relic of the previous dispensation in South Africa. Prior to 1994 and the accompanying political changes in the country, John would have been the kind of man who would have managed to get by quite comfortably in spite of his considerable interpersonal, intellectual and emotional deficits, by virtue of his position as a white, Afrikaans male. I started to wonder about how his entrenched feelings of inadequacy may have been exacerbated by the potency he was losing socially and politically as South Africa began to transition to a democratic society. John comes from a very conservative Afrikaans family that openly express their dissatisfaction with the changes in the country and do not attempt to conceal their racism. His mother complains bitterly every time she visits him in prison of how noisy the black prisoners are and expresses her wish for a separate visiting area. She stated that:

> I don't get a chance to speak to him in private when we visit him and I don't handle that very well. You know how they are [Black South Africans] – they bring all their millions of family members and they talk loudly and their food stinks. It really upsets me.

John's father was retrenched as part of restructuring initiatives to ensure more representation for population groups previously disadvantaged under apartheid. John was actively involved in the South African Police Force (now the SAPS) divisions that were deployed to manage riots and unrest in townships in the period leading up to the changes in legislation that did away with apartheid. John's criminal acts of rape and murder may have functioned as a means to compensate not only for his own inadequacy, but also for feelings of inadequacy

206 PSYCHODYNAMIC PSYCHOTHERAPY IN SOUTH AFRICA

he identified with and internalised from his father and grandfather. In addition, at an unconscious level, he may have identified with collective fears of annihilation and extinction among a smaller group of the South African population – a social, ethnic, political and cultural 'father' figure – who had dominated for many years during apartheid but whose omnipotence was waning.

John's first victim was a black female. The fact that he did not continue to target black South Africans, as the most obvious symbolised threat, may have been influenced by his intrapsychic dynamics relating to his relationship with his mother. His acts of murder and rape thus functioned to combine imperatives to compensate for inadequate male figures in his life – projected onto a collective father and fatherland, under threat of annihilation and impotent with regard to withstanding challenges to his prior omnipotence – as well as to displace rage and aggression towards a maternal figure who could not tolerate these feelings in him and retaliated in a persecutory fashion, coupled with shaming and humiliation.

John's relationship with his maternal grandfather warrants closer examination. It would appear that there was a triadic relationship between John, his grandfather and his mother. John's father, castrated by his father-in-law rival, retreated from his relationship with John's mother. Given the pre-Oedipal quality of the resulting triangle, it appears that John did not view his grandfather as a sexual rival for his mother, but rather as a source of competition for care and nurturance. Further, it appears that John's mother's attention was policed by both John and his grandfather through the manifestation of somatic complaints, which succeeded in drawing her closer to one and away from the other. John both idealised his grandfather and resented him for his seeming omnipotence over his mother and father. He could directly express only his idealisation towards such an omnipotent authority and had to express his rage indirectly or passive-aggressively, for example by denting his grandfather's car when borrowing it. John's grandfather was a heavy drinker, who became physically abusive towards his partner. One might hypothesise that John's identification with this grandfather part-object was enacted in his criminal acts.

CASE STUDY 2: Jacob

Jacob is a small, wiry black South African male in his early forties with keen, eager eyes and an abundance of energy. On first meeting, he presents as a charming, cooperative individual and this manner of presentation continues throughout our time together. In all our interviews, Jacob does not let his guard down and is the commensurate gentleman. Nothing is too much for him, and it is not long before he informs me that he, too, wishes to study psychology and would like my advice and input.

He is confident, self-assured and talkative, mostly on topics that centre on his own non-criminal exploits, but he is also often interested in me and frequently asks personal questions about my life and interests. Jacob is a storyteller. He spins long, elaborate tales about his early childhood, adolescence and adulthood that sound like they have been lifted from the pages of a Boy's Own adventure story. Initially, I am riveted and savour his words as he begins to tell me about himself. However, as his tales become ever more improbable and vehicles for his grandiosity and omnipotence, I am left with the unsettling feeling of having been conned or 'duped'. I notice how absorbed he becomes in his identification with this grandiose part of himself, basking in the amniotic fluid of his own self-importance, and I am struck by the libidinal cathexis and discharge he experiences as he revels in his fantasies. This enjoyment seems heightened by any perception on his part that I am a captive audience, mirroring him as important and heroic. I notice how he checks periodically to see whether he has captured my admiration and fascination and realise that I am of use to him solely in my capacity as audience and witness to his importance and grandiosity. In the absence of obtaining gratification for his narcissistic needs for grandiosity and omnipotence, as is typically hypothesised to be present in serial murderers (Burgess et al., 1986), in the usual form of the murder and rape of female victims, it appears that Jacob is compensating for this by having those needs met through his storytelling. I imagine that this must be highly unfulfilling for him and compare poorly with the gratification he might have obtained in committing his crimes. As a result, his pressing urge to tell his stories and silence any input from me is intense and another manner of exerting control over me – potentially heightened by my status as a female interviewer – and the process, thereby confirming his omnipotence in his own mind.

I am confused but I am also fascinated at his egocentricity and severe deficit in relating to an(other) as objective and subjective whole, which prevents him from acknowledging or anticipating the impact of his words on me as a separate thinking, feeling entity. It may speak to a severe deficit in his capacity for attachment or bonding or forming relationships in the mode theorised by Hickey (2006b). Perhaps it is his severe narcissism, his omnipotent and grandiose self, that cannot conceive that his tall tales might be transparent in any way. I am

not left with anger at being 'conned' but rather boredom at the inherent emptiness of his words and I wonder if I am identifying with some of his projections
around inner feelings of emptiness and lack of arousal. Perhaps my boredom is
my own defence against feelings of anger towards Jacob, which I am consciously
fearful of expressing in any way lest I evoke an aggressive response in him, an
individual with a history of violent and aggressive behaviour and a pronouncedly
brittle narcissistic construction. In spite of this, there are points in my interviews
with both John and Jacob where I identify with their grandiose and omnipotent projections in relation to my own vulnerability as a female (both of their
predominant victim types) and I become intent on not showing any fear. My
split-off vulnerable parts often return in dreams, however, where, on one occasion, I dream that John is strangling me and I struggle to pry his hands from
my neck. In my work with both John and Jacob I am acutely aware of needing
to compensate for, and deny, my vulnerability in relation to an omnipotent and
potentially dangerous other, and in that sense this may have contributed to an
unconscious power struggle for dominance, especially in the case of Jacob.

On one occasion that I arrive to interview Jacob, he is seated at a table
wearing reading glasses, a new addition, and looking intently at a psychology
textbook. I am not sure where he has procured this text, but am aware that
this is a prisoner who has managed to charm and convince prison authorities
and warders to allow him to keep a personal computer in his cell (donated by
a well-meaning religious organisation). Jacob is chameleon-like – able to adapt
and mould himself to expediently fit his circumstances and environment to the
service of his own needs. It later emerged that he was quite intent on having his
autobiography written and tried to convince me to do this with him, in spite of
it being against prison regulations. His initial mimicry was an attempt to flatter
and engage me narcissistically through favourable mirroring of me, as other; this
also symbolised a projection of Jacob's own intrapsychic dynamic and recreated a
compliant identified self-idealised object dyad.

I was always struck by how Jacob seemed so much younger than his chronological age and realised that I must have had something to do with his presentation which, albeit superficial, was often that of a charming, innocent boy next
door, who is eager to carry your schoolbags and attends choir practice. However,
Jacob is not a charming innocent schoolboy – he raped and murdered at least
38 women. He taunted and manipulated police authorities and was able to
evade capture for a considerable period of time. Jacob is an intelligent man – a
dangerous asset when used in the service of procuring victims. Jacob avoided

speaking of his crimes for most of our time together – he preferred spinning a tale of an idealised childhood and adolescence where he excelled at running and boxing and was the object of numerous girls' affections but always did the right thing. The fact that he is incarcerated in a maximum security correctional facility appears lost to him, as is the perception on his part that I might question why such a 'good boy' would have landed himself in such deep trouble. My countertransference is indicative of the power of denial and fantasy for Jacob, as I experience considerable anxiety and fear around confronting him on such issues, and feel more comfortable avoiding and colluding with his idealised grandiosity. The prevalence of powerful splitting in individuals who commit serial murder is again featured, as with John, in my interaction with Jacob, where it feels like any attempt to integrate split good and bad self part-objects will be met with considerable aggression and rage as a defence against annihilation. The result is a strong projective identification on my part with being a 'fraud' and deceiving Jacob into thinking that I believe his stories, thereby reinforcing his narcissistic, grandiose self.

Through the smoke and mirrors of Jacob's tall tales, I am able to tease out some of his early history. Jacob grew up in a crowded household and was one of seven siblings. As one of the youngest, he was subjected to severe physical abuse by his eldest sister, who beat him with an electric cord and threw boiling water at him. Both his mother and father were absent and spent large portions of the day at their respective places of work. Jacob's father was an alcoholic and spent most of his nights at the local tavern. Jacob was raised in a South African township amid considerable poverty and frequently went without food due to the family's financial constraints. He often ran away to his maternal aunt's place of residence to escape his harsh treatment at home. Jacob's household was characterised by considerable inconsistency and instability, with family members periodically moving in and out of the home. Jacob eventually ran away from home in his adolescence and began working on the mines, where he remained until launching his criminal career in his mid-twenties.

Jacob's retelling of his early history is disjointed and fragmented, with little continuity, mirroring his internal world. His defensive use of splitting is overwhelming, in line with the many theoretical expositions of serial murderers discussed above, specifically in Kohut's (1973) and Kernberg's (1984) work with malignant narcissists and aggression. The parts of his life which he recalls with greatest clarity are his experiences of aggression and violence at the hands of his eldest sister and his resilient omnipotence in overcoming his circumstances and experiences of deprivation. He has had no experiences of empathic attunement from a primary caregiver, and the lack of consistency with regards to the composition of the home and potential attachment figures has left Jacob with significant deficits in his capacity to form bonds with others. Jacob spoke strongly of the feelings of shame and humiliation he experienced when receiving beatings from his sister and the rage he felt towards her. This rage was coupled with a feeling of impotence and powerlessness in his ability to retaliate, and he was left to compensate in fantasy with detailed plans for revenge against her when older, or when the opportunity presented itself. The influence of cultural factors in the development of Jacob's personality was slightly different to that of John in that the male and female figures in Jacob's family were endowed with considerable potency with regard to cultural signifiers indicating hierarchies in the family structure. Consequently, older siblings possessed more power and authority than younger siblings, as did older males such as grandparents over parents and, ultimately, males over females. As with John, the theme of early experiences of humiliation, rejection and aggression on the part of caregivers compounded the excessive desire for revenge and displacement of aggression onto female victims (Hickey, 1991; Kohut, 1973).

In spite of a structurally derived and legitimated potency, because of his absence and alcoholism Jacob's father was inadequate in providing financially for his family and presenting a role model for character development. He also did not intervene to 'save' or rescue Jacob from the harsh treatment inflicted by his eldest sister, thus appearing castrated by a female in the family. This may have resulted in considerable anxiety and confusion in Jacob around a perceived violation of Oedipal and larger cultural norms. He may have displaced some of his anger towards an impotent father onto the castrator, in this case his sister, and then generalised this to all women. Raping and murdering female victims may have been an enactment of compensatory needs around reclaiming the potency he was deprived of by both his father and sister, as well as releasing considerable rage and aggression relating to a harsh, sadistic other.

Jacob's interpersonal style of relating through charm and seduction to both disguise underlying feelings of rage, aggression, entitlement and resentment, as well as to meet his needs to express such underlying feelings and exert control and omnipotence over others, was evident in his modus operandi. This involved luring potential victims to secluded locations under the guise of offering employment opportunities. Once he had succeeded in luring his victims to these locations, his aggression and rage would be unleashed and victims would be raped repeatedly and then strangled or stabbed. One can hypothesise that his method of killing varied according to the extent to which he was able to delay gratification of his need to annihilate and destroy the other. With strangling, he was able to delay gratification for longer and also satisfy needs for omnipotence and control over the other; the stabbing may have been the outcome of less robust defensive capacity and ego strength on the particular day. Jacob would frequently take souvenirs, transitional objects to stimulate his use of fantasy to gratify needs for omnipotence, control, aggression and revenge in the absence of a more suitable object. In this sense, the 'relational paraphilia' alluded to by Hickey (2006b) appears to come to the fore in the use of transitional phenomena as substitutes for integrated attachment and bonding with whole objects and persons.

Whereas John was predominantly identified with an inadequate and impotent self-object introject, Jacob was identified predominantly with a grandiose self-object, which can be seen in the differences in their modus operandi. Where John needed to surprise his victims and surreptitiously trespass into their homes, Jacob could charm, convince and gain his victims' trust in a more direct manner. John felt inadequate in terms of his interpersonal skills and more consciously related to a devaluing dismissive other part-object, whereas Jacob had more self-confidence and related more to an idealising other part-object, with his inadequate self-object repressed deeply in his unconscious. For Jacob, there was an undoing and reversal of early object relations with his sister, which saw him take the position of devaluing and powerful other in relation to a vulnerable and powerless victim. This extended to his relationship and communication with police during the time of his criminal acts, when he would frequently phone police officials and taunt them for their lack of efficiency and effectiveness in apprehending him. The police as a symbol of masculine, paternal social authority may have signified a manner in which Jacob could attack his own father for his inadequacy and impotence in protecting a victim (the young Jacob) from a harsh, punitive and violent aggressor.

Jacob's choice of victims is interesting – all were black females, mostly from poor socio-economic circumstances and unemployed. His consistency in victim choice may be a manifestation of his fantasy and his enactment of such fantasies, conforming to Hazelwood and Warren's (1995) description of the mechanism of fantasy in serial murder having distinct demographic, situational, relational and paraphilic elements. While one can see the parallels between his primary aggressor and sadistic tormentor in early childhood – his elder sister, a black female, also unemployed and from a poor socio-economic background – Jacob's victim choice reflects his unconscious repressed inadequacy in selecting victims who would have been relatively easy to 'seduce' and charm due to their desperation for employment and financial remuneration. One could also argue that his selection was expedient in making use of the socio-cultural and socio-economic context to facilitate his victim choice, and that this bears testament to his lack of empathy and his objectification of others as a means to an end. However, his choice of victims who were physically less imposing than himself, disempowered economically and frequently also culturally and socially in terms of their gender, indicates that as much as he was mostly identified with the grandiose self-object, his inadequate self-object still played a role in his object choice when it came to victim selection, and may have been activated strongly when these women spurned his advances once alone with him or attempted to run away, thus challenging his omnipotence and control. They may also have mirrored him with shock, horror and fear once he abandoned his ruse and became more aggressive, which possibly further stimulated his identification with an omnipotent, sadistic aggressor.

Jacob's victim choice also provides an opportunity to highlight intergenerational and cultural transmission of dynamic factors. As a black South African male, Jacob's cultural and political history is laden with experiences of castration and trauma at the hands of apartheid legislation. While political changes were manifesting at the time of his crimes to enable a restoration of political potency to black South Africans, challenges to the economic superiority of black males as primary breadwinners were being mounted by black women, who were increasingly seeking out employment and economic independence. Jacob's crimes may thus have signified an assault on both pre-existing 'fathers' in the form of apartheid agencies such as the South African Police Force (still largely associated with the apartheid government and its agendas during the time of Jacob's crimes) – by devaluing and attacking their omnipotence and authority through evading arrest and thereby highlighting police inadequacy – and on black women, who were emerging as a threat to the authority and historical superiority of black South African males.

Regarding the sexual nature of Jacob's crimes, one can hypothesise that his sexual development followed a similar trajectory to John's in that libidinal and aggressive components were linked sadistically as their psychosexual development was negotiated in the context of harsh and punitive treatment by a primary caregiver. While not alluded to in his conversations with me, erotic elements may have coloured Jacob's relationship with his elder sister.

CONCLUSION

On reflecting on the discussion in this chapter, the cases of John and Jacob both give insight into the psychodynamics of serial murder and effectively reflect theoretical arguments discussed in the earlier parts of the chapter. Both cases illustrate the prevalent role played by sadism, narcissism, fantasies of power, and feelings of shame and humiliation in response to narcissistic insults, as well as the ascendancy of an underlying sense of inferiority and the need for control over others with an explosive rage which overcomes weakened ego controls. However, both cases also highlight the important role played by contextual and cultural elements, for example in the way serial murder manifests with regard to victim selection and modus operandi. These factors have frequently been neglected by traditional psychoanalytic and psychodynamic theory in explaining the way in which behaviour of all types, particularly criminal behaviour and, in this case, serial murder manifests.

On examination and review of South African and international serial murder cases, it is evident that the composition and characteristics of the South African serial murder population differ greatly from American and European populations. Differences include the racial or ethnic composition of offender and victim, the prevalent victim type selected, the modus operandi, the level of organisation involved in planning and committing the rapes and/or murders, and the nature of offences. Such differences can be seen as strong evidence for the important role played by contextual factors, despite intrapsychic phenomena frequently remaining quite similar across populations. For example, differences in infrastructure between South Africa, as a developing country, and the United States, as a developed country, have resulted in differences in the modes of transport and methods of travel between murders and killing sites; socio-economic differences have influenced the modus operandi of serial murderers, as illustrated by the case example of Jacob, who used economic factors to source his victim pool.

The cases also illustrate the way in which political factors in the South African cultural landscape, specifically the changes that occurred alongside the 'emergence' of the serial murder phenomenon in South Africa, played a part in the intrapsychic dynamics of the individuals concerned, with both John and Jacob manifesting intergenerational 'ghosts' in their negotiation of shifts and upheavals in the societal milieu. While the South African context has been the focus of this discussion, it may be the case that similar processes take place in other countries and in different cultural contexts.

Serial murder remains a phenomenon that captures public attention and fascination. The discussion in this chapter has attempted to propose some ideas around what this fascination may be comprised of and how the mirroring of our own pre-Oedipal, unmediated and unmetabolised material is simultaneously frightening and fascinating in relation to the other, who is able to undo and surpass intrapsychic restrictions and adaptations to living empathically with others as a member of a cooperative collective. This exploration warrants further elaboration to tease out and understand the dynamics of serial murder.

Finally, serial murder continues to frustrate psychodynamic therapists and theorists alike in that it remains hard to prevent. As illustrated in the cases and in my experience, serial murderers' considerable lack of empathy or remorse, lack of capacity for reciprocal relationship or mentalisation, brittle and sensitive narcissistic organisation, and primitive defences such as splitting, denial and projection, make them almost impossible to treat. As succinctly put by John:

> the crimes…it was like a drug that you get addicted to…and it got bigger and bigger…and your mind gets corrupted and you do bigger crime – I could have gone on to rob banks [he meant that instead of becoming a serial murderer, he could have been a bank robber] but I didn't go that route. At the end, I wanted to get caught…because I knew…I knew that I couldn't stop myself…and it would just go on and on…without an end.

NOTES

1   See http://www.iss.co.za/uploads/National2010.pdf.
2   See http://www.saps.gov.za/statistics/reports/crimestats/2010/crime_situation_sa.pdf.
3   The following are examples of serial murder references in the press: *Rapport* (31 January 1999) ran an article titled 'Spanwerk los reeksmoord op' (Team work solves serial murder); the *Weekly Mail & Guardian* (9 September 1994) featured an article titled 'Station Strangler – Who's fooling whom?'; *City Press* (7 December 1997) featured an article titled ' "Electrician" may be next serial killer'; *Beeld* (14 August 1995) featured an article titled 'Reeksmoordenaars nie "dieselfde mens" ' (Serial murderers not the same person); and *The Star* (21 August 1997) featured an article titled '18 murders linked in hunt for serial killer'. Television programmes featuring serial murder have occurred on local series such as Carte Blanche and Third Degree, as well as in the form of documentaries such as Criminal Minds (2003), Psycho Factory (2004) and Solving It (2006–2011).

4   A mother who processes and makes sense of the infant's emotional experiences and makes him/her feel held, recognised and validated by modelling appropriate coping mechanisms for dealing with strong emotions.

REFERENCES

Abrahamsen, D (1973) *The Murdering Mind*. New York: Harper & Row.

Arendt, H (1994) *Eichman in Jerusalem: A Report on the Banality of Evil*. London: Penguin.

Bluestone, H & Travin, S (1984) Murder: The ultimate conflict. *American Journal of Psychoanalysis*, 44: 147–167.

Burgess, AW, Hartman, CR, Ressler, RK, Douglas, JE & McCormack, A (1986) Sexual homicide: A motivational model. *Journal of Interpersonal Violence*, 13(3): 251–272.

Claus, C & Lidberg, L (1999) Serial murder as 'Schahriar syndrome'. *The Journal of Forensic Psychiatry*, 10(2): 427–435.

Del Fabbro, GA (2006) A family systems analysis of serial murder. PhD dissertation, University of Pretoria, South Africa. Accessed from http://upetd.up.ac.za/thesis/available/etd-11222006-141729/unrestricted/00front.pdf on 4 November 2012.

De Wet, JA (2005) A psychological perspective on the personality development of a serial murderer. Master's thesis, University of Pretoria, South Africa. Accessed from http://upetd.up.ac.za/thesis/available/etd-10052005-101129/unrestricted/00dissertation.pdf on 4 November 2012.

Du Plessis, JJ (1998) Towards a psychological understanding of serial murder. Unpublished Master's thesis, University of Pretoria, South Africa.

Fenichel, O (1945) *The Psychoanalytic Theory of Neurosis*. New York: WW Norton.

Fitzpatrick, JJ (1976) Psychoanalysis and crime: A critical survey of salient trends in the literature. *The Annals of the American Academy of Political and Social Science*, 634(1): 67–74.

Freud, S (1917) *Mourning and Melancholia: Collected Papers, Volume 4*. London: Basic Books, by arrangement with Hogarth, 1959, pp. 152–170.

Fromm, E (1973) *The Anatomy of Human Destructiveness*. New York: Holt, Rinehart & Winston.

Gacono, CB (1992) Sexual, homicide and the Rorschach: A Rorschach case study of sexual homicide. *British Journal of Projective Psychology*, 37(1): 1–21.

Gorby, B (2000) Serial murder: A cross-national descriptive study. Unpublished Master's thesis, California State University, Fresno.

Guttmacher, MS (1960) *The Mind of the Murderer*. New York: Farrar, Straus, and Cudahy.

Hazelwood, RR & Warren, J (1995) The relevance of fantasy in serial sexual crime investigation. In RR Hazelwood & AW Burgess (eds) *Practical Aspects of Rape Investigation (second edition)*, pp. 127–138. New York, NY: CRC Press.

Hickey, EW (1991) *Serial Murderers and Their Victims*. Pacific Grove, CA: Brooks/Cole Publishing.

Hickey, EW (2006a) *Serial Murderers and Their Victims (fourth edition)*. Sydney: Thomas Wadworth.

Hickey, EW (2006b) *Sex Crimes and Paraphilia*. New Jersey: Prentice-Hall.

Hodgskiss, B (2001) A multivariate model of the offence behaviours of South African serial murderers. Master's thesis, Rhodes University, Grahamstown, South Africa.

Hodgskiss, B (2002) Serial killing in South Africa. Paper presented at the First International Conference on Criminal Analysis and Profiling, 3–5 June, Institute of Criminology, Paris, France.

Hodgskiss, B (2004) Lessons from serial murder in South Africa. *Journal of Investigative Psychology and Offender Profiling*, 1(1): 67–94.

Hook, D (2003) Reading Geldenhuys: Constructing and deconstructing the Norwood killer. *South African Journal of Psychology*, 33(1): 1–10.

Kernberg, OF (1984) *Aggression in Personality Disorders and Perversions*. New Haven, CT: Yale University Press.

Kernberg, OF (1992) *Severe Personality Disorders*. New Haven, CT: Yale University Press.

Kohut, H (1973) Thoughts on narcissism and narcissistic rage. *The Psychoanalytic Study of the Child*, 27: 360–400. New York: Quadrangle Books.

Labuschagne, GN (2001) Serial murder revisited: A psychological exploration of two South African cases. PhD thesis, University of Pretoria, South Africa. Accessed from http://upetd.up.ac.za/thesis/available/etd-03032006-131734/ on 4 November 2012.

Lane, B & Gregg, W (1992) *The New Encyclopaedia of Serial Killers*. Surrey: Headline.

Lanzkron, J (1963) Murder and insanity: A survey. *American Journal of Psychiatry*, 119: 754–758.

Liebert, J (1985) Contributions to psychiatric consultation in the investigation of serial murder. *International Journal of Offender Therapy and Comparative Criminology*, 29: 187–200.

Lowenstein, LF (1992) The psychology of the obsessed compulsive killer. *Criminologist*, 38: 26–38.

Marohn, RC (1987) John Wesley Hardin – adolescent killer: The emergence of a narcissistic behaviour disorder. *Adolescent Psychiatry*, 14: 271–296.

McCarthy, JB (1978) Narcissism and the self in the homicidal adolescent. *American Journal of Psychoanalysis*, 38: 19–29.

Meloy, JR (2000) The nature and dynamics of sexual homicide: An integrative review. *Aggression and Violent Behaviour*, 5(1): 1–22.

Menninger, K (1963) *The Vital Balance*. New York: Viking.

Myers, W, Burgess, A & Nelson, J (1998) Criminal and behavioural aspects of juvenile sexual homicide. *Journal of Forensic Sciences*, 43: 340–347.

Palermo, GB & Knudten, RD (1994) The insanity plea in the case of a serial killer. *International Journal of Offender Therapy and Comparative Criminology*, 38: 3–6.

Pistorius, M (1996) A psychoanalytic approach to serial murderers. Unpublished PhD dissertation, University of Pretoria, South Africa.

Podolsky, E (1956) The paranoid murderer. *Journal of Forensic Medicine*, 3: 149–151.

Pollock, GH (1978) Process and affect. *International Journal of Psycho-Analysis*, 59: 255–276.

Prentky, R, Burgess, A, Rokous, F, Lee, A, Hartman, C, Ressler, R & Douglas, J (1989) The presumptive role of fantasy in serial sexual homicide. *American Journal of Psychiatry*, 146: 887–891.

Reichard, S & Tillman, C (1950) Murder and suicide as defenders against schizophrenic psychosis. *Journal of Clinical Psychopathology*, 11: 149–163.

Satten, J, Menninger, K, Rosen, I & Mayhan, M (1960) Murder without apparent motive: A study in personality disorganization. *American Journal of Psychiatry*, 117: 48–53.

Schlesinger, LB (2001) The potential sex murderer: Ominous signs, risk assessment. *Journal of Threat Assessment*, 1: 47–72.

Smith, DL (1996) Psychodynamic therapy: The Freudian approach. In W Dryden (ed.) *Handbook of Individual Therapy*, pp. 19–25. London: Sage.

Stein, A (2000) Dissociation and crime: Abuse, mental illness and violence in the lives of incarcerated men. Unpublished PhD dissertation, City University of New York.

Tanay, E (1972) Psychiatric aspects of homicide prevention. *American Journal of Psychiatry*, 128: 815–818.

Turco, R (2001) Child serial murder – Psychodynamics: Closely watched shadows. *Journal of the American Academy of Psychoanalysis*, 29: 331–338.

UNODC (United Nations Office on Drugs and Crime) (2009) *Survey of International Homicide Rates 2009*. Accessed from http://www.unodc.org/documents/data-and-analysis/IHS-rates-05012009.pdf on 25 April 2010.

CHAPTER 9

SOME PSYCHOANALYTIC REFLECTIONS ON A PROJECT WORKING WITH HIV ORPHANS AND THEIR CAREGIVERS

Vanessa Hemp

South Africa is in the grip of an HIV crisis that is leaving many children orphaned at a very young age. A project was initiated in response to a growing awareness of the impact that these losses were having on a group of children attending a child psychiatry community clinic. The aim was to provide therapeutic groups for both the children and their caregivers. In this chapter, I explore these groups and consider a relational psychoanalytic understanding of how some of the central processes unfolded. It is hoped that the lessons learned and failures encountered in these groups could be useful to similar ventures. It is written from my clinical experience as a psychologist in both a state hospital and a community mental health clinic.

THE CONTEXT AND SETTING

During the time of these groups (2002–2007),[1] South Africa was in a difficult stage of its health policy relating to HIV. It was the Mbeki era (1999–2008), marked by AIDS denialism and ambivalent messages regarding the link between HIV and AIDS. Antiretrovirals were not readily available or part of the government healthcare programme, as they are today. For many people concerned about their HIV status, there did not seem to be a point to testing as the disease was considered untreatable. The common choice seemed to be to sit with not knowing rather than face the implications of being HIV+. In this context, being HIV+ was not simply about having contracted a terminal illness but was linked to shame, fear of exposure and vulnerability. The burden of these emotional states appears to have resulted in the emergence of manic defences, not just at an individual level but also at a broader societal level (Altman, 2005). In this chapter, I explore ways in which defences against unmanageable feelings emerged in both the project staff and the group members.

The setting was a children's community psychiatry clinic that operates as a satellite of a state psychiatric hospital. The community clinic was based in a neighbouring township where many families live in informal housing or shacks made of cardboard or corrugated iron. There are few resources available to this population. Levels of unemployment, poor education levels, deprivation, aggression and hopelessness are high among this strained community.

The staff were straddling two separate clinics, had high case loads and few resources available to them in order to conduct their work. Staff members' levels of frustration and burnout were high. A non-profit organisation was started to focus on the AIDS orphans. It was formed by clinicians trying to combat feelings of despondency and frustration due to the provincial health department's lack of support for the community clinic.

THE PROJECT

Project structure

One of the aims of the project was to facilitate the attachment and parenting skills of the caregivers. Another was to help the children process and deal with their grief and multiple adjustments. A variety of support and therapeutic groups were initiated. In structuring this programme, it was felt that interventions needed to incorporate not just the children but their support systems too. The aim was to provide a 'thinking space' for the caregivers and children to process and deal with their feelings.

Many of the caregivers were grandmothers (*gogos*) or aunts of the children and were going through their own grieving as a result of the deaths in their families. By directing interventions at both caregivers and children, it was hoped that the caregivers could be encouraged to provide a 'holding environment' for the children, a new home where attachments could be facilitated and difficult feelings processed, felt and thought through. Bion (1962) refers to adults or the 'other' providing a containing space where the emotional links can be maintained and alpha functioning can take place. In this way children are helped to think about and manage overwhelming emotions. The aim was to help the children psychologically process their grief and deal with their psychic pain rather than dissociating/disconnecting from it. We wanted to facilitate the *gogos'* capacity to contain the children's anxiety and find a way to help them to manage, digest and process both their own and the children's painful and unmanageable feelings in a functional way, as described by Fonagy et al. (2002).

In looking at loss, John Bowlby (1969) identified the three phases that occur when an infant or small child experiences the separation and loss of their primary caregiver as protest, despair and detachment: 'the phase of Protest raises the problem of separation anxiety; Despair that of grief and mourning; Detachment that of defense' (1969: 125). When considering the children attending the clinic, there was a concern that they had not had a space to experience protest or despair but that they had dissociated and disconnected from their emotional states. The clinicians involved were concerned about how to help the children emotionally integrate and continue on their developmental path as optimally as possible.

Therapeutic group structure

The children's groups included structured bereavement groups (according to age), support groups (following completion of the bereavement group) and a separate group for HIV+ children. The caretakers (*gogo* support groups) were in unstructured groups which focused on their own bereavement issues, helping the children with their grief, parenting input and general coping skills, for example anger management.

Families were allocated community care workers (CCWs). The CCWs case-managed the families, including conducting home and school visits to assess the quality of care that the children were receiving. The CCWs were also tasked with monitoring the children's progress and adjustment and conducting a needs analysis.

The AIDS orphans project also provided food relief (monthly food parcels) and income-generation opportunities (vegetable garden, sewing, choir and beading project).

EXPLORING THE BROADER DYNAMICS OF THE PROJECT AND THE BEREAVEMENT GROUPS

This section explores the impact of race and the use of translators and the psycho-analytic frame. One of the greatest difficulties with the bereavement groups was in creating a safe environment to facilitate therapeutic work. The group was framed as being a group for children who had all had someone important to them die. It was to be a space for them to talk and feel their feelings. Initially the children were very passive. When asked how they were feeling, they would all say that they were 'fine'. The idea of talking or thinking about feelings seemed to be a highly difficult concept for them.

Using translators

Discussing difficulties was further compounded by the fact that many of the children did not speak English and therefore communication was filtered through the CCW acting as translator. Working through a translator created a further barrier to connection and understanding between me (the therapist) and the children. Misunderstanding and misinterpretation were some of the difficulties experienced as part of the process. Lee (1997) identified two broad areas of difficulty in using translators in therapy: technical problems (such as distortion of meaning or inaccurate translation of words and concepts) and role conflicts (such as the patient's over-identification with the translator). Psychoanalytically, the communication between therapist and patient is filtered through another person's unconscious and conscious communication. 'Understanding and being understood must be the prerequisites of any therapeutic interaction…interpretation is not simply translation; it is the process to ensure that the full linguistic and cultural meaning of what is said is truly conveyed' (Farooq, 2009: 104).

The impact of race on group dynamics

It is important to consider the role that racial differences and unconscious racial prejudices may have played in attempting to create a therapeutic space in the children's group (Altman, 2000). The group consisted of 10 black children, a black female CCW (who translated and co-facilitated) and me, a white female.

The 'new' South Africa, as it has been termed, finds it hard to discuss issues of race or racism in an open and transparent manner. The guilt of apartheid has left many white South Africans feeling the need to make reparations for the ills of the past but denying that they might still bear some racist thoughts or feelings towards the 'other' in society. Bearing Altman's words in mind, 'we should expect to find racism in our countertransference and in our thoughts and feelings generally, and that reflection on our countertransference is an essential element if we wish to deal with race in our therapeutic work' (2000: 591). During my time at the clinic I was constantly aware of my 'otherness'. My skin colour spoke before I could open my mouth, evoking assumptions and expectations about who I was and what I could or couldn't offer. At times I made an effort to unpack these thoughts and assumptions, but it felt like an awkward and ungainly conversation. My concern was that by naming race it might create damage and trauma in the room, the dilemma that Swartz (in press) discusses. Whose preoccupation and concern was it, mine or the patients'? This failure to address the issue of race shut down certain conversations that might have been very useful as part of the therapeutic process (Swartz, in press). Most of the time, I dealt with this difference by trying to deny it – engaging and immersing myself in the culture of the community, eating 'slaaiwatwat' (a traditional township fast food) from the local spaza shop with the clinic staff. It was an attempt to diminish and disavow my alien otherness, rather than opening up a space to think about and play with possibilities and identities.

'Shh…don't tell anyone there is an *umlungu* in the room.' Many of the children in the group did not have close contact with white people, making me very strange and other to them. Initially, the children were curious about the *umlungu* (a term used for a white person, with slightly derogatory connotations). I tried to use humour by jokingly referring to myself as the *umlungu* in an attempt to reduce their anxiety about my strangeness to them: 'I am sure you are wondering what this strange *umlungu* will ask us to do today?' In my attempts to equalise some of the power dynamics, I may have taken on a self-denigrating attitude. Straker (2004), discussing Eng and Han (2000), refers to this process as racial melancholia. The children wanted to look at my car and assess how I differed from their broad perception of white people. I attempted to open up conversation in the group by saying, 'I think it must feel quite strange for you to be in a room with a white person. You might have questions you want to ask me but feel too shy to ask.' The children found this quite amusing and giggled openly. I vacillated between open discussion and avoidance. In my need to connect with the children and make them feel safe, there were times when I avoided talking or thinking about my 'otherness'. Speaking about these issues was further compounded by the language barrier and the complications inherent in using the CCW as translator throughout the process. My attempts to address racial issues all had to be filtered through the translator, evoking a bizarre image of a black woman talking about race issues from a white perspective in the first person. Race and views of the 'other' remained alive in the room in various ways. At times this could be raised but I missed many opportunities to deal with both my and the children's racist conceptions in my striving to be non-racist. Difficulty in talking about racism can be a denial of our innate racism and inability to bring it to consciousness (Altman, 2000).

One of the psychic wounds of apartheid was a paternalistic attitude towards black people, where whites took on the mantle of parents who would take control and fix it all. This attitude emerged in the group through the children's treatment of me as an 'idealised object' who could omnipotently fix all problems. I was very aware of my lack of omnipotence in 'fixing these children's pain'. This difficulty was amplified by the split between the children and the adults in the group. Culturally, black children in this community are expected not to make eye contact with or talk back to adults. My stance in the group of wanting them to engage and share difficult thoughts and feelings left them feeling quite lost and torn between different sets of expectations – those of their families and mine as their therapist.

I felt that to deny race and the impact that it had on me and the group members would be to deny the reality of the South African past and place certain topics into the category of subjects that are unspoken. As Altman noted, '[I]f we said that racism is "out there", in racist society, and not "in here", in our own psyches, we would be splitting off and denying an important "bad object" experience between us' (2000: 596). In short, by naming and recognising these racist elements within, we are able to work with them and think about their impact on the group dynamics. As the relationships within the group were developed over time, my personal sense of otherness subsided.

Meeting material and emotional needs

One of the frequent conversations held at the clinic was about the impact that providing material support had on the psychological work done in the project. Providing some material assistance to a seriously deprived population seemed to leave the community with the feeling that their needs had been heard (Shoshani et al., 2010). It did, however, create tensions in the project. I felt that the participants were being bribed into attending the groups. It emerged that some of the *gogos* thought that receiving their monthly food parcels was contingent on their and the children's attendance at therapeutic groups. They had been forcing the children to come to the clinic for fear that they would lose their food parcels should they not attend the groups. At times this may have impacted on the children's sense that they could choose if they wanted to come or not. This became a matter of some debate within the clinic, where some staff members agreed that there should be a link between the food parcels and group attendance. Although it was decided that it was not going to be the policy of the project, this link may still have been inadvertently expressed by some staff members to the *gogos*. Clarity that the two were unrelated did not affect attendance of the children or adults in the programme.

The children were given peanut butter sandwiches before the start of each group, as many had not eaten any lunch. We felt that they would not be able to engage and think if they were hungry. Meeting certain material needs in this manner brought to the fore some problematic interactions between the children and adults involved in the programme. Many material difficulties and needs were brought to the group in the form of requests for soccer boots, stationery and money for school trips.

An awkward dynamic developed in the group I ran. It started with handmade cards as expressions of affection from one of the girls. This was then adopted by another young girl who was quite manipulative. She would create a card expressing her love for me and then add a request for something material. The children were encouraged to directly express their needs to the CCWs. However, they seemed to feel that if they came directly to me they were more likely to have the request heard. This process led to splits in the group, where some children were more able to ask for material goods and would receive them, leaving others feeling envious and excluded. The focus then became on meeting material needs as something concrete and tangible that could lead to a feeling of some achievement, thus allowing me to maintain my sense of competence and agency in the world (Shoshani et al., 2010).

In an attempt to describe the impact that this highly deprived environment had on the staff working there, one staff member said, 'The deprivation and neediness is like a huge black hole that is infinite and can never be filled.' In the face of this deprivation, it is easy for therapists to become overwhelmed and disinvested, feeling that nothing they do will make any difference. Many conversations were held in the clinic to try to process the staff members' overwhelming feelings and sense of helplessness. While omnipotence needs to be monitored, it is also vital that staff and the community find a way to negotiate a sense of impotence without falling into despair and disengagement. This was a constant negotiation that I personally experienced.

Dealing with the psychoanalytic frame

Psychoanalytic work with groups and individuals prizes the notion of the frame. Community work pushes the therapist to examine ways of maintaining a therapeutic frame in order to facilitate therapy without alienating the clinic population. Community clinics in South Africa generally do not function with appointments and set times. Patients are told what day they need to attend the clinic and when they arrive they sit in a queue until their turn. In the bereavement groups, a set time and day of the week was assigned. However, lateness, which would classically be considered resistance to therapy, could not immediately be interpreted as such in this setting. As a whole, the children were usually compliant and arrived as close to the designated time as logistics would allow. All of the children came to the clinic unaccompanied by adults. Missing their transport, or being kept after school for additional school work, at times impacted on their attendance. Lateness due to factors beyond their control could not be interpreted as unconscious communication to the therapist or the group, but was rather a function of their life circumstances. However, it still disrupted the group and I tried to process these difficulties in the group. There was also a small group of children who missed groups or came to them extremely late as a way of indirectly expressing some difficulty with the group. The CCW and I spent time after the groups thinking about these children and trying to tease out if we were dealing with resistance or logistics beyond the children's control. Adhering to the frame in this manner in order to monitor unconscious communication can be useful in a community setting where children struggle to express frustrations or disappointment. It is important, though, that adherence to the frame and sticking too rigidly to the times of appointments are not used defensively to avoid engaging in community work. This was the case with a number of trainee psychologists attending the clinic, who felt so overwhelmed by the trauma, loss and deprivation of the community that they started to avoid running groups or seeing individual patients, quoting their adherence to the psychoanalytic frame as the reason. The trainees blamed the unreliable, irresponsible patients for not arriving on time for their therapy. This often had unacknowledged racist undertones ('these people' don't have a sense of time), resulting in an empathic disconnection from the patient and therefore a disavowal of overwhelming feelings (Altman, 2000). My frustrations as their supervisor mounted in the face of their avoidance and resistance to doing the work, laced with racist overtones that were difficult to confront. Eagle (2005) addresses the emotional strain and secondary traumatisation that occurs when working therapeutically with trauma and loss, which can lead to burnout and avoidance.

A great deal of the work revolved around trying to create a consistent, containing space. Just keeping the children all in the group room was sometimes a challenge. Boundaries were hard to maintain. This was made harder by the shortage of space at the clinic. I would sometimes arrive for the group to find that the room was being used for another purpose. This had a very disruptive effect on the group as we scrambled around trying to find a private space to meet. These confusions regarding the room at times appeared to be the result of veiled hostility due to difficulties between staff members. These toxic staff dynamics played a definite role in the disruptions and undertones of sabotage. One group had to meet outside under a tree. Children ended up climbing the tree and the group was totally disrupted.

In my view, community work in townships requires some flexibility and creativity around the frame. A containing, safe place was essential for the children, but at times when the room had to be moved, the children could draw on the consistency of the therapist and the CCW to manage feelings of displacement. Rituals were put in place to mark the beginning and end of the group, so framing the therapeutic work. As mentioned, the disruptions to the group were often more diagnostic of destructive staff dynamics than of resistance in the children. Unsuccessful attempts were made to address these staff dynamics.

Exploring the dynamics more specifically

The project was initiated by the head nurse and the child psychiatrist who headed the clinic prior to my employment. Shortly after I started at the clinic, the clinic head resigned unexpectedly. Her loss was devastating to the project at a variety of levels: emotionally, she was one of the 'parents'; professionally, she was a highly skilled, experienced child psychiatrist; administratively, she was involved in all the organisation and funding. Her departure left many staff members, particularly the CCWs, feeling uncontained and anxious about their positions. I do not think that there was adequate mourning and processing of her loss and the feelings it evoked. This was ironic as our project's focus was on dealing with loss, but self-reflectively we struggled to visit those places in ourselves.

On reflection, the genesis of the project bore some of the seeds of its defensive difficulties. The project was born out of the community clinic staff's frustration and feelings of helplessness around the immensity of the HIV crisis. In contrast to the health department's denial and avoidance of the pandemic, action became vital for the staff. It is my sense that in order to fight against their feelings of helplessness in the face of this human tragedy, the staff involved themselves in manic activity that helped to maintain a degree of omnipotence. There was no space for vulnerability or impotence in the clinic. This had the effect of shutting down valuable conversations that could have provided support and containment for the overwhelmed staff (Shoshani et al., 2010).

The community care workers

The CCWs were mostly drawn from the community and came from similarly deprived and traumatised backgrounds as our patient population. Part of the task of the project was to train, supervise and contain the CCWs to enable them not only to translate for the groups but also to act as co-facilitators. With the limited resources in our community clinics, it is vital that professionals help to train other staff to work with bereaved children and their families. When engaging in this work, however, it is important to be aware of the internal processes and dynamics of the staff. In the case of the project, secondary traumatisation and burnout depleted the staff's internal resources, reducing the barriers to acting out.

The therapist

I started my work at the community clinic very shortly after qualifying. I felt totally overwhelmed and daunted when the task of running the bereavement group for the children was given to me. I would have to work through translation with a group of children living in very deprived surroundings who had all lost their mothers. I did not know where to start. Thinking about their pain and circumstances left me feeling helpless and barely skilled. How could I, a white middle-class psychologist, begin to imagine what their lives and struggles felt like? My personal struggles felt infinitesimal in the face of their circumstances.

The question of how to be a good-enough therapist to contain and help process the children's unmanageable feelings felt impossible. My struggle became harder when the clinic head resigned, resulting in the staff turning to me for guidance and containment at a time when I felt unsure and overburdened.

Nandi, a community care worker

The relationship between me and Nandi, the CCW who translated and assisted in the group, played a significant role in the group dynamics. We shared an uneasy and tenuous working relationship. She reported to me and I was responsible for doing her work evaluations and supervising her involvement in the children's bereavement group. It probably did not feel safe for her to be personally vulnerable when I was evaluating her performance. She was an anxious woman who had lost her own sister to HIV and was fostering her niece. She was both a CCW and a recipient of food parcels and support for her niece. This dual relationship placed her in a vulnerable situation, the extent of which I only became aware of quite far into the process. She tended to be quite harsh and strict with the children and required a great deal of mediation from me in an attempt to soften her attitude towards them. In private supervision and discussion with me, I encouraged her to allow the children to have their feelings and not to expect them to just behave and 'be good'. Within the group her harsh attitude towards the children elicited equally harsh judgemental feelings in me towards her. I found myself struggling to contain my frustration with her. It felt as if I was an overburdened single parent to the children in the group. In my vulnerability as an inexperienced, newly qualified therapist, I did not feel safe to expose my struggles to Nandi.

My capacity to remain empathically connected to Nandi fluctuated, largely dependent on my own internal resources and feelings of depletion. There was no space within the programme to be vulnerable and to struggle – a split occurred where we had to disavow our own struggles in order to address the huge well of pain in the community. The staff and I were in desperate need of containment and support but felt too depleted to think about how to get that need met. The trauma experienced by the staff was profound and there was not enough emotional space for debriefing and containment. I felt personally depleted and unable to adequately contain the rest of the staff.

In retrospect, I realise that Nandi was being asked to perform a function for the group that she was not emotionally able to manage at the time. I was expecting her to hold and contain the children's difficult feelings when she was struggling to perform this psychic function for herself and her family. I was also struggling to emotionally process the loss and trauma that we were encountering. It emerged later that she was emotionally overwhelmed by the cases that she had to manage at the clinic. The cases were also eliciting her own personal concerns about her HIV status and fear that her own child might be orphaned. Rather than face the shame of exposure regarding her possible HIV status and her emotional vulnerability, she disavowed and disconnected from those parts of herself and retreated into an omnipotent space where she was invested in her job and in being helpful and knowing what to do. In addition, Nandi's dual relationship as CCW and recipient of food parcels had put her in an awkward situation with the other CCWs. She was perceived as being singled out and favoured, evoking the envy of some of her colleagues. As a consequence, she was verbally attacked and ostracised by one of the staff members, adding to her emotional burden. Her emotionally brittle presence made it difficult to create a safe space for the children. How could they be expected to feel safe to express their feelings when one of the group facilitators sent direct messages of sanction against doing so? Nandi encouraged the children to avoid and deny their feelings, telling them to 'be positive and just smile'. Feeling good with a thumbs up sign ('sharp, sharp') was a state that she encouraged and praised. Nandi appeared to be using a manic defence to protect herself from her feelings of impotence, shame and vulnerability (Shoshani et al., 2010).

The extent of this disconnection was revealed when one of the children in the group died over the December holidays. M was 12 years old and had been sick on and off during the year. No one had suspected her of being HIV+. When I entered the clinic for the first time in the new year, I asked if anyone had heard how she was doing. Nandi glanced up from filing and said, 'Oh, her aunt came to tell us that she died before Christmas.' This comment was given in an offhand manner and she continued filing. The news hit me in the solar plexus like a sharp blow. Then my sadness turned to anger with Nandi for her apparent lack of distress. Nandi seemed totally disconnected and unaffected by the loss that had struck me very personally. This child had had a warm and endearing manner; in addition, she had been the most emotionally engaging child in the group. My feeling was that her input and engagement in the group had helped to facilitate the other children's process by showing that it was safe to express a range of feelings. I took this loss to heart in a number of ways, questioning why I had not known or guessed that she might be HIV+, and imagining how I could have helped her by trying to access treatment if I had known. This is an example of how I needed to guard against a sense of omnipotence as a way of denying my helplessness and fallibility (Shoshani et al., 2010). In effect, it shook my confidence in being able to manage the group and the therapeutic work. I realised that I had viewed this child as being one of the group facilitators who made the group seem manageable. I spent a great deal of time thinking about how to deal with the loss in the group, the impact that it might have on the members and ways to use it to facilitate the group process. I also had to spend time processing my personal loss and powerlessness in the face of this child's death.

Before the next group I took Nandi into my office to talk about what had happened. When she saw how upset I was about the child's death, she became distressed. A real space opened up for us to share our pain and loss, to debrief. The rupture in our relationship healed in our sharing of pain and vulnerability. We agreed on performing a little ritual in the group where candles would be lit while we thought about M and others whom we missed. The candles would then be blown out, with a goodbye. The children could take the candles home and ask caregivers to light them when they thought about their deceased parents. During this group, one of the girls got distressed and started to cry. The others were initially sombre and then seemed to disconnect and started playing with the candles and giggling. Considering this a number of years later, I realise that the process was too intense and overwhelming for the majority of the children to engage in. To acknowledge the loss of M would involve acknowledging the other losses they had experienced and would be emotionally overwhelming. In order for them to remain relatively intact faced with multiple losses and dramatic adjustments, these children needed to engage in a massive denial of their affect and the result was an absence of grief. On the one hand, perhaps the group had not been as attached to M as I had been. Alternatively, perhaps her death was too close, bringing death with all its reality and inevitability into the room. M's death was possibly perceived as a huge impingement on the group that Nandi and I had not been able to prevent. It is my understanding that the severe deprivation and scourge of HIV left members of this community feeling besieged in a way that mirrored the impact of armed conflict. As Shoshani et al. (2010) wrote, this external reality posed a constant threat to my ability to create a safe, insulated environment – a reliable container – in which to work. M's death fractured this already imperfect container, leaving the children feeling emotionally overwhelmed and unsafe. They took flight into a manic state as they became overwhelmed, disconnecting from the situation and their grief.

Despite the disruption that M's death caused in the group, it also resulted in a more constructive healing process, both in the group and between Nandi and me.

I made a decision to engage using an interrelational perspective. Expressing my own sadness in the group, in a contained way, regarding the loss of M provided a mirror of ways in which to talk about and deal with mourning. I was upset but not out of control, thus perhaps showing the children that painful feelings did not have to be avoided and denied but could be survived and felt. This was contrary to the messages of denial and avoidance that had been given to many children in the face of their losses. In processing and feeling our feelings rather than dissociating from them, our psyche is strengthened rather than depleted by numerous splits, giving us the sense that we can manage and survive strong emotional states.

Containing and supporting staff

Weekly meetings/trauma counselling sessions were scheduled after this group with Nandi and other CCWs, both individually and in a group, to provide them with a space to reflect on their own process and unconscious dynamics and to offer containment in a highly overwhelming environment. The work that Nandi was doing was literally too close to home. In thinking about her vulnerability and trying to understand her dynamics, I was able to deal with and process my own uncomfortable feelings towards her. My pausing to process and think about my reactions to Nandi opened up a space where I could regain an empathic connection to her. I could also recognise my own burnout and how it had led to my empathic failure towards Nandi.

This is one of the values of engaging in psychodynamic thinking within community work. It provides a way of dealing with countertransference feelings and the threat of burnout by drawing links and thinking about emotional states (Bion, 1963). This helps one to deal with staff dynamics in a thoughtful way and to manage countertransference feelings and emotional states.

UNDERSTANDING DIFFICULTIES IN PROCESSING OVER-WHELMING FEELINGS

In this disempowered township community, faced with the multiple strains of unemployment, poverty, high crime rates, and HIV/AIDS leaving numerous children orphaned, a wide-scale disconnection and denial occurred, mirroring the Mbeki government's AIDS denialism and lack of action in the face of the pandemic (Altman, 2000).

A common difficulty that emerged in many of the families and children that were seen in the clinic was dealing with and processing the deaths that they had experienced. The refrain heard repeatedly was, 'I must move on and not think about it.' The underlying concern seemed to be that if the bereaved focused on the loss of their loved ones, the pain would become overwhelming and intolerable, and their ability to function in the world would collapse. This concern was echoed in the grandmothers (*gogos*) who had been left to care for their deceased families' children. 'Moving on' was a highly prized skill, but ineffective in healing their pain. Asking the group members to get in touch with their feelings was contrary to much of the input that they had received from family and community members. It appeared that denial of the pain of loss and avoidance of their feelings were defences that were drawn on. Knox explores the dual nature of defences, on the one hand to 'fragment painful meaning, rendering it less unbearable by the process of dissociation and compartmentalization', and on the other hand 'as attempts at repair, constructing new and less distressing symbolic significance which renders trauma less threatening to one's personal sense of worth and identity' (2003: 226).

Children's mourning process is different to that of adults due to their ongoing development. As children are dependent on their caregivers for their continued survival, the death of a loved one leaves them confronted not only with the task of grieving the loss, but also with how to process it in order to survive and proceed with the necessary developmental tasks, including making new attachments. Factors to consider when assessing children's developmental ability to mourn include their ability to distinguish fantasy from reality, their capacity for object constancy, their abstract thought processes, and their limited ego resources (Silverman & Worden, 1993).

In the bereavement groups, the children generally presented with very little affect. The group seemed to be a fun extramural activity where they received peanut butter sandwiches and engaged in various activities. Initially, many of the children presented as being quite emotionally blunted and disconnected. As time passed and they began to feel safer and more comfortable in the group, the children appeared less wooden and more alive and connected. The group was made up of latency-aged children, who have been identified as using massive denial of both reality and affect to manage situations that feel overwhelming (Nagera, 1970). Some children failed to exhibit grief, for various reasons. One was children having, as Wolfenstein (1966) discussed, a 'short sadness span', where developmental imperatives pushed them to engage with curiosity in the world around them. Another group of children emerged as being attachment impaired, possibly as a result of long parental illness and the resultant neglect.

Ways of understanding the children's inability to deal with feelings

Dissociation

Many of the children in the group were unable to deal with the immensity of the loss that they had experienced. It seems that coping with the loss of their mothers was further exacerbated by the difficulty the adults around them had in dealing with both the death and the cause of the death. Not one of the children said that their mother had died of AIDS. However, it could be inferred from the caregivers that AIDS had been the major reason for the deaths. A great deal of shame was connected to the notion that you may have lost a parent/child to AIDS (Nagler et al., 1995). Rather than staying connected to these shameful feelings and fears of contracting HIV, the death and its cause were denied and the shameful feelings avoided through dissociation. This distanced the individual from their experiences and depleted their internal resources. This splitting resulted in their losing the opportunity to feel and process their depressive pain. Some of the children had also been traumatised by watching the gradual deterioration of their parents as a result of AIDS. Some post-traumatic stress was evident and debriefing occurred. The children were filled with fear that they might become contaminated by the disease and die in the same painful way (Miller & Murray, 1999). HIV education was presented to the groups to alleviate some of their anxiety. Children's feelings of responsibility for their parent's death were also addressed. The children were not used to discussing their thoughts and feelings and there was an expectation that I was a teacher and would tell them what to do, that there was a right and a wrong answer. They seemed to feel that they needed to comply and behave well throughout the process. This involved presenting a brave face and not being shamed by becoming overwhelmed and exposing their feelings. In time the group found a way of holding some of these tensions and experiencing the group as a containing space. Feedback from the children's caregivers suggested that they seemed more content and able to continue their lives.

An eight-year-old girl in the group, S, had nursed her dying mother for a number of months prior to her death. She had been abandoned by her extended family due to their fears of contagion. S was highly traumatised by having seen the deterioration and wasting away of her mother. She found it hard to remember how her mother had been before the illness. As part of the group process, the children compiled memory boxes to help them restore a more intact image of their dead mother. Assisting the children in finding photographs to place in their boxes was difficult in this impoverished community. S engaged enthusiastically in the process and some of her trauma features started to subside. We had to directly address her fear that she was responsible for her mother's death and that she could have done something to save her.

Failure to mourn

Some theorists (Freud, 1960; Wolfenstein, 1966) suggest that when a child under the age of six experiences a loss, that child is at great risk of permanent psychological damage because their cognitive and language development reduces the likelihood of them being able to process and deal with death. There is a failure to mourn. Some of the children in the group had lost their mothers very early and might therefore fall into this category. Two young brothers accompanied their older sister S, described above, to the group. They were five and six years old at the time of the group. L and Sp came to the group happily and engaged in the exercises in a practical but emotionally detached way. Although both boys were very quiet, they did not seem distressed when difficult feelings were discussed. I had the sense that their loss was unreachable. It was locked away, inaccessible through language.

Attachment difficulties

Many of the children who formed part of the group seemed to have pre-existing difficulties. This was identified by them having been patients at the child psychiatry clinic prior to the loss of their parents. When considering the cases, attachment difficulties were among some of the presenting problems of these children. The children were particularly vulnerable as they came from poor socio-economic circumstances and their parents had sometimes been sick for protracted periods, during which time they would not have been available as secure attachment figures. In addition, family members tended to rally around the sick parents and the children were left to fend for themselves. Early self-sufficiency is encouraged in this population, largely due to parents being overburdened and having to work long hours. A brother and sister who had had behaviour problems prior to their mother's death struggled to engage in the group. They came to the clinic intermittently and on occasions when they knew from the other children that some treat had been organised by the project. Their attachment history was marked by early abandonment by their alcoholic mother and multiple caregivers. Despite many efforts to bring them into the group, they remained on the periphery. It was my sense that they had attachment difficulties that made it hard for them to sustain relationships. The other children reported that the brother and sister were constantly making and losing friends and were not interested in what happened in the group.

With these difficulties in mind, it was important to facilitate the relationships between the children and their new caregivers. It was decided that caregivers who were closest to the children and had the most genuine concern for them should be allocated as foster parents, rather than those who could best financially support them. The children needed caregivers who would love them and facilitate the expression of their painful feelings. Bowlby (1969) posits that the proximity to the attachment figure provides the child with a safe haven from threat. The accessibility of the attachment figure provides a secure base from which a child might more confidently confront challenge, and separation from the attachment figure triggers separation anxiety. Hence, while the loss of a major attachment figure in childhood can and usually is devastating, the presence of substitute attachment figures or of other secure attachments can facilitate the bereavement process in children. If the death followed a long illness, it could mean that the child is likely to have endured months of neglect, which might have had a negative impact on their attachment to the primary caregiver (Grollman, 1995; Harris & Bifulco, 1991).

When dealing with and understanding the processes of the groups, it was sometimes hard to distinguish between symptoms which were manifestations of the children's grief and those which were a reflection of children with attachment difficulties. These attachment difficulties could have been a result of having a sick, distracted parent or, alternatively, could have been due to parental pathology, such as personality disturbance or attachment problems that inhibited their ability to attach to their own children.

CULTURAL INFLUENCES ON PSYCHOLOGICAL PROCESSES

In South Africa, ancestors play an important part in many people's culture. They are vested with mystical power and retain a jural role in the world of the living, particularly in the lives of their descendants (Brain, 1973). In the community clinic, children referred to their parents as being with the ancestors, in the same way that children in other cultures might refer to deceased parents being with angels in heaven. This seemed to provide a sense of comfort and containment for the children. Psychologically, it provides the child with an ongoing sense of contact with the parent, of being watched and protected by them. This relationship enables the child to accept the reality of the parent's death, in part by finding a way for the parent to keep on living, in some sense, in the child's life (Nagera, 1966). In more Kleinian terms, the parents become internalised as good objects that can be drawn upon to strengthen the psyche. In order to work successfully within any community, it is vital that the therapist pay appropriate respect to the belief systems. In my experience, therapeutic work can be furthered by drawing on an understanding of the culture of ancestors to express psychological states in an accessible way to the child, for example: 'I think your mother would want you to know that it is alright for you to be having these sad or angry feelings. That she loves you and can understand that you are cross that she died and left you. She won't be upset with you for feeling this way.' Issues of self-blame could be handled in a similar manner.

As an aside, one of the psychological drawbacks of the child retaining a relationship with the parent in this way is the tendency for the deceased parent to be idealised. This idealisation can make it difficult for the foster/replacement caregivers to form a good attachment with the child. When disciplined or disappointed by any of the new caregivers' actions, rather than understanding and accepting them, the child may feel that 'she' is not their real mother or that all these unpleasant things happen because they are not really loved since they are not their 'real' children. The child may feel that their real mother would have been so much nicer, more tolerant and understanding. Nagera (1966) speaks about the danger of the idealisation of the dead parent resulting in a tendency to split the ambivalence, with the positive feelings being directed to the idealised dead parent and the negative ones to the substitute parent. The substitute parent's behaviour is then viewed as emerging from the fact that they are not their 'real' parent and are therefore harsher with them. In the *gogo* groups, concerns and difficulties of this nature were common areas of discussion. Many *gogos* reported being told, 'You can't tell me what to do; you are not my "real" mother.' *Gogos* were advised to acknowledge the children's feelings and explain that they knew they could not replace their parents but they loved them as if they were their real parent. Discipline emerged as a common struggle with the *gogos*.

Two of the 10 children in the group, as well as many others attending the clinic, reported that their mothers had been bewitched. M, the group member who later died, stated that her mother had been bewitched and struck by unseen lightning. Her mother had been greatly respected in the community as a professional nurse who had done well in her life. For her family it was unthinkable and unbearable that she could have contracted HIV. Witchcraft enabled the family to retain an idealised image of her after her death.

CONCLUSION

The AIDS orphan crises poses a crucial challenge to South African society. How are we going to address and deal with generations of children growing up as orphans? If this population is not provided with adequate foster/substitute parents, we will end up with, as Burnett suggests, 'a new "lost generation" of dysfunctional and delinquent…youth who have been inadequately (nurtured), cared for, educated and socialized' (2000: 20). Rutter et al. (2008) found a fivefold increase in childhood psychiatric disorder in bereaved children as compared to the general population, especially in relation to depression and anxiety. These findings are supported by Harris and Bifulco's work (1991; Bifulco et al., 1992) exploring the link between childhood loss of a parent, later depression, and attachment difficulties.

When working with a highly strained population such as these children, it is important to recognise that defences, while having negative long-term consequences, can serve to protect the child from overwhelming situations that would damage their sense of self-worth and identity (Knox, 2003). However, a developmental lens is always important in recognising what may be currently adaptive but will require mediation so as not to result in long-term personality difficulties.

In this chapter I explored some of the pitfalls that were experienced in one such attempt to put together a programme to deal with orphaned children. Looking at the process through a psychodynamic lens assists us in understanding and making sense of some of the destructive elements and defences that make engaging in this work challenging. In order to retain staff and continue to build similar programmes, it is vital that unconscious elements are explored so that the valuable work done in our community clinics is not undermined and can be taken forward. Secondary traumatisation and burnout need to be guarded against through debriefing, supervision and therapy. Providing containment for staff working under these desperate conditions is vital (Eagle, 2005). In my experience, this began with a space to make mistakes, to look at my failures and to express my vulnerability. As Benjamin states, 'if we are mindful of our failures, gradually we will learn to recover from ruptures in attunement, and thus become sensitive to and use more effectively the inexplicable gaps created by the patient's unintegrated or warring self-parts and the analyst's failure to contain them' (2009: 441). Psychodynamic thought provides a useful framework to make sense of destructive forces on both a societal and an individual level that prevent us from 'getting the job done'.

The far-reaching and overwhelming nature of the AIDS pandemic can leave mental health professionals, as well as society at large, feeling overwhelmed and inadequate. This threat to our narcissism can result in manic defences, as described by Altman (2005), where, rather than staying engaged and processing the shame that results from our impotence, we dissociate from these uncomfortable feelings and project this sense of helplessness and inadequacy into the 'other'. In this case, the 'other' constitutes HIV orphans and people affected by HIV/AIDS, or other staff members. This split enables mainstream society to place these children and their caregivers into a group for whom they do not need to feel socially responsible (Altman, 2005). This failure to act can have devastating consequences. Patrick Burnett (2008), reporting on the findings of a commission by the Harvard School of Public Health, states that, 'More than 330,000 lives were lost to HIV/Aids in South Africa between 2000 and 2005 because a "feasible and timely" antiretroviral (ARV) treatment program was not implemented'. In research published online in October 2008 in the *Journal of Acquired Immune Deficiency Syndromes*, the Harvard researchers (Chigwedere et al., 2008) state that an estimated 35 000 babies were born with HIV during the same period because of delays in implementing a mother-to-child programme using the anti-AIDS drug Nevirapine.

This splitting is described in Sue van Zyl's (1999) interview with psychotherapist Gill Straker. They discuss the Truth and Reconciliation Commission and attempt to understand white complicity in apartheid injustices. Straker provides a useful description of the dynamic processes at play and describes the ability of the white population to dissociate and compartmentalise aspects of apartheid and racism that they were exposed to. This ability to dissociate is facilitated by the defence mechanism of splitting. This allows all the good to be vested in one object (inner representation of the in-group) and all the bad to be vested in another (inner representation of the out-group). Projective identification aids this splitting, with both interpersonal and intrapsychic implications.

> The use in the external reality of one group by another as the receptacle for projective identifications is a familiar notion, and it is this projective

identification which I believe is fundamental to racism, as is the failure to develop the broad-based empathy/concern associated with the depressive position. Racism/apartheid is predicated both upon an internal process of splitting as well as on a complete lack of empathy on the part of one group for another, which is an end product of such splitting. (Van Zyl, 1999: 253)

The facilitation of a move towards a more depressive position functioning is required in our society, both in dealing with the victims and those affected by HIV/AIDS, and with those at risk of infection. Similar processes of splitting lead to people engaging in risky behaviours under the guise of a manic defence and thereby not being able to protect themselves from infection or from facing the possibilities of being HIV+.

Finally, professionals working in the field can benefit from understanding psychodynamic processes that may be interfering with their community-based interventions. This understanding can hopefully provide containment for their difficult countertransference feelings, as well as guidance around the destructive mechanisms that may be at play in clinics or projects. A psychodynamic understanding can also help in neutralising the personal nature of some attacks between staff or patients, enabling professionals to feel less threatened or personally wronged. This knowledge could then hopefully be used to work with staff dynamics and facilitate constructive work environments, with containing support systems.

NOTE

1   The work at the community clinic took place between 2002 and 2007. The specific child bereavement group ran from 2002–2003.

REFERENCES

Altman, N (2000) Black and white thinking: A psychoanalyst reconsiders race. *Psychoanalytic Dialogues*, 10: 589–605.

Altman, N (2005) Manic society: Toward the depressive position. *Psychoanalytic Dialogues*, 15(3), 321–346.

Benjamin, J (2009) A relational psychoanalysis perspective on the necessity of acknowledging failure in order to restore the facilitating and containing features of the intersubjective relationship (the shared third). *International Journal of Psychoanalysis*, 90: 441–450.

Bifulco, A, Harris, T & Brown, GW (1992) Mourning or early inadequate care? Reexamining the relationship of maternal loss in childhood with adult depression and anxiety. *Development and Psychopathology*, 4(3): 433–449.

Bion, W (1962) *Learning from Experience*. London: Tavistock.

Bion, W (1963) *Elements of Psycho-Analysis*. London: William Heinemann Books.

Bowlby, J (1969) *Attachment and Loss, Volume 1. Attachment*. London: Basic Books.

Brain, JL (1973) Ancestors as elders in Africa: Further thoughts. *Journal of the International African Institute*, 43(2): 122–133.

Burnett, P (2000) Gateway to care. *The Big Issue*, Cape Town, November, 40(4): 20–21.

Burnett (2008) *Hundreds of Thousands Died Due to Lack of Aids Programmes, Harvard Research Says*. Accessed from http://westcapenews.com/?p=193 on 10 November 2012.

Chigwedere, P, Seage, GR, Gruskin, SJD, Lee, T & Essex, M (2008) Estimating the lost benefits of antiretroviral drug use in South Africa. *Journal of Acquired Immune Deficiency Syndromes*, 49(4): 410–415.

Eagle, G (2005) Grasping the thorn: The impact and supervision of traumatic stress therapy in the South African context. *Journal of Psychotherapy in Africa*, 15: 197–207.

Eng, D & Han, S (2000) A dialogue on racial melancholia. *Psychoanalytic Dialogues*, 10: 667–701.

Farooq, S (2009) Shooting the messenger, the problem is widespread. *British Journal of Psychiatry*, 195: 553.

Fonagy, P, Gergely, G, Jurist, E & Target, M (2002) *Affect Regulation, Mentalization and the Development of the Self*. New York & London: Other Books.

Freud, A (1960) Discussion of Dr John Bowlby's paper. *Psychoanalytic Study of the Child*, 15: 53–62.

Grollman, EA (ed.) (1995) *Bereaved Children and Teens: A Support Guide for Parents and Professionals*. Boston: Beacon Press.

Harris, T & Bifulco, A (1991) Loss of parent in childhood, and attachment style and depression in adulthood. In CM Parkes & J Stevenson-Hinde (eds) *Attachment Across the Lifecycle*. London/New York: Tavistock/Routledge.

Knox, J (2003) Trauma and defences: Their roots in relationship. An overview. *Journal of Analytic Psychology*, 48: 207–233.

Lee, E (1997) *Working with Asian Americans: A Guide for Clinicians*. New York: Guilford Press.

Miller, R & Murray, D (1999) The impact of HIV illness on parents and children, with particular reference to African families. *Journal of Family Therapy*, 21: 284–302.

Nagera, H (1966) *Early Childhood Disturbances: The Infantile Neurosis, and the Adulthood Disturbances*. New York: International Universities Press.

Nagera, HMD (1970) Children's reactions to the death of important objects: A developmental approach. *The Psychoanalytic Study of the Child*, 25: 360–400.

Nagler, SF, Adnopoz, J &Forsyth, BWC (1995) Uncertainty, stigma and secrecy: Psychological aspects of AIDS for children and adolescents. In S Geballe & W Andiman (eds) *Forgotten Children of the AIDS Epidemic*, pp. 71–82. New Haven, CT: Yale University Press.

Rutter, M, Bishop, D, Pine, D, Scott, S, Stevenson, JS, Taylor, EA & Thapar, A (2008) *Rutter's Child and Adolescent Psychiatry (fifth edition)*. New Jersey: Wiley-Blackwell Publishers.

Shoshani, M, Shoshani, B & Shinar, O (2010) Fear and shame in an Israeli psychoanalyst and his patient: Lessons learned in times of war. *Psychoanalytic Dialogues*, 20: 285–307.

Silverman, PR & Worden, JW (1993) Children's reactions to the death of a parent. In MS Stroebe, W Stroebe & RO Hansson (eds) *Handbook of Bereavement: Theory, Research, and Intervention*, pp. 300–316. New York: Cambridge University Press.

Straker, G (2004) Race for cover: Castrated whiteness, perverse consequences. *Psychoanalytic Dialogues*, 14: 405–422.

Swartz, S (in press) Naming and otherness: South African Intersubjective Psychoanalytic Psychotherapy and the Negotiation of Racialized Histories.

Van Zyl, S (1999) An interview with Gillian Straker on the Truth and Reconciliation Commission. *Psychoanalytic Dialogues*, 9: 245–248.

Wolfenstein, M (1966) How is mourning possible? *The Psychoanalytic Study of the Child*, 21: 93–123.

CHAPTER 10

RECLAIMING GENEALOGY, MEMORY AND HISTORY: The psychodynamic potential for reparative therapy in contemporary South Africa

Michael O'Loughlin

Gone.
Buried.
Covered by the dust of defeat – or so the conquerors believed
But there is nothing that can be hidden from the mind.
Nothing that memory cannot reach or touch or call back
(Don Mattera, 1987, quoted in Delport, 2001a: 31)

The expression 'Whereof one cannot speak, thereof one cannot stay silent', which appears as an epigraph on the title page of the work *History Beyond Trauma* by psychoanalysts Davoine and Gaudillière (2004), underscores a key theme of this chapter – and indeed of psychoanalysis – that there is much beneath the surface: the silenced, the erased, the unspeakable have ways of making their presence felt. Taken at an individual level, this is a truism of psychoanalytically oriented approaches to clinical practice. However, if individuals are understood as socio-historically constituted, situated in genealogy and history, ancestrally located, the possibility of life narratives animated by spectral presences, or what Garon (2004) calls 'skeletons in the closet', takes on new significance.

I share the concern of Nuttall and Coetzee, and many of the contributors to their book *Negotiating the Past: The Making of Memory in South Africa*, that 'the push to forget the past and to look to a new future' (1998: 1) runs the risk of creating a privileged version of history that will leave stories untold, many citizens severed from their socio-historical and ancestral lineages, and skeletons lurking in the nation's closet. A key thesis of psychoanalysis is that ghostly presences inevitably return in some form, and this *revenant* (cf. Derrida, 1994) can be highly consequential both for individuals and for societies. The eruption of war in the Balkans in the early 1990s, predicated in part on a resurrection of the humiliation of the Serbian people at the Battle of Kosovo in 1389, serves as a salutary reminder of the longevity and mischief-making capabilities of unacknowledged or suppressed spectres, particularly those that involve some combination of loss, trauma, humiliation and shame. In arguing for a psychoanalysis of the social, I am, therefore, arguing for a psychoanalysis of the spectral.

There is great anxiety in South Africa about reopening the wounds of apartheid. The rhetoric of a 'rainbow nation' offers hope for unity and national identity. The problem, as De Kok (1998) reminds us, is that the custody of memory is highly contested. She talks, for example, of the 'amnesiac rhetoric' of the National Party, which supported the Truth and Reconciliation Commission (TRC) in hopes of 'getting the past out of the way' (Schutte, quoted in De Kok, 1998: 59). She notes, however, a similar imperative in the frequent exhortations of the TRC to close 'this chapter of our history' (1998: 59), and certainly a similar inference might be drawn from Tutu's rhetoric of forgiveness in *No Future without Forgiveness* (1999). On the other hand, De Kok notes there are those who advocate for the reclamation of traumatic memory as a form of national catharsis – and clearly the TRC served this function in part – and those who refused to see value in 'truth' or 'reconciliation' unless those concepts were tied to some form of retributive justice.

The question I wish to address here is how psychoanalytically oriented psychotherapy might contribute to a critical debate about the formation and reformation of South Africa as a nation, and particularly how these considerations might lead to changes in both the practice of psychodynamic therapy and the dissemination of psychodynamic ideas throughout mental health and community care structures in South Africa. The challenge, as De Kok notes, here addressing the role of cultural institutions, is:

> ...of permitting contradictory voices to be heard as testimony or in interpretation, not in order to 'resolve' the turbulence but to recompose it. This involves resistance to increasing pressure on art and the public institutions to contribute directly to the psychic requirement of 'settlement' and nation building. If yoked to these imperatives, art too will become victim to the pressure to 'forgive and forget'...It is in the multiplicity of partial versions and experience, composed and recomposed within sight of each other, that truth 'as a thing of this world', in Foucault's phrase, will emerge. In this mobile current, individuals and communities will make and remake their meanings. This constant reconstitution is difficult labour, equivalent perhaps in individual narratives to the personal experience of mourning, recovery, and remembrance, and in aesthetic terms to the elegiac imperative. (1998: 61)

In what follows I will begin with some autobiographical work that lays bare my interest in the psychodynamics of intergenerational trauma transmission – in the possibilities of working through, and in the consequences of silence and the entombment of secret or shameful events. I will then sketch the outlines of a psychoanalytic conceptualisation that respects genealogy, history memory, intergenerational trauma, spectral memories, and ancestral lore. I will make brief reference to the District Six Museum as offering a theorisation and practice of active memory work that is congruent with my understanding of a therapy that seeks to repair the fabric of socio-historical continuity and to reconnect shattered social linkages in people's experiences. I should note here that my notion of memory work is not restricted to memories of apartheid-era wounds only, but includes the sweep of history that has come to constitute the South Africa of today. This includes the consequences of migrations, colonisations, enslavement, displacements, diasporic shifts, and so on.[2] Finally, in view of the dearth of clinicians in South Africa, I will offer some indications of how the way of working I outline might be adaptable for use by educators, artists and community workers to promote a socially conscious psychodynamic approach to collective memory work and individual therapy that opens up new conversational possibilities within educational and therapeutic spaces for members of the diverse communities of South Africa.

REFLECTION ON ORIGINS

The requirement that I enter a personal analysis caused me great trepidation when I began psychoanalytic training. I felt profoundly vulnerable. Throughout my life, as I noted elsewhere (O'Loughlin, 2007a), I have had a feeling akin to what Bion (1984) terms 'nameless dread'. The possibility of confronting unformulated and dreaded aspects of my own experience made me very anxious. Gradually, however, I made the transition from intellectual curiosity about psychoanalysis to an interest in exploring my own experience. The culmination of this work was the completion of a book of essays, *The Subject of Childhood*, part of which is devoted to an exploration of my own childhood history (O'Loughlin, 2009a). At first I was interested only in the specifics of my own childhood and the origins of my own personal anguish. I talk in the book, for example, about my protracted struggle with writing, and how this appeared to be related to my father's lack of facility in reading and writing, and the terrible shame that he felt because he never received the education necessary to learn to read and write comfortably. I speak too of the abject poverty and emotionally harsh climate in which both of my parents were raised. While working on the book I decided to speak with my mother about my childhood and, inevitably, this turned into a conversation about her own childhood. What follows is a brief fragment.

> During my mother's childhood tuberculosis was rampant in Ireland. Since the disease was highly contagious, and since this was prior to the development of a vaccine, contraction of the disease was a death sentence, and sufferers were isolated in facilities known as workhouses.[3] At the youthful age of 30, having three children under 10, my mother's mother went to hospital to deliver her fourth baby, and was then transferred from there to the workhouse, where she died in due course from tuberculosis. My mother had one recollection of her mother prior to her illness. That was when she baked a cake for the children for some occasion. 'I can't remember her face,' she said, 'but I remember pure kindness.' She also recalls one visit to see her mother in the workhouse, but all she can remember is tears. My mother's older sister, aged 10, having eavesdropped on her father making plans to put the children in an orphanage after their mother's death, smuggled a letter into the workhouse to inform their mother of his intentions. Her mother then made their father swear to raise the children himself. In view of what we have since learned about Irish orphanages of the period, that was a most fortunate outcome.[4]

The children were never told of their mother's impending death. Rooting through a chest of clothing at home one day, the children found what they thought was a brown dress. When they asked their father about it, he told them to ask their grandmother. She harshly told them it was the habit in which their mother was to be buried. When their mother finally died, the children were not even informed. When I asked if any process was put in place to assist the children in mourning, my mother looked at me in amazement for making such a naïve inquiry: 'It was awful hard...I can't think of anything like it...Every time we heard that someone died I felt like I was going to vomit...It had an awful effect on us... Don't talk of it.' The regimen of domestic servitude and deprivation only intensified thereafter until finally she and her sister were old enough to enter domestic service for other families.

On my mother's side, we have generations of a family of rural Irish people, victims of severe deprivation and suffering in the present, bearers of untold trauma from a genocidal famine, and apparently incapable of providing any kind of psychological sustenance for my mother and her siblings who had suffered such immediate catastrophic losses. There was a certain hardness in the Ireland of my youth and earlier when it came to children's emotions. This is evident, for example, in Frank McCourt's widely read *Angela's Ashes* (1996), a work that was received in parts of Ireland with considerable resentment. Anthony Clare, one of Ireland's leading psychiatrists, characterised Irish culture as, 'A culture heavily impregnated by an emphasis on physical control, original sin, cultural inferiority and psychological defensiveness' (1991: 14). He quotes an Irish psychiatrist writing on Irish child-rearing practices in 1976:

> The family home in Ireland is a novitiate for violence. Even from the cradle the child is made to feel rejection, hostility, and open physical pain. The infant is left to cry in his cot because his mother does not want to 'give in to him.' Later he is smacked with the hand or a stick. He is made to go to bed early. He is not allowed to have his tea. He is put in a room by himself...and in order to invite this morale breaking treatment from his parents, all the Irish child has to do is to be *normal.* It is the normality of childhood that sets parents' teeth on edge. They take no joy in childishness. (in Clare, 1991: 15–16)
>
> Sitting with my mother and attempting to wrap my mind around the indescribable nature of her unmourned losses was an unforgettable experience for me. Part of my heaviness of heart undoubtedly

came from my empathy with my mother's legacy of suffering, and part no doubt came from the indubitable realisation that my subjectivity was formed in the crucible of my mother's losses. I also marvel that, despite her upbringing, and contrary to my father's more incommunicative and heavy-handed approach, my mother managed to transcend her pain and raise her children with fortitude, love and empathy. (O'Loughlin, 2009a: 55–56)

I had set out simply to fill in some of the missing gaps in my own childhood history. However, listening to my mother's resigned acceptance of suffering, and wincing at her stoic philosophy that you just bury the pain and go on – a posture on pain that is achingly familiar to me – I began to wonder if indeed there was larger meaning in her story. I also began to ruminate about my father's frightening panic attacks, and about the alcoholism and mental disturbance in his family. Could there be more to these events than meets the eye? My thoughts turned to the Great Hunger, a catastrophic famine that swept through Ireland from 1845 through 1847. This awful catastrophe was not a famine, properly speaking. There is well-established evidence that the British colonial rulers exported Irish livestock and wheat while a million Irish peasants died terrible deaths from starvation due to failure of the potato crop on which they depended. Two to three million people fled Ireland at that time, and many died in steerage in the coffin ships that bore them to the New World. It was a genocide of catastrophic proportions that sliced the population in half.[5]

I explore the traumatic legacy of the Great Hunger at length in a recent article (O'Loughlin, 2012a). Here is a brief extract which poses four-square the struggle with spectral memory and unresolved mourning:

Irish-American author Tom Hayden (1997a) addresses this silence in a book he edited, *Irish Hunger: Personal Reflections on the Legacy of the Famine*. He speaks of the 'ocean of silence' that washed over the trauma, characterizing himself as 'an orphan from history' because of his parents' failure to share that history with him, though he recognizes they may not have been conscious of this knowledge because of the likely abject silence of their forebears (Hayden, 1997b). The book is premised on the notion that Ireland is a traumatized nation (e.g. Lloyd, 1997; Waters, 1997) and that tremendous damage is being done by a 'culture of amnesia,' the product of 'three generations of horrified silence' (Waters, p. 29).

In the context of the workings of malignant shame, the collection is remarkable in its acknowledgement of ghostly echoes of past trauma in our unconscious.

To take just one illustrative story, consider the case of Irish-American journalist, Carolyn Ramsay. She offers a visceral account of the workings of hungry ghosts in her daily life. Having discussed how her grandmother, an emigrant child of Famine survivors, developed an obsession for feeding sandwiches to imaginary people in her old age, Ramsay begins to ruminate on her own 'need to feed':

> I don't know another working mother who worries about feeding people the way I do... It has taken me years, on the other hand, to focus on just feeding my family – not the whole world. On late nights when I've pounded chicken and chopped vegetables alone in my kitchen while my family sleeps, I've wondered precisely what my problem is… Part of me passes off the feeding urge as a slightly embarrassing compulsion, although its emotional depth and power indicate otherwise. After dropping food at a soup kitchen for the first time a decade ago, I had to steer my car to the side of the street because I was sobbing so hard I couldn't see. There's such unremitting sadness at the root of this drive to feed people that I've come to assume that it links me somehow to the dark events in Ireland in the mid 1800s. I can't know this. No famine stories made their way from my migrating great-grandparents to me, or even to my parents. 'The Irish aren't real talkers,' my mother once said. When I consider how my grandmother's need to feed imagined ghosts has followed me for thirty years though, it seems likely her famine-surviving parents' attitudes towards food made a deep impression on her. How could they not? (O'Loughlin, 2012a: 240–241)

A conspiracy of silence by the Irish government and Irish historians substantially buried knowledge of the Great Hunger until dissident scholars raised the issue at the 150th anniversary of that event in 1995.[6] Since a great majority of people of Irish descent on the planet today are descended from surviving victims of that catastrophic trauma, I wondered what possible long-term effects such people might have suffered from the burial of this trauma. Could there be a link from the trauma of the Great Hunger to my father's panic attacks, and to the mental illness and alcoholism in his family? Could my mother's stoicism and difficulty expressing pain be traced back that far? Indeed, could the unusually high rates of schizophrenia, depression and alcoholism in Ireland today have their origins in this – *and* other – buried traumas?

For my purposes here, suffice it to say that I am convinced that silence around historically traumatic events can have deleterious effects both for individuals and for whole societies. Once the silence is established, however, breaking the pattern is not easy. I learned this, to my cost, when I sent copies of *The Subject of Childhood* to my mother and my siblings, only to be met with reproach and criticism for having told tales out of school.

> Refrain from an(y) Irish childhood:
> Mind your own business.
> A closed mouth catches no flies.
> What you don't know won't trouble you.
> What's it to you anyway?
> What do you want to know that for?
> Sure isn't that all in the past?
> What are they talking about that for, anyway?
> Can't you just be happy with the life you have now?
> (O'Loughlin, 2012a: 238)

My belief is that the past is never past. Whether we acknowledge the past or deny it, it is with us daily in our lives as a silent, spectral presence. The challenge, therefore, is not just in exhuming secrets from the past. We need to seize the initiative to retell old stories in new ways so that new possibilities for expressing our identities as individuals, groups and whole nations become possible and so that we can mourn our pasts and transcend the parts of our pasts that prevent us from imagining how to live our lives otherwise. As the earlier discussion of De Kok's work indicated, the power of resurrecting narrative lies not in the retelling, but in the possibility of recomposition that is entailed. This is a truism in individual intrapsychic psychoanalytic work. My point here is that the possibilities of working through are enhanced when socio-historical and spectral aspects of experience are taken into consideration. In addition, attention to the collective aspects of socio-historical and ancestral experience opens up a window for psychodynamic clinicians to contribute to the discussion about the psychological state of society and the possibilities of working through societal trauma in ways that can produce social healing.

THE RUINS OF MEMORY AND THE INTRACTABILITY OF SILENCE

Langer (1991) presents an analysis of the complexities of traumatic memory. His analysis of Holocaust survivor transcripts reveals the different ways that tensions between the imperatives 'You won't understand' and 'You must understand' (1991: xiv) play out for different survivors. While silence is a well-established consequence of Holocaust trauma (cf. Auerhahn & Peskin, 2003; Danieli,1998; Felman & Laub, 1992; Pisano, 2012), Langer illustrates the layers of complexity and difficulty entailed in bringing narrative coherence to what he calls the 'the ruins of memory'. He quibbles with the notion that traumatic memories need to be reawakened, suggesting that Holocaust memory is 'an insomniac faculty' (1991: xv), and what is needed is to conceptualise the complex relationship between past and present that traumatic memory embodies.

From an intensive study of Holocaust survivor narratives, Langer identified five postures toward memory and recollection that different survivors embodied. The first of these, 'deep memory', represents cases where there is a profound split between everyday life in the present and the highly traumatised experience of a past where 'moral distinctions crumble' (1991: 27). This disjuncture produces a dissociation in which the survivor feels an incommensurability between the trauma events that they experienced and what is comprehensible by current moral standards. The split-off memory manifests as a form of silence. The 'choiceless choice' faced by a starving concentration camp survivor who felt obligated to steal a fellow inmate's hidden piece of bread in order not to die of starvation, or the desperation of another who stole the working shoes needed for hard labour from a fellow inmate who was attempting to perform elementary ablutions – and who faced certain death from hard labour without the shoes – created a lesion in the psyche that was unbridgeable. This gap then produced corrosive shame that led to silence – the survivor being certain in the knowledge that their actions could not be understood within any normalised frame of reference.

'Anguished memory', Langer tells us, comes from the split produced by a chasm between a remembered trauma and the normality of everyday present life:

> I feel my head is filled with garbage: all these images, you know, and sounds and my nostrils are filled with the stench of burning flesh. And it's...you can't excise it, it's like – like there's another skin beneath the skin and that skin is called Auschwitz, and you cannot shed it... (survivor testimony, quoted in Langer, 1991: 53)

Failing both at integration and at dissociation, such survivors are 'in futile search for a physician of memory' (1991: 52). Langer notes that memory can be conceptualised as 'not only a spring, flowing from the well of the past', but also as 'a tomb, whose contents cling like withered ivy to the mind' (1991: 69). Speaking of 'humiliated memory', Langer invokes Nietzsche's statement that 'an excess of history is detrimental to life' (1991: 79). Reminiscent of the poignant situation of my own mother, as described earlier, Langer again draws from Nietzsche to capture the burden of unsymbolised experience: '[M]odern man (sic) drags an immense amount of indigestible knowledge stones around with him which on occasion rattle around in his belly' (quoted in Langer, 1991: 81). The end result is unspeakability: 'The only way out of the inner sanctum of dark revelation, in this and similar moments of testimony, is avoidance. We may call it inaccessible, but what we really mean is that it is not *discussable*' (1991: 118).

'Tainted memory' refers to the even more appalling situation where the only way the traumatised person could survive the trauma was through annihilation of the self – the suspension of all humanity. Drawing on Maurice Blanchot, Langer refers to this kind of traumatic memory as 'unexperienced experience', and he describes the disintegration of one such survivor as memory returned and her narrative proceeded:

> [She] begins her testimony with perfect composure, a model of the integrated self. Slowly, as her narrative unfolds, her facial gestures and head movements, the stretching of her neck and licking of her lips, her uncontrollable perspiring, and deep sighs reveal a woman increasingly possessed by rather than possessing her story. (1991: 137)

This kind of memory is 'the reverse of redemptive' (1991: 157), and any attempt at recuperative memory work with such survivors must proceed with great care. Finally, Langer speaks of 'unheroic memory' as representing the difficulty of survivors who were traumatised by being poised on the brink of extinction: 'In a milieu where living was dying, where existence was a death sentence worse than anything that even Camus was ever able to imagine, where today seemed *always* better than tomorrow because freedom was unthinkable and death a certainty, the self functioned on the brink of extinction…' (1991: 183).

The therapeutic response to traumatic silence, therefore, needs to be nuanced, as many forms of unspeakableness may lie beneath the surface and the capacity for speech may be severely compromised.

Last night, after writing these words, the dogs came back. My childhood dreams had been peopled with 'wicked' (i.e. fearsome and vicious) dogs, reminiscent of the Neapolitan Mastiffs in the Harry Potter movies, or the marauding dogs in Ari Folman's movie *Waltz with Bashir*. In this dream I am visiting my brother. He whistles and summons two snarling and fearsome dogs. He has them simulate an attack on his arm so I am in no doubt as to their ferocity. They have the run of his house and I awake suffused in anxiety as to how I can sleep there.

Now I have insomnia, and a dark cloud hangs by the door. Why do I tell you this? Why should I not tell you this?

GRAPPLING WITH MEMORY AND HISTORY[7]

Revenants or returning spirits have a long history in many different cultures, and the capacity for psychoanalysis to offer a space for spectral presences, hauntings and ancestral memory in its practice creates an intersection with indigenous beliefs and ways of knowing that holds important possibilities for dialogue around healing. Derrida (1994) coined the term 'hauntology', and he contrasts it to 'ontology' as the difference between an emphasis on ' being' in the present as opposed to an acknowledgement of spectral presences that haunt our very existence. This is reminiscent of Bollas's (1987) notion of the 'unthought known', except that here the unthought known refers to the silent intrusion of socio-historical and genealogical legacies in our intrapsychic preoccupations. As Gordon notes, 'The ghost is not just simply a dead or missing person, but a social figure, and investigating it can lead to that dense site where history and subjectivity make social life' (1997: 8).

Abraham and Torok (1994) devoted much of their work to understanding secrets. Rand notes that:

> For Abraham and Torok, silence is an independent clinical and theoretical entity. Whether it characterizes individuals, families, social groups, or entire nations, silence and its varied forms – the untold or unsayable secret, the feeling unfelt, the pain denied, the unspeakable and concealed shame of families, the cover-up of political crimes, the collective disregard for painful historical realities – may disrupt our lives. (1994a: 21)

They speak of phantomic memory as 'memory they buried without legal burying place' (1994: 141) and their work is replete with images of the psyche as containing tombs, crypts, sealed-off places in which secrets are buried. There are echoes in their work of Ferenczi's (1988) notion of trauma as an alien transplant. With respect to the mechanisms by which secrets are transmitted, Abraham and Torok's theory is consistent with recent research on intergenerational trauma (e.g. Danieli, 1998; Emery, 2002; Fraiberg et al., 1975; Kaplan, 1995) in highlighting how a child, drawn to secrets or to encapsulated – and hence unsymbolised – experiences in the parent, develops a parentifying impulse, redirects their libidinal investments to the parent's unsymbolised need, and ends up with a gap, a black hole, or a negative (cf. Green, 1999) at the core of their being. Abraham and Torok express the mechanism this way:

> Should a child have parents 'with secrets,' parents whose speech is not exactly complementary to their unstated repressions, the child will receive from them a gap in the unconscious, an unknown, unrecognised knowledge – a *nescience* – subjected to a form of 'repression' before the fact.

> The buried speech of the parent will be (a) dead (gap) without a burial place in the child. The unknown phantom returns from the unconscious to haunt its host and may lead to phobias, madness, and obsessions. Its effects can persist through several generations and determine the fate of an entire family line. (1994: 140)[8]

A phantom, for Abraham and Torok, therefore results from the child's empathic identification with 'rejected psychic matter' in the crypt or split-off part of the parental unconscious. They refer to this process as 'endocryptic identification'. In clinical terms, Abraham and Torok suggest that this often takes the form of psychosomatic illnesses, phobias, etc., where the material that is unspeakable seeks expression in a symptom. Rather than seeing somatic symptoms as direct expressions of psychic need, Abraham and Torok view them as 'the return of the dead who are in mourning' (1994: 162) through their incorporation in bodily symptoms. Torok, drawing on Freud's discussion of the 'prejudice of the "I" ', notes that when we listen to a patient, or observe psychosomatic symptoms in a patient, we should not assume that we are dealing with the first person singular, nor should we make the assumption that, as she puts it, ' "I" really means the legal identity of the subject' (in Abraham & Torok, 1994: 180), since the patient may be voicing – or being spoken by – inherited phantomic trauma.[9]

Rand states that the notion of phantom widens the discussion beyond the intrapsychic concerns of the individual to include the collectivist origins of experience:

> The concept of the phantom redraws the boundaries of psychopathology and extends the realm of possibilities for its cure by suggesting the existence within an individual of a collective psychology comprised of several generations, so that the analyst must listen for the voices of one generation in the unconscious of another. (1994a: 166)

Later, Rand rather elegantly refers to the psychoanalytic treatment of an individual as, in effect, 'psychoanalysis *in absentia* of several generations (parents, grandparents, uncles, et al.) through the symptom of a descendant' (1994b: 168). Rand goes on to note the political implications of Abraham and Torok's thinking, suggesting, much as I did earlier with the example of the Battle of Kosovo, that humiliation, shame and traumatic memory can be transmitted covertly from generation to generation until eventually the phantom finds a new mode of expression. We witness this recursiveness, for example, in the persistence and periodic resurgence of Nazi ideology in contemporary Germany. Contrary to the original Derridean formula that spectral presences are part of our being, Abraham and Torok take a more conventional psychoanalytic view that phantoms lose their force once they become speakable (cf. Rogers, 2006), and they also suggest that the phantomic potency of spectral memory declines in successive generations.

Drawing on Ferenczi's *Clinical Diary* (1988), Garon (2004) elaborates an understanding of phantomic trauma – what she calls 'skeletons in the closet' – that is quite congruent with the conceptualisation of Abraham and Torok. Garon worries that unless analysts are aware of their own socio-historical constitutedness, they are likely to be incurious about their patients' histories and they will fail to recognise what such patients may be unconsciously seeking to communicate. She says that it is not the trauma, per se, that causes the symptom in the child. Rather, it is the disavowal of the trauma by the parent, or an earlier ancestor, that leaves the child with what Ferenczi calls 'an alien transplant'. 'Both analyst and analysand,' Garon notes, 'are then faced with a *psychic blank*, an alien abode of what has not been taken account [of] by language' (2004: 85). The difficulty in analysis is that such elements, producing trauma that is not directly traceable to an experienced traumatic event, contain elements 'refractory to any metabolisation or representation' (2004: 86).

Garon postulates that the splitting that is inherent in intergenerational trans-mission changes form across generations. She says that it begins with negation in the first generation, and then proceeds to denial and, by the third generation, the secrets are foreclosed. In therapy, Garon (2004) says, this is manifested in a progression from the unspeakable to the unnameable to the unthinkable. Such children are destined to live in silence, and they are perpetually oriented towards offering a parentifying response to the foreclosed other. Speaking of children – and this is a topic to which I will return below – Garon conceptualises the therapeutic challenge in terms of the restoration of narrative capacity: 'If every child is confronted with the internal necessity to create their own story, the task is particularly harsh for children who carry alien transplant. They are stuck with family secrets that generate anxiety and the simple fact of thinking about it is forbidden' (2004: 91).

In therapy, Garon suggests, the object is not necessarily to reconnect the adult patient with the facts of the historical trauma or lack they experienced, because indeed such connections may be well hidden. Rather, it is to engage the patient in awareness of the foreclosure of their experience, the blanks in their psyche, the naming of the very possibility of skeletons rattling in their closet and producing disquiet. Crucial to this process, as Ferenczi emphasised, is the analyst's awareness of the gaps and lacks in their own experience, the foreclosure of their own language, and the nameless dread produced by their own inherited unsymbolised parts.

THE CONSEQUENCES OF BEING BORN OUTSIDE OF GENEALOGY

> I think it is of the utmost importance that in his (sic) countertransference the analyst should be able to bear the anxiety of not knowing and even of not knowing that he does not know. Only when, against this background of anxiety and ignorance, something as yet unrevealed in the patient's history is mobilized, *to solve an enigma posed by this transference*, do we reach the clinical quasi-certainty *that this history is part of the patient's psyche*. (Faimberg, 2005: 7)

The difficulty in mobilising history in therapy patients is that some patients may have been severed from social linkages, or they may have inherited severed social links from their ancestors. This is true, for example, of people in indigenous communities throughout the world who have suffered displacement, genocide and cultural erosion as a result of the expansion of colonial and imperial powers across the globe. Lear (2006) discusses the catastrophic consequences of westward expansion in the United States for the Crow nation. The Crow was a warrior nation, and their defeat at the hands of the US Cavalry ensured that the men of the tribe could no longer maintain their warrior status. Thus, a core aspect of their subjectivity had to be abandoned, raising what in earlier times would have been an unthinkable question: 'Among the Crow, is there a Crow?' (2006: 46).[10] Likewise, Erikson (1976) explores the consequences of the dispersal of the community at Buffalo Creek, Virginia, following a mine disaster. Erikson sums up the loss of communality and social collectivity that arises from collective trauma this way:

> By collective trauma, I mean a blow to the tissues of social life that damages the bonds linking people together and impairs the prevailing sense of communality. The collective trauma works its way slowly and even insidiously into the awareness of those who suffered from it; thus, it does not have the quality of suddenness usually associated with the word 'trauma,' It is, however, a form of shock – a gradual realization that the community no longer exists as a source of nurturance and that a part of the self has disappeared. 'I' continue to exist, although damaged and maybe even permanently changed. 'You' continue to exist, although distant and hard to relate to. But 'we' no longer exist as a connected pair or as linked cells in a larger communal body. (1976: 302)

Apfelbaum (2002) also addresses the psychic consequence of uprootings and displacements by exploring the consequences of severance of genealogical links. She notes that people who are torn from their origins through wars, displacements or social upheaval become 'cultural orphans'. All humans are inscribed in familial and genealogical filiations and any rupture to that genealogical continuity leaves a child bereft of context. In the words of Janine Altounian, such a child 'faces an eclipse of his/her origins…[and becomes] a human being without "a shadow" ' (quoted in Apfelbaum, 2002: 81). The silence we often witness in displaced and uprooted people, Apfelbaum suggests, comes from the lack of 'a collective framework of intelligibility' within which their actions might be understood. She suggests that the lack of an understanding listener causes a retreat into silence and shame, and the suffering thus becomes unspeakable.[11]

My understanding of the role of history, ancestry and genealogy in human subjectivity, and particularly the role of ruptures in social linkages in the production of psychosis and other deeply dysregulative responses, has been greatly enhanced by reading *History Beyond Trauma*, Davoine and Gaudillière's (2004) important book. Contrary to current biomedical and pharmacological approaches to mental disorders,[12] these authors are frank that socio-historical factors are at the forefront of their minds in seeking to understand madness: 'Thus, in our experience, the successive shocks that constitute the rhythm of an analysis of madness always lead us back to the same region, the field of historical and social traumas' (2004: xxiii). They suggest that suffering from war, displacement and conquest is an inescapable part of the history of most people in the world, and large numbers of our patients, inevitably, are descended from ancestors who fled ruined worlds. Rather poetically, they suggest that the work of analysis is to 'bring into existence zones of nonexistence wiped out by a powerful blow that actually took place' and they note that sometimes a symptom such as madness 'tells us more than all the news dispatches about the left-over facts that have no right to existence' (2004: xxvii). Echoing the quote from Faimberg (2005) that serves as epigraph to this section, Davoine and Gaudillière argue that 'moments excised from history' – 'pieces of frozen time' – that may have travelled down generations, are actualised in the transference and become available for analysis for the first time.

A key concept for Davoine and Gaudillière is a notion of social linkage that is reminiscent of Apfelbaum's notion of genealogical filiation. The task of analysis is to detect ruptures in social linkages because these are the moments that have produced the unsymbolised material – the unspoken and unspeakable events – that leave us with only the cryptic communication of the symptom as remnant. The process of recreating social linkages, reweaving ancestral and narrative threads of continuity, is one of taking 'a piece of history that has escaped History' (2004: 11) and assisting the patient in inscribing it into his or her personal history. Davoine and Gaudillière suggest that this is the most vital moment in clinical work, the moment when the therapist can create conditions for the return of the real, the feeling of 'nameless dread', the encounter with the ghost. They propose that the therapist become an 'annalist', that is, a chronicler of the moment when 'the thread of speech may be radically cut' (2004: 71), leaving the patient with unsymbolised experience. As Bollas (1987) noted, in discussing 'the unthought known', our work is to bring patients for the first time to visit familiar places where they have dwelt for a very long time. 'Regaining a foothold in history' (Davoine & Gaudillière, 2004: 47) is the antidote to dissociated or unsymbolised experience. Elsewhere Davoine and Gaudillière refer to the primary influence of the therapist as that of a curious other who reignites a process of 'subjectivation', the possibility of becoming a subject, in the patient. For therapists who work with psychotic or severely dissociated patients, this capacity to 'reopen the question' (2004: 70) is a core function of psychodynamic therapy.

Truth telling by the therapist is vital to healing and that is why this kind of work cannot thrive unless, as the earlier quote from De Kok indicated, we speak 'not in order to "resolve" the turbulence but to recompose it' (1998: 61). In terms of treatment, Davoine and Gaudillière point out that it is not so much the unspeakability of trauma that is at issue, because, after all, the trauma speaks covertly through symptoms. Rather, it is the *inaudibility* of the trauma to the therapist. Our task is to create conditions for the reception of speech and the animation of moribund subjectivity. Davoine and Gaudillière return to the Salmon principles, an approach developed by Salmon (1917) for the treatment of shell shock, to articulate the core elements of therapy. The four Salmon principles are expectancy, immediacy, proximity and simplicity, and while the authors explore these principles at length, I will extract some general therapeutic considerations.

It is vital, according to Davoine and Gaudillière, that the analyst expect authentic communication from the patient: 'The abolition of pretense, unvarnished access to the truth of situations, and tearing the veil from the weakness of adults free up an energy usually held back by repression' (2004: 218). I am reminded of the moving work that Peciccia and Benedetti are accomplishing in Perugia, Italy, with persons suffering from psychosis who are mute. Using the entirely silent dialogue involved in Progressive Mirror Drawing, they animate the patient's deepest dynamics and invite the patient into a wordless dialogue of deep human significance (Peciccia & Benedetti, 1998). Davoine and Gaudillière also address the conundrum of time. Here the authors explore the complexity of working in a chronological, time-bound world, with someone for whom part of their experience may be suspended in time and for whom concepts such as past and present may be essentially meaningless. Most of all, perhaps, as many of the authors reviewed here note, the therapist needs to be working on his or her 'own stuff' in order to fine-tune the unconscious attunement to gaps, blockages, obscure signifiers, history, phantoms and, indeed, *nescience*, that makes the invitation to re-enter subjectivity possible:

> We might as well name our hobbyhorses, since the patient guesses that they are there. 'You're working on your own stuff,' he says to the analyst, who is surprised to be seen through. Is this hobbyhorse a stuffed horse? 'But it isn't

yours any more than mine,' the patient continues, seizing hold of the object that thus becomes an agreement between them. And what might 'your own' mean in this case? 'Neither you nor I exists, in this regard, as owners of well-delimited egos or of well-trained chargers, when you and I are struggling on a path this is strewn with pitfalls – what's more a path on which we are always in the same place. Right?' (Davoine & Gaudillière, 2004: 162)

TELLING GHOST STORIES: Inscribing and re-inscribing memory

Having traversed the realm of secrets, ghosts, phantoms, spectres and other haunting shadows, it remains to ask how to embark on human-scale projects that allow the weaving together of narrative possibilities that enable people and communities to (re)find themselves – to tell again, and for the first time, the story of their being. The problem with national solutions such as the rhetoric of a 'rainbow nation', or the sanctification and sanitising of sites such as Robben Island as icons of an official story of liberation, is that they create a univocal master narrative – a new official story – and thereby risk instituting a new form of silence.[13] Can one fight silence with silence? Can one fight erasure with erasure? Where will all of the atrocities, the displacements, the bereavements and the losses go if they are driven underground? When will they rear their ugly heads again? And what of the people who live their lives with gaps in their subjectivities, haunting echoes in their dreams of disappointed ancestors, lost lands, lost affiliations and missing loved ones?

This is not to suggest that memory work is easy. Families are fractious. Tribal groups are fractious. Nation states are fractious. The architects of colonisation and apartheid engineered division and hierarchy in South Africa to seal their dominance through the rationing of privilege and the exploitation of difference. The response to Pippa Skotnes's *Miscast*[14] suggests that the debate will be fractious and good intentions cannot protect us from embodying privilege, from tearing the scars off old wounds, and from wounding each other. But the conversation begins (cf. Long, 2011; White, 2002). The 'working through' begins. New collective memories can only be forged from the reclaiming of past lives. Otherwise we are left with the dilemma of silence. Robins describes it thus:

My early childhood exposure to knowledge about the Shoah was the official Zionist version in which Holocaust memory is appropriated to legitimize

Israeli nationhood. It was only in my thirties that I was able to begin to experience the Shoah at a personal level. That happened after years of submerging my Jewish identity and understanding the Shoah as an event that happened to other people, at another time, on another planet. Like my father's silence about the Holocaust, it seems likely that millions of black parents are unable to express what they feel about the humiliations and pain of their everyday experiences of racism under apartheid. Perhaps the rage about systemic racism will only be expressed in future generations. Like my father, millions of black South Africans may be too concerned with survival, and perhaps only their sons and daughters will be in a position to revisit their parents' and their own traumas. (1998: 125)

Delport (2001b) describes the District Six Museum[15] in Cape Town as a 'living museum', though expressing discomfort with the term 'museum' with its connotations of fossilised knowledge, singular viewpoint and privileged storytelling. She struggles with redefining the term to include the grand, activist ambition of the District Six project:

Thinking back on this problematical notion of a 'museum', with all its connotation of collections and displays, the term seems at odds with the intense six-year life of the museum project as a living space and place for working with memory. Recalling that time, I believe that the term 'museum' may have been evoked as something that suggested solidity, a continuity and permanence that could withstand even the force of the bulldozer and the power of a regime committed to the erasure of place and community. The common impulse in the call, however, was for a place of memory, not a monument, but a focus for the recovery and reconstruction of the social and historical existence of District Six. (Delport, 2001b: 11)

What is compelling about the District Six project is the dynamic nature of the work, the idea that people come there to inscribe their memories through 'rituals of remembrance' (Forbes, 2001: 27). An outstanding example of such work is the process by which members of the displaced District Six community return to the Museum and write their thoughts publicly on sheets of paper. Volunteers then take those inscriptions and embroider them onto yards of cloth in a process of memory retracing whereby the 'grooving and re-grooving confirm value' (Forbes, 2001: 27).

In their timeline for the Museum, Prosalendis et al. (2001) repeatedly empha-sise that while the Museum has few physical artefacts – the bulldozers did their work with resolute finality – the substance of the Museum is about 'abstract issues, about loss, memory, and recovery' (2001: 93). Could a psychoanalyst state the fundamental purpose of our work any better? In discussing the exhibition *Digging Deeper*, Delport captures the dynamic nature of this process:

> I see significance in the term *Digging Deeper* as an indication of those mo-ments when individuals, not only those affected by forced removals, allow the contents of the Museum to lead them further into an examination of their own historical experience, attitudes and capacities. It is a labour, an aspect of working with memory, that may uncover and connect the fragment of self within the broad mosaic of our collective and interrelated, past and potential experience. (2001c: 157)

ADDRESSING GENEALOGICAL RUPTURES AND SEVERED SOCIAL LINKS: The possibility of reparation

With some notable exceptions (e.g. Altman, 2009), analysts seem more comfort-able in their consulting room than engaging in social change projects. It has not always been so. Freud's free clinics (Danto, 2005), and the continuing work of the Tavistock Clinic in London, are reminders that social activism and commu-nity service have important roots in our field. Stepansky (2009), however, argues that in the United States psychoanalysis has become increasingly marginal as time-limited, 'evidence-based' practices increase their hegemony. I share Stepansky's view that psychoanalytic practices could preserve their relevance by demonstrating a capacity for addressing complex social problems. Against the backdrop of enormous recent social upheaval, a dearth of clinicians, and a nation on the cusp of charting a new course for its future, this would appear to be an ideal moment for South African therapists to contribute to expanding the role of psychoanalysis in creating national mental health policy and in developing psychoanalytically informed community mental health practices.

With respect to South Africa, recent discussions (e.g. Hook, 2011; Hook & Long, 2011, Long, 2011; Shefer & Ratele, 2011; Straker, 2011; Truscott, 2011) illustrate the continuing complexity of the debate around memory, race and difference and they offer provocative illustrations of the uses of psychoanalysis in the work of the Apartheid Archive Project.[16] Here I would like to conclude by focusing on the capacity for psychoanalytically informed therapists to not only work directly with persons who have suffered trauma, but to extend their influence in the social arena to address the severance of social links, the denial of memory, the erasure of generational and ancestral wisdom, and the rupture of genealogical continuity.

Narrative is a key concept in the rehabilitation of memory and the restoration of genealogical filiation. Aboriginal Australian writer Judy Atkinson explores how the structural violence inflicted on Aboriginal Australian people produced continuing patterns of violence transgenerationally among Aboriginal groups because the original wounds live on in *trauma trails* that move across generations. Recognising how indigenous societies are constructed around oral traditions and ancestral spirit wisdom, Atkinson (2002) says that trauma resulting from physical and cultural annihilation leads to a collapse of lore – a condition of *lorelessness* that leaves people bereft of social linkages and communal bonding of the kind documented by Lear (2006) among the Crow nation. While physical violence takes its toll, Atkinson suggests that cultural annihilation produces the most profound traumatic sequelae: 'In cultural genocide, people come to believe that they themselves are of no value, that their cultural practice and traditions are inferior, and hence so are they, that they are non-persons with no value' (2002: 72). The movement across generations of suffering produced by colonialism and other forms of structural violence (e.g. forced resettlement; erasure of language, culture and religious beliefs and practices) that wilfully destroyed ancestral links, family bonds and links to the land as source of spiritual sustenance, produces a traumatic residue. Tragically, as Atkinson notes, this unnamed and unmetabolised violence becomes internalised and can lead to an escalation of self-destructive violent acts as well as to an increase in domestic and societal violence. This tragic outcome is depicted, for example, in Tamahori's film *Once were warriors*,[17] which explores generationally embedded patterns of domestic violence among the Māori of Aotearoa/New Zealand.

ENGAGING IN A DIALOGUE AROUND REPARATION IN SOUTH AFRICA

In societies such as South Africa, where citizens have endured events that have produced mass trauma, is it possible to initiate dialogue that might lead to reparation and that could stave off the potential return of spectral trauma remnants that have the potential to destabilise South African society? Given the paucity of mental health resources in the country, a community-based approach that utilises key community stakeholders is essential. Rather than viewing psychoanalysis or psychodynamic psychotherapy as a singular solution, to be administered directly by psychologists to individuals and groups, South African mental health professionals might consider themselves as catalysts for change who offer assistance to community professionals (e.g. child-care workers, teachers, community workers, community nurses, religious leaders, indigenous healers) to build spaces for local dialogues around trauma, reparation and reconciliation. Psychodynamically skilled clinicians can infuse into that discussion concepts we hold dear, such as embracing history, valuing narrative, ensuring containment and safety in the therapeutic space, facilitating working through and so on. As noted earlier, the analyst in such a context becomes an *annalist*, assisting communities in developing means for recuperating narrative, re-establishing social linkages, reclaiming genealogy, and retelling their stories with a view to laying ghosts to rest, giving voice to traumatic experience, and finding a renewed energy for moving forward.

A pedagogical illustration: Evocative pedagogy and regenerative curriculum

In my own work I have conceptualised the problem as one of assisting trauma survivors – individually and collectively – in creating frameworks of intelligibility for their experiences. The challenge is partly the psychodynamic problem of 'bringing into existence zones of nonexistence' – of connecting people with unnamed, foreclosed, or spectral aspects of their own experience. It is also in part the socio-historical challenge of mobilising history, reweaving ancestral narrative threads, and reigniting more expansive notions of subjectivity. What unites both of these missions is an interest in cultivating conditions for the reception of full speech,[18] and generating with people questions that might animate their capacity to seek to know and hence to symbolise their experience.

One area of my own professional work is preparing professionals who work with children. With appropriate training, teachers, school psychologists and child-care professionals can play an influential role in providing culturally grounded, psychodynamically informed emotional education to groups of children. School professionals can speak to unconscious losses by using narrative-based approaches to working with children that are informed by principles of depth psychology (e.g. Atkinson, 2002; Britzman, 1998, 2009; O'Loughlin, 2009a).[19] In an ideal world, education would seek to transcend instrumental goals such as imparting socially sanctioned knowledge and dispositions and would allow children to imagine themselves otherwise (cf. O'Loughlin & Johnson, 2010). Schools have the potential to be ideal places for the kind of emotional work and narrative exploration that are central to pathways to healing for children and communities. This is only possible, of course, if schools are not exclusively cognitively focused and test-driven. A fundamental commitment to the notion of schools as places for socio-emotional growth is required, as is a commitment to the kind of dialogue that leads history to be understood as a nuanced, complex, contested, multilayered narrative rather than a single pseudo-unifying master narrative to be absorbed and regurgitated.

Two key principles of imagining schools as places that might engage in reparative dialogue are the concepts of 'evocative pedagogy' and 'regenerative curriculum'.[20]

Evocative pedagogy

This notion is based on the idea that each child has a culturally constituted unconscious of the kind discussed above, and that an important part of depth pedagogy is engaging children with losses, ancestral memory, phantoms, ghosts, silences and so on, so that they may begin to stitch themselves into the larger quilt of the familial and collective narratives from which they have come. As I noted:

> Psychoanalysts have long recognized that a powerful agent of change in therapy is the presence of the analyst as witness and receiver of unconscious knowledge. Teachers, too, ought to be prepared to receive such knowledge, and should understand how to evoke the unconscious in children through their own evocative presences. A teacher with a passion for myth, storytelling, drama, memory, and the wisdom of elders will draw these evocative knowledges into the classroom, and will elicit evocative responses from students that allow students to experience their own inner knowledges as nameable and addressable. (O'Loughlin, 2009c: 160)

This, of course, is a radical departure from what we often think of as schooling. Instead of privileging didactic, conformist or cognitive ways of being, the argument here is for a pedagogy that evokes each child's latent historical subjectivity and calls it forth as a central component of a child's coming to be.

Regenerative curriculum

This is built around the idea that '[i]f severance of the social link comes from the foreclosure of history, then a major focus of curriculum ought to be on the regeneration of those links by assisting children in experiencing their latent historical subjectivities and in claiming a specific indigenous identity' (O'Loughlin, 2009c: 162–163). Children come from communities which embody particular epistemologies, ancestral narratives and a particular lore. In the unforgettable words of Fraiberg and colleagues, for each child the ghosts of the past 'take up residence and conduct the rehearsal of the family tragedy from a tattered script' (1975: 165). Curriculum, therefore, rather than consisting of inert ideas designed to infuse sanitised official narratives of a society, might fruitfully be considered as a regenerative process of bringing to life the origins, aspirations and possibilities of particular communities of people. In this scheme, teachers, as well as being analysts, might consider themselves as 'annalists', documentarians of the individual and collective unconscious of specific communities of children.

> Speaking in terms of narrative, this kind of teaching privileges the active construction of narrative. However, the epistemological and identificatory possibilities of narrative are enhanced by introducing children to multiple modes of narrating, privileging particularly narrative modes that embody the ancestral lore, rituals, and worldviews that particular indigenous children have inherited. Curriculum, in this conceptualisation, is an organic process that gets constructed with children and with community stakeholders for the children of that particular community. Teachers might then consider themselves as documentarians of the collective unconscious of the community; documentarians of existing lore; and documentarians of the processes and products involved in constructing new forms of lore with children and community members. (O'Loughlin, 2009c: 162)

It is my sincere conviction that we can accomplish much more together than separately. If psychodynamically oriented therapists view indigenous healers, spiritual leaders, community workers, educators and health workers as partners, the reparative possibilities are limitless. A first step, perhaps, might be for psychodynamically oriented therapists to initiate a dialogue with the various groups that hold power in South Africa about infusing the national debate with a consideration of the importance of reparation, and working through to the safeguarding of future civility and the preservation of the important democratic experiment that is South Africa today. Perhaps this volume can contribute to that process.

NOTES

1   Throughout this chapter I use the terms 'psychoanalytic psychotherapy', 'psychodynamic psychotherapy' or simply 'psychotherapy' interchangeably to refer to approaches to therapy that are informed by the dynamic orientation typical of clinical psychology preparation.

2   See Nandy (1983) and DelVecchio et al. (2008) for further discussion of the psychic legacy of colonialism.

3   In what amounts to a Freudian slip, in my book I referred to these facilities as 'workhouses'. Workhouses were facilities in which many of the victims of Ireland's Great Hunger (to be discussed below) were sent to die. The facility in which Irish tuberculosis victims died was actually called a sanatorium.

4   The reference here is to the prevalence of sexual abuse of children by clergy in Irish orphanages during the 20th century (see Finnegan, 2001, and Raftery & O'Sullivan, 1999, for an overview).

5   See Woodham-Smith (1962) for the first comprehensive account of the Great Hunger. For contemporary accounts, see Kinealy (1997, 2006).

6   For critical scholarship on the psychological consequences of the Great Hunger and the official silence concerning its effects, see Valone and Kinealy (2002).

7   For extended discussion of the material that follows, see O'Loughlin (2007b, 2008, 2009b, 2010, in press a).

8   Davoine and Gaudillière, whose work I discuss below, describe the role of the child who has been turned into *therapôn* this way: 'As we have seen, a baby may be assigned the role of *therapôn*, keeper of the mind, for its parents, the boundary of their irrationality, remaining welded to them by a bond that may prevent any other attachment' (2004: 157).

9   This notion of being 'spoken through' is similar to Bakhtin's (1981) notion of ventriloquation.

10   For an application of Lear's analysis to the plight of Aboriginal peoples in Australia, see O'Loughlin (2008, 2009b).

11   Langer (1991), a Holocaust scholar, reminds us how difficult it is for those among us, having been spared trauma and thus possessing 'normal memory', to receive memory of atrocity. On the one hand, there is the difficulty for the narrator in conveying appalling suffering in everyday language:

Like Primo Levi, Delbo contends that as a result of the camp experience the word as well as the self had achieved a form of doubling: 'cold,' 'filthy,' and 'gaunt' meant one thing to her and another thing to the 'you' she is addressing. Because a language of Auschwitz has never emerged, an interpreter is constantly at work in the texts of deep memory to remind us of the need to collaborate with all efforts at redefinition. Witnesses themselves are hounded by this predicament – the dual thrust of the words. 'Otherwise,' Delbo conceded, 'someone [in the camps] who has been tormented by thirst for weeks would never again be able to say: "I'm thirsty. Let's make a cup of tea."… "Thirst" [after the war] has once more become a currently used term. On the other hand, if I dream of the thirst I felt in Birkenau [the locale of the extermination facilities in Auschwitz] I see myself as I was then, haggard, bereft of reason, tottering. I feel again physically that *real* thirst, and it's an agonizing nightmare.' (Langer, 1991: 8)

Conversely, sometimes the anguish pours forth without any symbolising restraint, and then it is the hearer who refuses to bear witness and thereby silences the speaker. Langer offers an example of a Holocaust witness who had already narrated such awful events that his wife had left the interview room deeply distressed.

Shortly after his wife leaves, one of the interviewers says to the witness, 'This is a nice place to stop.' Then we hear whispering off camera. Meanwhile, Moses S. is saying to himself aloud, 'And more, and more, and more. Do you want to hear more?' One of the interviewers replies, 'No. Let's end here.' He insists. 'One more story.' She persists. 'No, no. We'll stop here.' But he overrides her objection and tells the story of the prisoner choked to death by a Kapo for having eaten his friend's bread. And here the interview ends – but it is the interviewer's choice, not his…In his efforts to make us witnesses too, Moses S. grows *too* graphic thus alienating various members of his audience and vividly illustrating their difficulty in becoming active collaborators in the ordeal of testimony. (Langer, 1991: 28)

12 See O'Loughlin (2012b) and O'Loughlin and Charles (2012) for a critique of pharmacological approaches to treatment for psychological disorders.

13 See Davison (1998) for critical discussion of Robben Island.

14 *Miscast: Negotiating Khoisan History and Material Culture* was presented at the South African National Gallery (SANG), Cape Town, 13 April–15 September 1996. Davison describes *Miscast* and the ensuing controversy this way:

The concept of 'Miscast' was in keeping with the overall mission of the gallery to redress past inequalities. The aim of Skotnes' project was to illuminate the colonial practices that had mediated perceptions of people classified as Bushmen and Hottentots, and cast them as objects of scientific study. Harrowing images and artefacts of human suffering, humiliation, and objectification formed the visual burden of the installation, while transcribed texts from oral San literature, finely crafted objects, and rock art evoked the sense of a heritage lost. No redemption from shame was offered; no affirmation of survival. On the contrary, one gallery was designed so that viewers could not avoid walking on images of KhoiSan people, signifying inescapable complicity with past oppression. But who was Skotnes implicating? What reactions did she anticipate from people of KhoiSan descent? And what of her own position as curator? If unequal power relations characterized the colonial past, surely this continued to be so in the present. Far from applauding the exhibition, angry KhoiSan descendants contested the authority of the curator to represent their history and accused SANG of perpetuating the colonizing practices of the past. (1998: 158–159)

For additional commentary, see Douglas and Law (1997), Jackson and Robins (2011), and Lane (1996). See also http://web.uct.ac.za/depts/sarb/X0034_Miscast.html.

15 See http://www.districtsix.co.za/ for details. For discussion of the Museum's origins and purpose, see Rassool and Prosalendis (2001). For a discussion of the District Six Museum as a site of witness, see O'Loughlin (2007b).

16 See http://www.apartheidarchive.org/site/ for details.

17 Tamahori, L *Once Were Warriors*. DVD, New Line Home Video, 1995.

18 Lacan distinguishes *parole pleine* (full speech) from *parole vide* (empty speech) to capture the difference between speaking from a place of desire versus a place of hollowness. See the discussion in O'Loughlin (2009a).

19 For a wide variety of examples of creative applications of psychoanalysis in educational and child-related contexts, see the essays in my forthcoming books (O'Loughlin in press a, b).

20 See O'Loughlin (2009c) for an extended discussion.

REFERENCES

Abraham, N & Torok, M (1994) *The Shell and the Kernel* (edited, translated and with an introduction by N Rand). Chicago: University of Chicago Press.

Altman, N (2009) *The Analyst in the Inner City: Race, Class, and Culture through a Psychoanalytic Lens (second edition)*. New York & London: Routledge.

Apfelbaum, E (2002) Uprooted communities, silenced cultures and the need for legacy. In V Walkerdine (ed.) *Challenging Subjects: Critical Psychology for a New Millennium*, pp. 78–87. New York: Palgrave.

Atkinson, J (2002) *Trauma Trails, Recreating Song Lines: The Transgenerational Effects of Trauma in Indigenous Australia*. Melbourne, Australia: Spinifex Press.

Auerhahn, NC & Peskin, H (2003) Action knowledge, acknowledgment, and interpretive action in work with Holocaust survivors. *Psychoanalytic Quarterly*, 72: 615–659.

Bakhtin, M (1981) *The Dialogic Imagination*. Austin, Texas: University of Texas Press.

Bion, W (1984) *Elements of Psycho-analysis*. London: Routledge.

Bollas, C (1987) *The Shadow of the Object: Psychoanalysis of the Unthought Known*. New York: Columbia University Press.

Britzman, D (1998) *Lost Subjects, Contested Objects: Toward a Psychoanalytic Inquiry of Learning*. Albany, NY: SUNY Press.

Britzman, D (2009) *The Very Thought of Education: Psychoanalysis and the Impossible Professions*. Albany, NY: SUNY Press.

Danieli, Y (ed.) (1998) *International Handbook of Intergenerational Trauma Transmission*. New York: Plenum.

Danto, E (2005) *Freud's Free Clinics: Psychoanalysis and Social Justice, 1918–1938*. New York: Columbia University Press.

Davison, P (1998) Museums and the reshaping of memory. In S Nuttall & C Coetzee (eds) *Negotiating the Past: Making Memory in South Africa*, pp. 143–160. Cape Town: Oxford University Press.

Davoine, F & Gaudillière, J (2004) *History Beyond Trauma*. New York: Other Press.

De Kok, I (1998) Cracked heirlooms: Memory on exhibition. In S Nuttall & C Coetzee (eds) *Negotiating the Past: Making Memory in South Africa*, pp. 57–74. Cape Town: Oxford University Press.

Delport, P (2001a) Signposts for retrieval: A visual framework for enabling memory of place and time. In C Rassool & S Prosalendis (eds) *Recalling Community in Cape Town*, pp. 31–46. Cape Town: District Six Museum Foundation.

Delport, P (2001b) Museum or place for working with memory? In C Rassool & S Prosalendis (eds) *Recalling Community in Cape Town*, pp. 11–12. Cape Town: District Six Museum Foundation.

Delport, P (2001c) Digging deeper in District Six: Features and interfaces in a curatorial landscape. In C Rassool & S Prosalendis (eds) *Recalling Community in Cape Town*, pp. 154–165. Cape Town: District Six Museum Foundation.

DelVecchio, M, Hyde, S, Pinto, S & Good, B (2008) *Postcolonial Disorders: Ethnographic Studies in Subjectivity*. Berkeley: University of California Press.

Derrida, J (1994) *Specters of Marx: The State of the Debt, the Work of Mourning, and the New International*. New York: Routledge.

Douglas, S & Law, J (1997) Beating around the Bush(man!): Negotiating Khoisan history and material culture. *Visual Anthropology*, 10: 85–108.

Emery, E (2002) The ghost in the mother: Strange attractors and impossible mourning. *Psychoanalytic Review*, 89(2): 169–194.

Erikson, K (1976) Loss of communality at Buffalo Creek. *American Journal of Psychiatry*, 133: 302–305.

Faimberg, H (2005) *The Telescoping of Generations: Listening to the Narcissistic Links between Generations.* London: Institute of Psychoanalysis & Routledge.

Felman, S & Laub, D (1992) *Testimony: Crises of Witnessing in Literature, Psychoanalysis, and History.* New York & London: Routledge.

Ferenczi, S (1988) *The Clinical Diary of Sándor Ferenczi* (J Dupont, ed.). Cambridge, MA: Harvard University Press.

Finnegan, F (2001) *Do Penance or Perish: Magdalen Asylums in Ireland.* London: Oxford University Press.

Forbes, D (2001) A museum for the city. In C Rassool & S Prosalendis (eds) *Recalling Community in Cape Town*, pp. 25–30. Cape Town: District Six Museum Foundation.

Fraiberg, S, Adelson, E & Shapiro, V (1975) Ghosts in the nursery. *Journal of the American Academy of Child Psychiatry*, 14: 387–421.

Garon, J (2004) Skeletons in the closet. *International Forum of Psychoanalysis*, 13: 84–92.

Gordon, A (1997) *Ghostly Matters: Haunting and the Sociological Imagination.* Minneapolis: University of Minnesota Press.

Green, A (1999) *The Work of the Negative.* New York: Free Association.

Hook, D (2011) Narrative form, 'impossibility' and the retrieval of apartheid history. *Psychoanalysis, Culture & Society*, 16(1): 71–89.

Hook, D & Long, C (2011) The Apartheid Archive Project, heterogeneity, and the psychoanalysis of racism. *Psychoanalysis, Culture & Society*, 16(1): 1–10.

Jackson, S & Robins, S (2011) Miscast: The place of the museum in negotiating the Bushman past and present. *Critical Arts*, 13(1): 69–101.

Kaplan, L (1995) *No Voice is Ever Wholly Lost: An Exploration of the Everlasting Attachment between Parent and Child.* New York: Simon & Schuster.

Kinealy, C (1997) *A Death-dealing Famine: The Great Hunger in Ireland.* London: Pluto Press.

Kinealy, C (2006) *This Great Calamity: The Irish Famine 1845–52.* Dublin: Gill & Macmillan.

Lane, P (1996) Breaking the mould? Exhibiting Khoisan in South African museums. *Anthropology Today*, 12(51): 10–14.

Langer, L (1991) *Holocaust Testimonies: The Ruins of Memory.* New Haven, CT: Yale University Press.

Lear, J (2006) *Radical Hope: Ethics in the Face of Cultural Devastation.* Cambridge, MA: Harvard University Press.

Long, C (2011) Transitioning racialized spaces. *Psychoanalysis, Culture & Society*, 16(1): 49–70.

McCourt, F (1996) *Angela's Ashes.* New York: Scribner.

Nandy, A (1983) *The Intimate Enemy: Loss and Recovery of Self under Colonialism.* Delhi: Oxford University Press.

Nuttall, S & Coetzee, C (eds) (1998) *Negotiating the Past: The Making of Memory in South Africa.* Cape Town: Oxford University Press.

O'Loughlin, M (2007a) On losses that are not easily mourned. In B Willock, L Bohm & R Curtis (eds) *On Deaths and Endings: Psychoanalysts' Reflections on Finality, Transformations and New Beginnings*, pp. 103–120. London: Routledge.

O'Loughlin, M (2007b) Bearing witness to troubled memory. *Psychoanalytic Review*, 94(2): 191–212.

O'Loughlin, M (2008) Radical hope or death by a thousand cuts: The future for indigenous Australians. *Arena Journal*, 29/30: 175–201.

O'Loughlin, M (2009a) *The Subject of Childhood*. New York: Peter Lang Publishing.

O'Loughlin, M (2009b) An analysis of collective trauma among indigenous Australians and a suggestion for intervention. *Australasian Psychiatry*, 17: 33–36.

O'Loughlin, M (2009c) Recreating the social link between children and their histories: The power of story as a decolonizing strategy. In M O'Loughlin *The Subject of Childhood*, pp. 143– 164. New York: Peter Lang Publishing.

O'Loughlin, M (2010) Ghostly presences in children's lives: Toward a psychoanalysis of the social. In M O'Loughlin & R Johnson (eds) *Imagining Children Otherwise: Theoretical and Critical Perspectives on Childhood Subjectivity*, pp. 49–74. New York: Peter Lang Publishing.

O'Loughlin, M (2012a) Trauma trails from Ireland's Great Hunger: A psychoanalytic inquiry. In B Willock, R Curtis & L Bohm (eds) *Loneliness and Longing: Psychoanalytic Reflections*, pp. 233–250. New York: Routledge.

O'Loughlin, M (2012b) Countering the rush to medication: Psychodynamic, intergenerational, and cultural considerations in understanding children's distress. In US Nayar (ed.) *International Handbook on Mental Health of Children and Adolescents: Culture, Policy & Practices*. Delhi, India: Sage.

O'Loughlin, M (in press a) *Psychodynamic Perspectives on Working with Children, Families and Schools*. Lanham, MD: Jason Aronson.

O'Loughlin, M (in press b) *The Uses of Psychoanalysis in Working with Children's Emotional Lives*. Lanham, MD: Jason Aronson.

O'Loughlin, M & Charles, M (2012) Psychiatric survivors, psychiatric treatments, and societal prejudice: An inquiry into the experience of an extremely marginal group. In G Cannella & S Steinberg (eds) *Critical Qualitative Research Reader*, pp. 500–511. New York: Peter Lang Publishing.

O'Loughlin, M & Johnson, R (eds) (2010) *Imagining Children Otherwise: Theoretical and Critical Perspectives on Childhood Subjectivity*. New York: Peter Lang Publishing.

Peciccia, M & Benedetti, G (1998) The integration of sensorial channels through progressive mirror drawing in the psychotherapy of schizophrenic patients with disturbances in verbal language. *Journal of the American Academy of Psychoanalysis*, 26: 109–122.

Pisano, NG (2012) *Granddaughters of the Holocaust: Never Forgetting What They Didn't Experience*. New York: Academic Studies Press.

Prosalendis, S, Marot, J, Soudien, C & Nagia, A (2001) Punctuations: Periodic impressions of a museum. In C Rassool & S Prosalendis (eds) *Recalling Community in Cape Town*, pp. 74–95. Cape Town: District Six Museum Foundation.

Raftery, M & O'Sullivan, E (1999) *Suffer the Little Children: The Inside Story of Ireland's Industrial Schools*. Dublin: New Island Books.

Rand, N (1994a) Introduction: Renewals of psychoanalysis. In N Abraham & M Torok *The Shell and the Kernel*, pp. 1–22. Chicago: University of Chicago Press.

Rand, N (1994b) Introduction & Editor's Note. In N Abraham & M Torok *The Shell and the Kernel*, pp. 165–169. Chicago: University of Chicago Press.

Rassool, C & Prosalendis, S (eds) (2001) *Recalling Community in Cape Town*. Cape Town: District Six Museum Foundation.

Robins, S (1998) Silence in my father's house: Memory, nationalism, and narratives of the body. In S Nuttall & C Coetzee (eds) *Negotiating the Past: Making Memory in South Africa*, pp. 120–142. Cape Town: Oxford University Press.

Rogers, A (2006) *The Unsayable: The Hidden Language of Trauma*. New York: Random House.

Salmon, TW (1917) *The Care and Treatment of Mental Diseases and War Neuroses (Shell Shock) in the British Army*. New York: War Work Committee of the National Committee for Mental Hygiene.

Shefer, T & Ratele, K (2011) Racist sexualization and sexualized racism in narratives on apartheid. *Psychoanalysis Culture & Society*, 16(1): 27–48.

Stepansky, P (2009) *Psychoanalysis at the Margins*. New York: Other Press.

Straker, G (2011) Unsettling whiteness. *Psychoanalysis, Culture & Society*, 16(1): 11–26.

Truscott, R (2011) National melancholia and Afrikaner self-parody in post-apartheid South Africa. *Psychoanalysis, Culture & Society*, 16(1): 90–106.

Tutu, D (1999) *No Future Without Forgiveness*. New York: Doubleday.

Valone, D & Kinealy, C (2002) *Ireland's Great Hunger: Silence, Memory, Commemoration*. Lanham, MD: University Press of America.

White, K (2002) Surviving hating and being hated: Some personal thoughts about racism from a psychoanalytic perspective. *Contemporary Psychoanalysis*, 38: 401–422.

Woodham-Smith, C (1962) *The Great Hunger*. London: New English Library.

Afterword

Many of the chapters in this volume address a common theme: the need for a new kind of psychoanalytic theory and practice in South Africa which is relevant to its unique problems. The authors are attempting to develop a new form of psychoanalytically oriented psychotherapy which is inflected by, appropriate for and relevant to post-colonial South Africans. They are trying to develop a new hybrid theoretical framework which interrogates the assumptions of current psychoanalytic theory and expands its scope to include non-Western collectivist notions of self and community. Taken together, the chapters are a clarion call for a radical transformation of psychoanalytic praxis, an invitation for the heretofore invisible African, non-Western third to be acknowledged and welcomed into the analytic consulting room. These chapters are part of a new wave in psychoanalytic thinking which interrogates the implicit, hidden assumptions about class, gender, race, sexual orientation, culture and Western standards which are embedded in psychoanalytic theories (see Cushman, 2012; Dimen, 2011; Layton et al., 2006; Lobban, 2011). In our opinion psychoanalysis needs an infusion of such thinking if it is to remain a viable option for people from a variety of classes and cultures.

Addressing the decline of psychoanalysis in the United States, Paul Stepansky (2009) noted in *Psychoanalysis at the Margins* that it is vital that the field shed its elitism and make a commitment to technical pluralism and to encouraging psychoanalysts to develop applications that demonstrate that psychoanalysis has something useful to offer to society. As Stepansky noted, psychoanalysis has often cloaked itself in elitism and snobbery and in doing so has reinforced the perception that it is only a bourgeois therapy for bourgeois problems. This is unfortunate, as psychoanalysis had a long history of social activism, particularly in its earliest days, that has continued into the present (Altman, 1995; Danto, 2005; Moskowitz, 1996; O'Loughlin, 2010, 2012; Watkins & Shulman, 2008). Particularly now, with increasing pressure from market-based and evidence-based reforms, it is essential that psychoanalysis make the case for the utility and even efficiency of psychoanalytic and psychodynamic approaches to addressing particular societal problems. We believe that the contributors to this book have laid out many of the parameters for such a case, and we hope the book will contribute to a vigorous debate within South Africa as to how psychodynamic approaches might be a part of providing comprehensive mental health services to the highly under-resourced populations of South Africa.

A key characteristic of the book is the insistence of the authors in locating their work self-reflexively in their own socio-historical and socio-cultural origins, as well as their willingness to acknowledge the extraordinary legacy of apartheid and the ways in which the racial divide, the legacy of institutional violence, the complexities of gender and the lingering presence of unsymbolised intergenerationally transmitted trauma make their presences felt in the therapeutic process. What distinguishes psychodynamic thinking from alternatives such as cognitive behavioural therapy, for example, is the emphasis on transference, the recognition of the relation between symptoms and origins and an understanding that individual development and change always occur within a relational matrix. These three notions, as well as the notion of a racial shadow as an active third in any therapeutic relationship in South Africa, are key insights that underline the contribution of psychodynamic thinking to clinical practice and clinical training, as many of the authors in this collection illustrate. Conceptualising new modes of therapy in such a way that these elements are included could be a key contribution of South African psychoanalysis as a new mental health infrastructure emerges.

The authors in this volume have highlighted some of the issues which a new, hybrid praxis should address. First, in a country as epistemologically diverse as South Africa, where citizens draw on a variety of sources for meaning making, including indigenous worldviews and indigenous notions and practices of healing, in addition to Western understandings of mental health, it is vital that a dialogue take place across these differences and that common ground be articulated that does not privilege a singular view, but creates a space for the formation of collaborative and complementary models of mental health service delivery. There will be points of commonality, for example around notions of narrative, unconscious, ancestral and inherited trauma, as well as points of significant divergence. An additive model, in which complementarity of modes of healing is explored, is much more likely to be well received than a subtractive model with the echoes of colonial dominance and the spectre of cultural erasure it inevitably entails. This could lead to the development of hybridised modes of treatment that are informed by psychoanalysis, by other modes of psychotherapy and by indigenous beliefs and practices.

Second, this praxis should make space for reworking some of the trauma which is the fallout from the apartheid system and the AIDS epidemic. Domestic violence, serial murder, unmourned losses, institutional violence and structural inequality can all be considered trauma sequelae, as perhaps can some of the comorbid symptoms of HIV/AIDS. If these are considered within the rubric of intergenerational trauma and the severance of social linkages caused by forced relocation, civil strife, murder and the other atrocities that accompanied apartheid, then it would seem timely to engage in a discussion about the possibilities of reparative therapy that would allow people to restore ancestral continuity, reclaim their places in genealogy, and promote reconciliation through dialogue and sharing, much as the Truth and Reconciliation Commission aspired to do. The alternative to silence is the creation of dialogical spaces in communities that promote mutual understanding bound by mutual suffering. Trauma therapists and therapists with an understanding of group dynamics have invaluable expertise to offer to such a process. Since these issues have more to do with the state of the national psyche than with individual pathology, they provide an ideal space in which to work across disciplines in the construction of culturally relevant spaces for working through mass trauma and rebuilding community bonds. Community workers, teachers, nurses, ministers and other key community stakeholders can serve to initiate dialogue to break the silence and begin the work of reparation. Psychodynamic psychologists could well take the lead in facilitating training for such workers, much as DW Winnicott and others contributed to the creation of support services for the many children who fled London during the Blitz in 1940.

Ultimately, we hope that as the new mental health structure develops in South Africa, the debate will centre on the development of locally grown models of mental health delivery that take account of the socio-historical situatedness of particular groups of people; that address the specific mental health needs of the community; that recognise the presence of collective and intergenerational trauma in communities; and that are cognisant of the availability of local caregivers, who can become partners in reparative therapy and community-building processes. South African psychoanalytic therapists are in a unique position to straddle Western and non-Western formulations of self, other, community and culture and formulate a new hybrid theoretical framework which includes the African, non-Western third which is applicable to other multicultural countries.

It goes without saying that the considerations advanced by the authors in this collection are applicable also to other African societies grappling with post-colonial legacies, displacements and the HIV/AIDS epidemic in diverse episte-mological and multicultural contexts.

Glenys Lobban and Michael O'Loughlin

REFERENCES

Altman, N (1995) *The Analyst in the Inner City: Race, Class and Color Through a Psychoanalytic Lens.* Hillsdale, NJ: Analytic Press.

Cushman, P (2012) Why resist? Politics, psychoanalysis and the interpretive turn. *Division Review*, Spring: 11–13.

Danto, E (2005) *Freud's Free Clinics: Psychoanalysis and Social Justice, 1918–1938.* New York: Columbia University Press.

Dimen, M (ed.) (2011) *With Culture in Mind: Psychoanalytic Stories.* New York: Routledge.

Layton, L, Hollander, N & Gutwill, S (eds) (2006) *Psychoanalysis, Class and Politics: Encounters in the Clinical Setting.* New York: Routledge.

Lobban, G (2011) Li-an: Wounded by war. In M Dimen (ed.) *With Culture in Mind: Psycho-analytic Stories*, pp. 25–30. New York: Routledge.

Moskowitz, M (1996) The social conscience of psychoanalysis. In R Perez Foster, M Moskow-itz & R Javier (eds) *Reaching Across Boundaries of Culture and Class: Widening the Scope of Psychotherapy*, pp. 21–47. New Jersey: Jason Aronson.

O'Loughlin, M (2010) Reclaiming a liberatory vision for psychoanalysis. In symposium The Psychologies of Liberation: Clinical, Critical and Pedagogical Perspectives presented at the Annual Meeting of Association of Psychoanalysis, Culture & Society, Rutgers University, New Jersey, October.

O'Loughlin, M (2012) Countering the rush to medication: Psychodynamic, intergeneration-al, and cultural considerations in understanding children's distress. In US Nayar (ed.) *International Handbook on Mental Health of Children and Adolescents: Culture, Policy & Practices*, pp. 275–288. Delhi, India: Sage.

Stepansky, PE (2009) *Psychoanalysis at the Margins.* New York: The Other Press.

Watkins, M & Shulman, H (2008) *Toward Psychologies of Liberation.* New York: Palgrave Macmillan.

Index

Printed and bound by CPI Group (UK) Ltd, Croydon, CR0 4YY

09/06/2025

14685798-0001